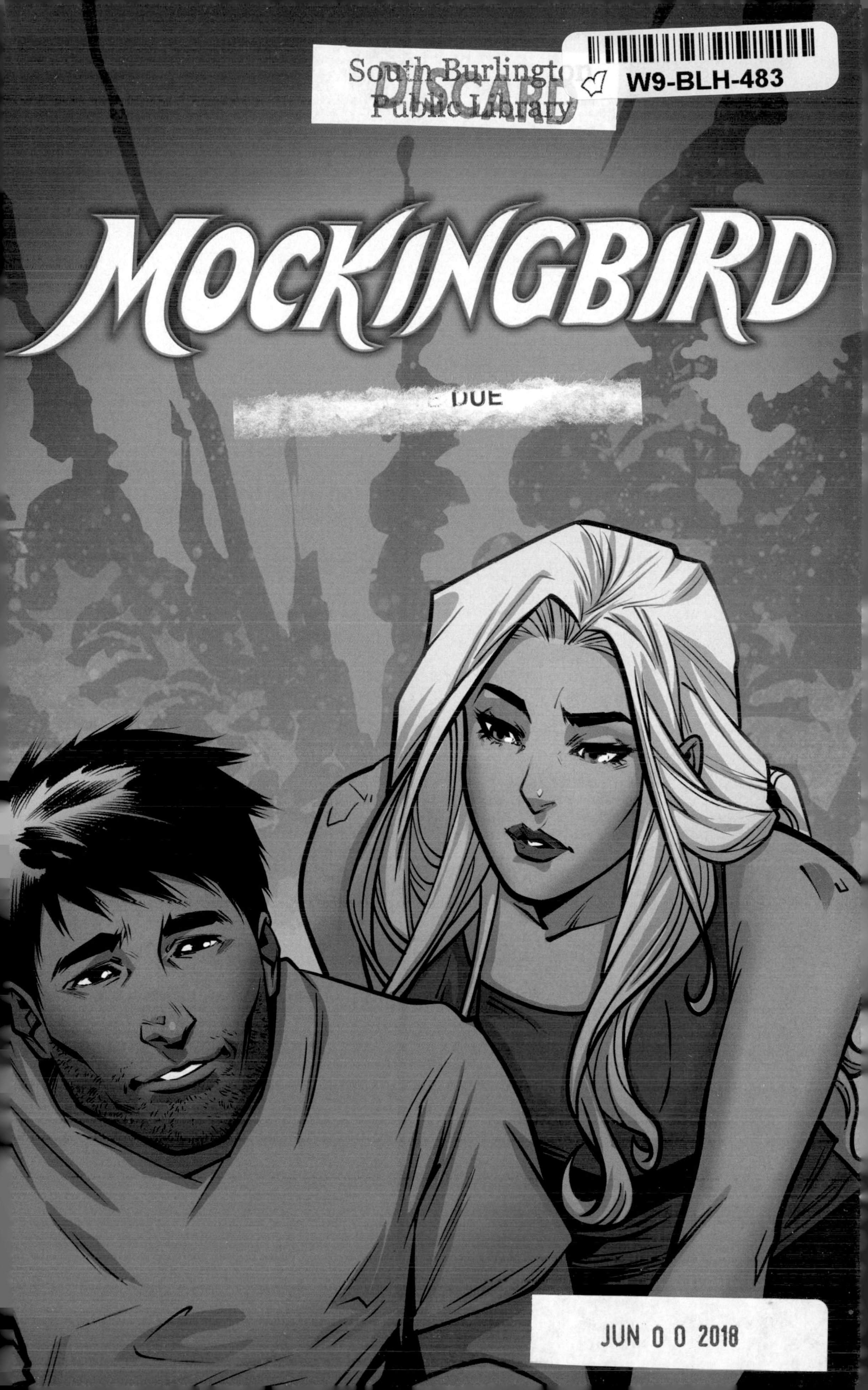
MOCKINGBIRD

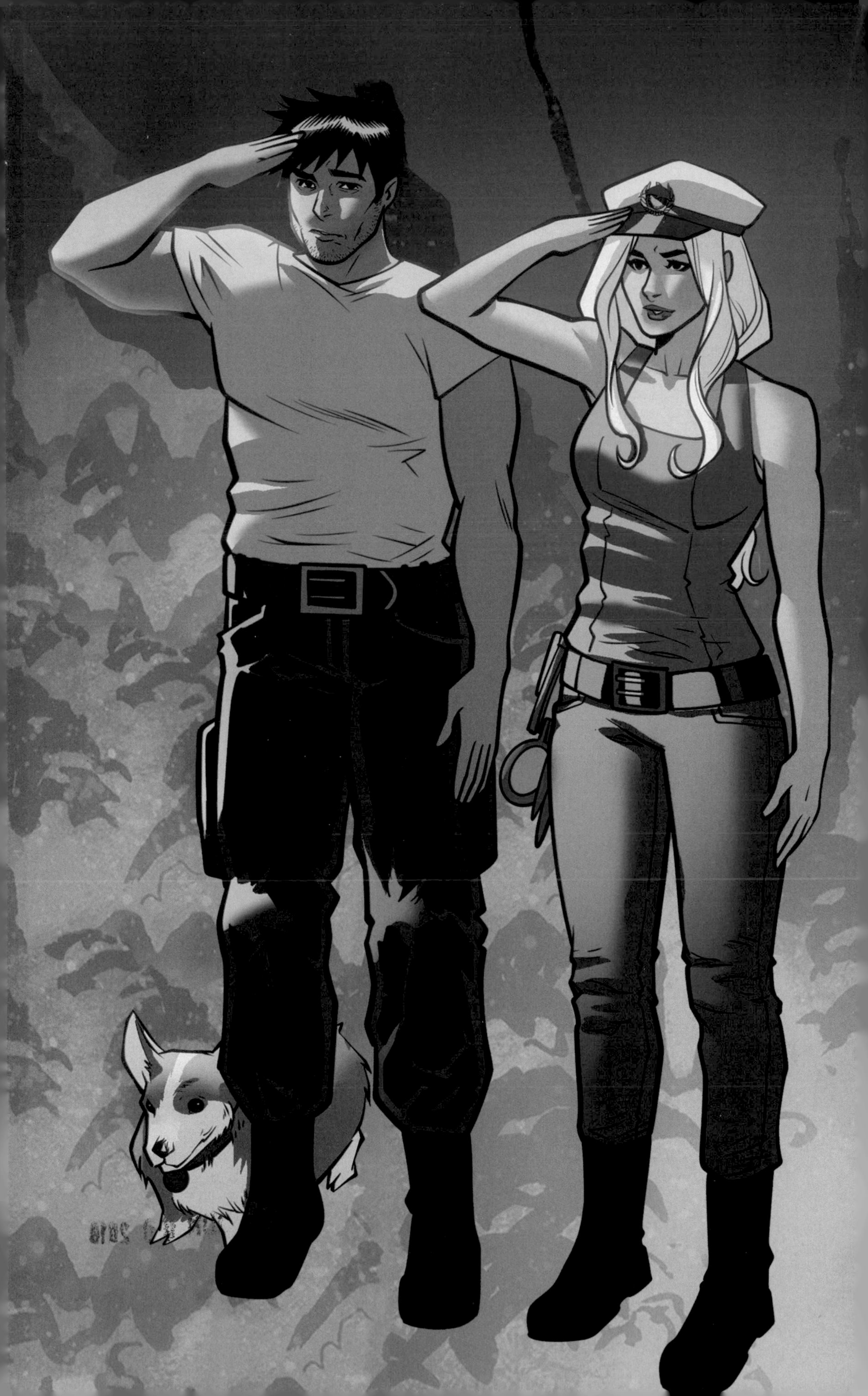

MOCKINGBIRD

MY FEMINIST AGENDA

Chelsea Cain
WRITER

Kate Niemczyk
PENCILER

Sean Parsons
INKER

Rachelle Rosenberg
COLOR ARTIST

VC's Joe Caramagna
LETTERER

**Joëlle Jones &
Rachelle Rosenberg**
COVER ART

Christina Harrington
ASSISTANT EDITOR

Katie Kubert
EDITOR

Tom Brevoort
EXECUTIVE EDITOR

COLLECTION EDITOR: JENNIFER GRÜNWALD
ASSISTANT EDITOR: CAITLIN O'CONNELL
ASSOCIATE MANAGING EDITOR: KATERI WOODY
EDITOR, SPECIAL PROJECTS: MARK D. BEAZLEY
VP PRODUCTION & SPECIAL PROJECTS: JEFF YOUNGQUIST
SVP PRINT, SALES & MARKETING: DAVID GABRIEL
BOOK DESIGNER: JAY BOWEN

EDITOR IN CHIEF: AXEL ALONSO
CHIEF CREATIVE OFFICER: JOE QUESADA
PRESIDENT: DAN BUCKLEY
EXECUTIVE PRODUCER: ALAN FINE

JUN 0 0 2018

MOCKINGBIRD VOL. 2: MY FEMINIST AGENDA. Contains material originally published in magazine form as MOCKINGBIRD #6-8 and NEW AVENGERS #13-14. First printing 2017. ISBN# 978-1-302-90123-3. Published by MARVEL WORLDWIDE, INC., a subsidiary of MARVEL ENTERTAINMENT, LLC. OFFICE OF PUBLICATION: 135 West 50th Street, New York, NY 10020. Copyright © 2017 MARVEL No similarity between any of the names, characters, persons, and/or institutions in this magazine with those of any living or dead person or institution is intended, and any such similarity which may exist is purely coincidental. **Printed in Canada.** DAN BUCKLEY, President, Marvel Entertainment; JOE QUESADA, Chief Creative Officer; TOM BREVOORT, SVP of Publishing; DAVID BOGART, SVP of Business Affairs & Operations, Publishing & Partnership; C.B. CEBULSKI, VP of Brand Management & Development, Asia; DAVID GABRIEL, SVP of Sales & Marketing, Publishing; JEFF YOUNGQUIST, VP of Production & Special Projects; DAN CARR, Executive Director of Publishing Technology; ALEX MORALES, Director of Publishing Operations; SUSAN CRESPI, Production Manager; STAN LEE, Chairman Emeritus. For information regarding advertising in Marvel Comics or on Marvel.com, please contact Vit DeBellis, Integrated Sales Manager, at vdebellis@marvel.com. For Marvel subscription inquiries, please call 888-511-5480. **Manufactured between 2/24/2017 and 3/28/2017 by SOLISCO PRINTERS, SCOTT, QC, CANADA.**

10 9 8 7 6 5 4 3 2 1

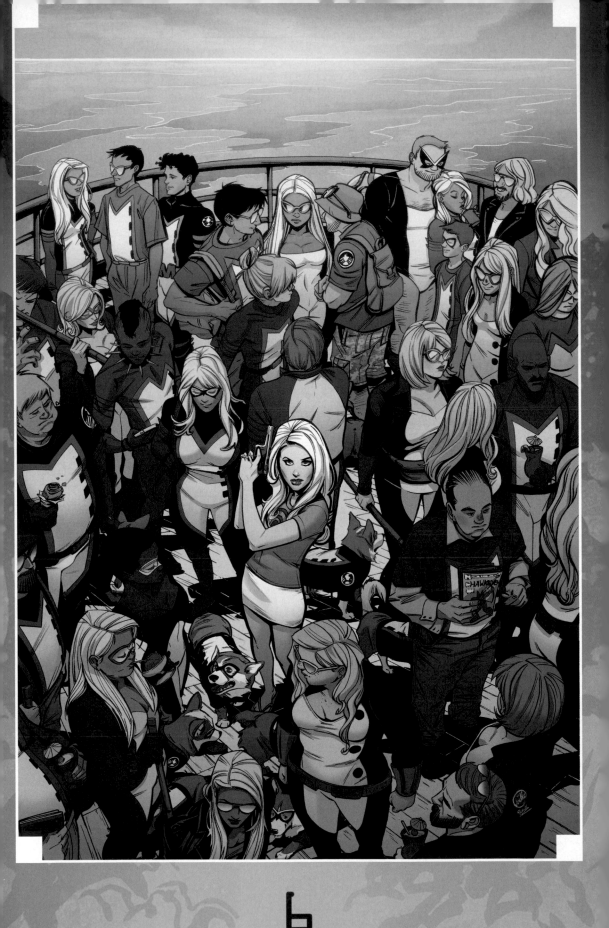

THE DAILY BLOWHOLE

Your source for news aboard the *Diamond Porpoise!*

DAY 1

FORECAST

Ahoy!

Welcome aboard. We're expecting you. The *Diamond Porpoise* is excited to be hosting this year's annual Nerd Cruise. Accordingly, sunscreen will be available free of charge on deck at all times. Please be aware that there has been a schedule change: Hawkeye will not be appearing as Saturday's keynote speaker. Instead, John Roderick will host a seminar on ascot-tying.

There will be no refunds.

I'm looking forward to meeting you all at tonight's mandatory lifeboat drill.

Yours sincerely,
Captain Katie Kubert

 Sunrise: 7:54 A.M.

 Sunset: 8:45 P.M.

☠ Chance of pirates: MEDIUM

FAQ

Q: Will the the magnetic abnormalities of the Bermuda Triangle affect my pacemaker?

A: Yes! Defibrillators are located near the Cinnabon™ on level two.

Q: How long does it take to travel to the Bermuda Triangle?

A: 3-11 days, depending on ripples in spacetime.

The wi-fi password is: IVMLMJWFT

Join us Sunday for poolside *Game of Thrones* rerun bingo hosted by celebrity game designer Keith Baker! (Swimsuits required.)

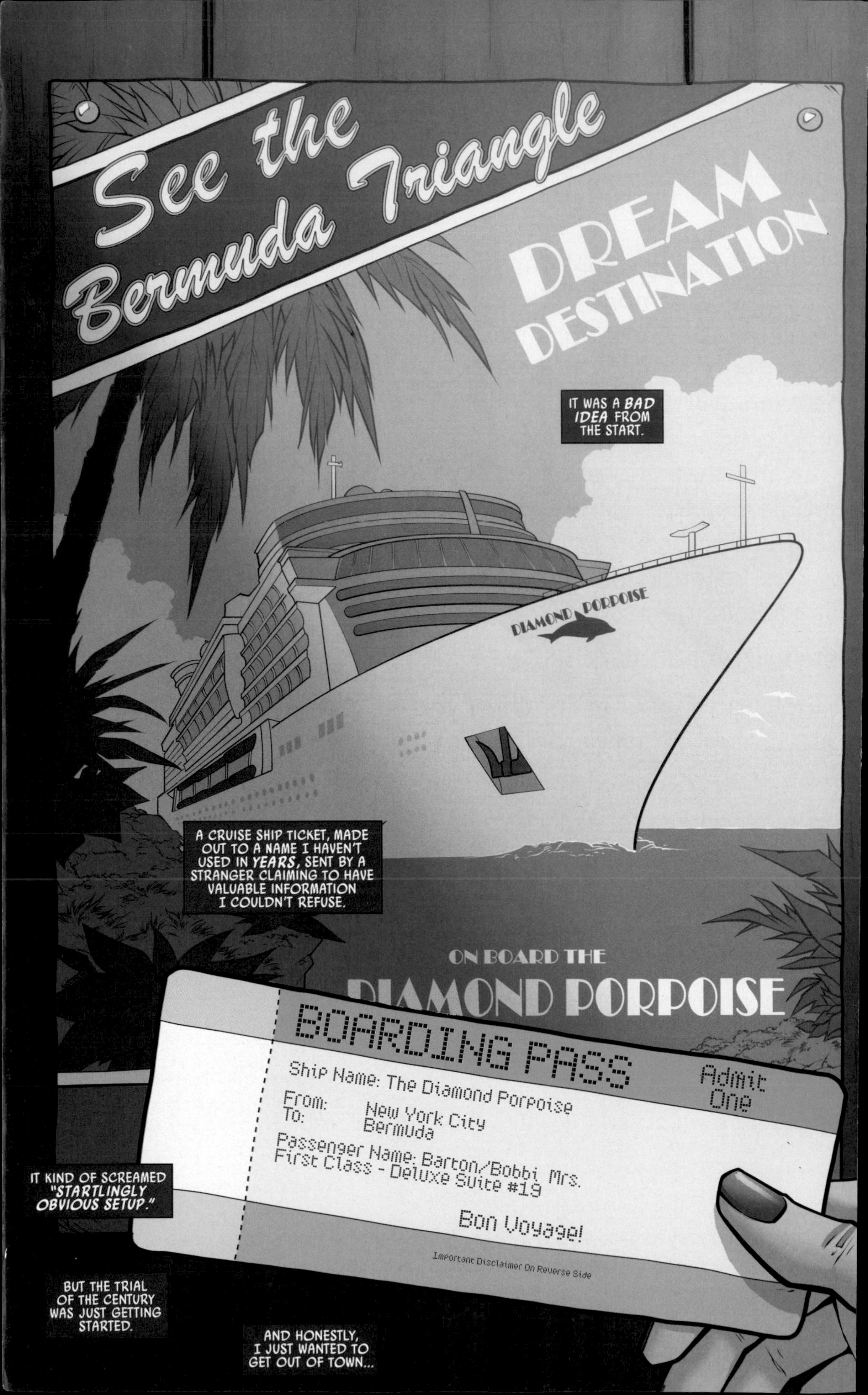

See the Bermuda Triangle
DREAM DESTINATION
IT WAS A BAD IDEA FROM THE START.
DIAMOND PORPOISE
A CRUISE SHIP TICKET, MADE OUT TO A NAME I HAVEN'T USED IN YEARS, SENT BY A STRANGER CLAIMING TO HAVE VALUABLE INFORMATION I COULDN'T REFUSE.
ON BOARD THE
DIAMOND PORPOISE
BOARDING PASS
Ship Name: The Diamond Porpoise
Admit One
From: New York City
To: Bermuda
Passenger Name: Barton/Bobbi Mrs.
First Class - Deluxe Suite #19
Bon Voyage!
Important Disclaimer On Reverse Side
IT KIND OF SCREAMED "STARTLINGLY OBVIOUS SETUP."
BUT THE TRIAL OF THE CENTURY WAS JUST GETTING STARTED.
AND HONESTLY, I JUST WANTED TO GET OUT OF TOWN...

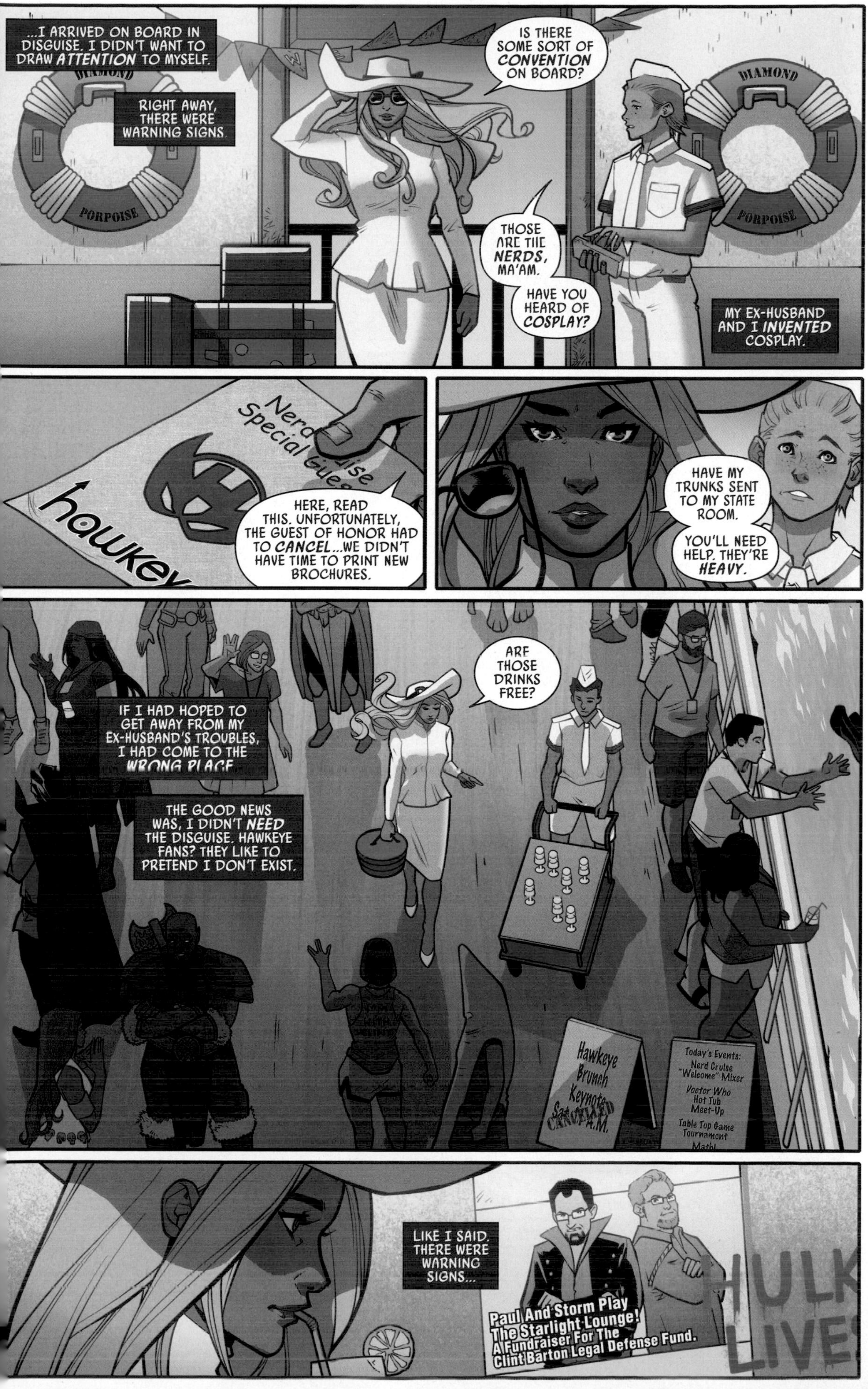
...I ARRIVED ON BOARD IN DISGUISE. I DIDN'T WANT TO DRAW ATTENTION TO MYSELF.
RIGHT AWAY, THERE WERE WARNING SIGNS.
DIAMOND
PORPOISE
IS THERE SOME SORT OF CONVENTION ON BOARD?
THOSE ARE THE NERDS, MA'AM.
HAVE YOU HEARD OF COSPLAY?
DIAMOND
PORPOISE
MY EX-HUSBAND AND I INVENTED COSPLAY.
HERE, READ THIS. UNFORTUNATELY, THE GUEST OF HONOR HAD TO CANCEL...WE DIDN'T HAVE TIME TO PRINT NEW BROCHURES.
HAVE MY TRUNKS SENT TO MY STATE ROOM.
YOU'LL NEED HELP. THEY'RE HEAVY.
IF I HAD HOPED TO GET AWAY FROM MY EX-HUSBAND'S TROUBLES, I HAD COME TO THE WRONG PLACE.
THE GOOD NEWS WAS, I DIDN'T NEED THE DISGUISE. HAWKEYE FANS? THEY LIKE TO PRETEND I DON'T EXIST.
ARE THOSE DRINKS FREE?
Hawkeye Brunch Keynote
CANCELLED
Today's Events: Nerd Cruise "Welcome" Mixer
Doctor Who Hot Tub Meet-Up
Table Top Game Tournament
LIKE I SAID. THERE WERE WARNING SIGNS...
Paul And Storm Play The Starlight Lounge! A Fundraiser For The Clint Barton Legal Defense Fund.
HULK

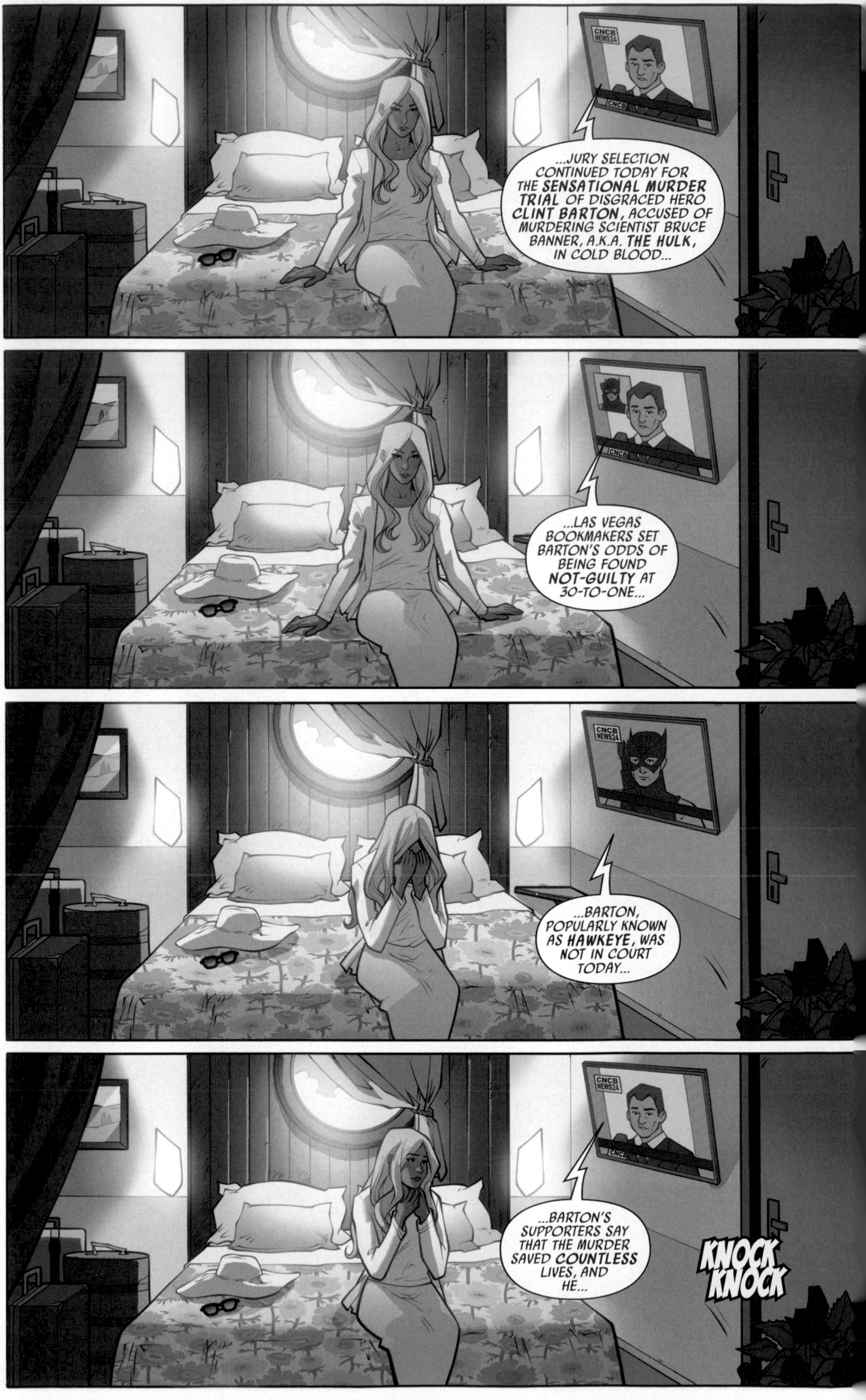
CNCB NEWS24
...JURY SELECTION CONTINUED TODAY FOR THE SENSATIONAL MURDER TRIAL OF DISGRACED HERO CLINT BARTON, ACCUSED OF MURDERING SCIENTIST BRUCE BANNER, A.K.A. THE HULK, IN COLD BLOOD...
...LAS VEGAS BOOKMAKERS SET BARTON'S ODDS OF BEING FOUND NOT-GUILTY AT 30-TO-ONE...
...BARTON, POPULARLY KNOWN AS HAWKEYE, WAS NOT IN COURT TODAY...
...BARTON'S SUPPORTERS SAY THAT THE MURDER SAVED COUNTLESS LIVES, AND HE...
KNOCK KNOCK

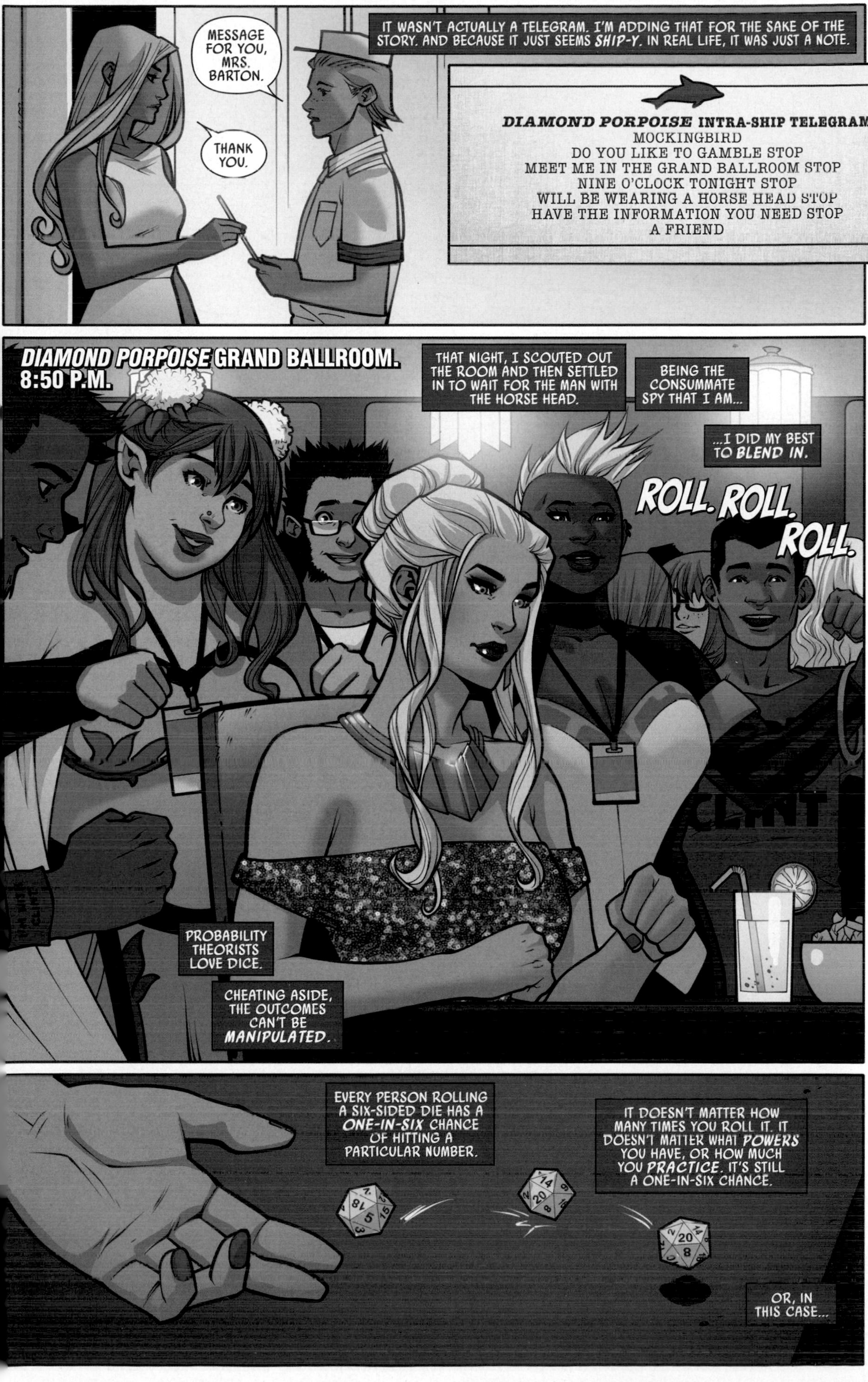
IT WASN'T ACTUALLY A TELEGRAM. I'M ADDING THAT FOR THE SAKE OF THE STORY. AND BECAUSE IT JUST SEEMS SHIP-Y. IN REAL LIFE, IT WAS JUST A NOTE.
MESSAGE FOR YOU, MRS. BARTON.
THANK YOU.
DIAMOND PORPOISE INTRA-SHIP TELEGRAM
MOCKINGBIRD
DO YOU LIKE TO GAMBLE STOP
MEET ME IN THE GRAND BALLROOM STOP
NINE O'CLOCK TONIGHT STOP
WILL BE WEARING A HORSE HEAD STOP
HAVE THE INFORMATION YOU NEED STOP
A FRIEND
DIAMOND PORPOISE GRAND BALLROOM. 8:50 P.M.
THAT NIGHT, I SCOUTED OUT THE ROOM AND THEN SETTLED IN TO WAIT FOR THE MAN WITH THE HORSE HEAD.
BEING THE CONSUMMATE SPY THAT I AM...
...I DID MY BEST TO BLEND IN.
ROLL. ROLL. ROLL.
CLINT
PROBABILITY THEORISTS LOVE DICE.
CHEATING ASIDE, THE OUTCOMES CAN'T BE MANIPULATED.
EVERY PERSON ROLLING A SIX-SIDED DIE HAS A ONE-IN-SIX CHANCE OF HITTING A PARTICULAR NUMBER.
IT DOESN'T MATTER HOW MANY TIMES YOU ROLL IT. IT DOESN'T MATTER WHAT POWERS YOU HAVE, OR HOW MUCH YOU PRACTICE. IT'S STILL A ONE-IN-SIX CHANCE.
OR, IN THIS CASE...

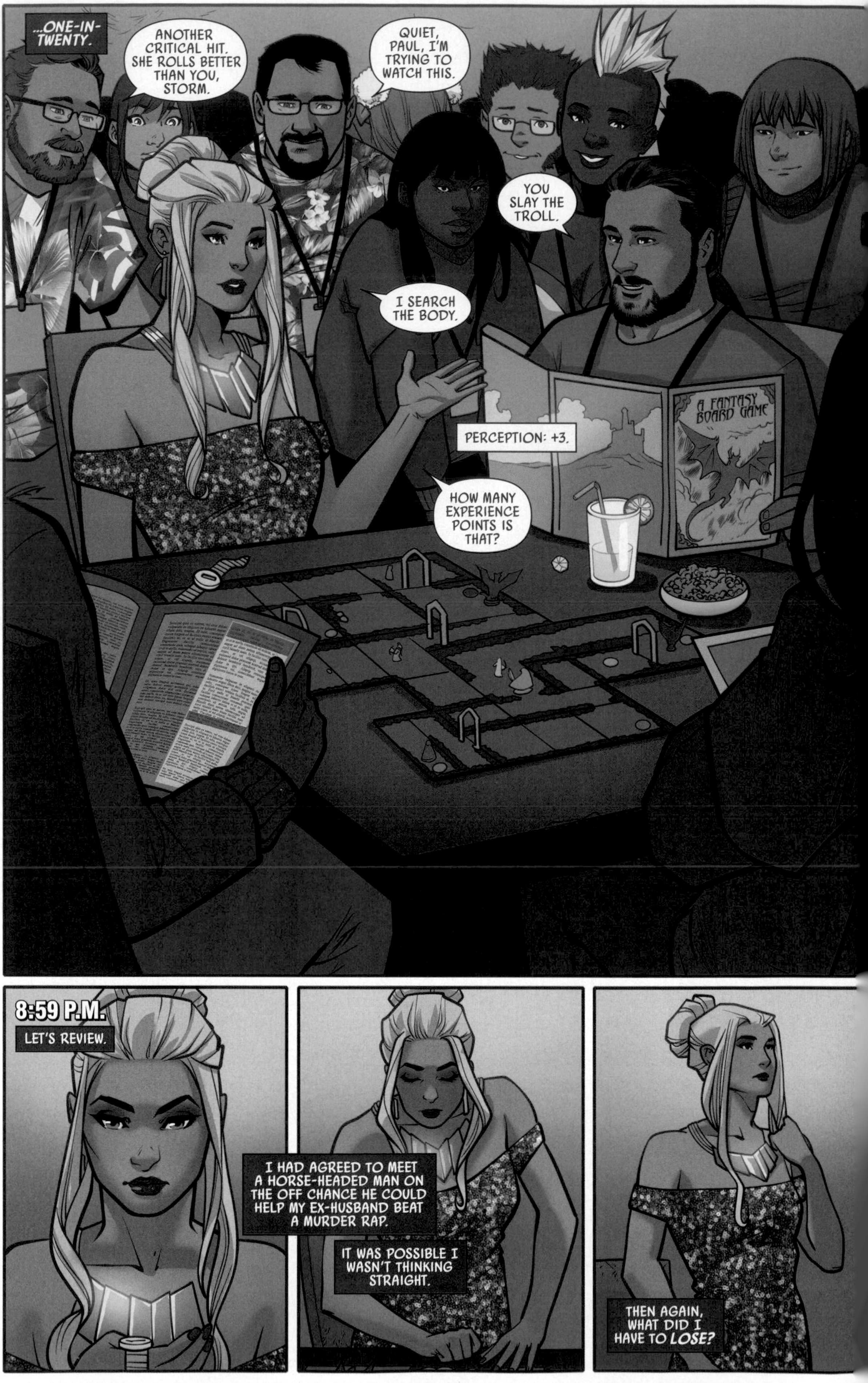
...ONE-IN-TWENTY.
ANOTHER CRITICAL HIT. SHE ROLLS BETTER THAN YOU, STORM.
QUIET, PAUL, I'M TRYING TO WATCH THIS.
YOU SLAY THE TROLL.
I SEARCH THE BODY.
A FANTASY BOARD GAME
PERCEPTION: +3.
HOW MANY EXPERIENCE POINTS IS THAT?
8:59 P.M.
LET'S REVIEW.
I HAD AGREED TO MEET A HORSE-HEADED MAN ON THE OFF CHANCE HE COULD HELP MY EX-HUSBAND BEAT A MURDER RAP.
IT WAS POSSIBLE I WASN'T THINKING STRAIGHT.
THEN AGAIN, WHAT DID I HAVE TO *LOSE?*

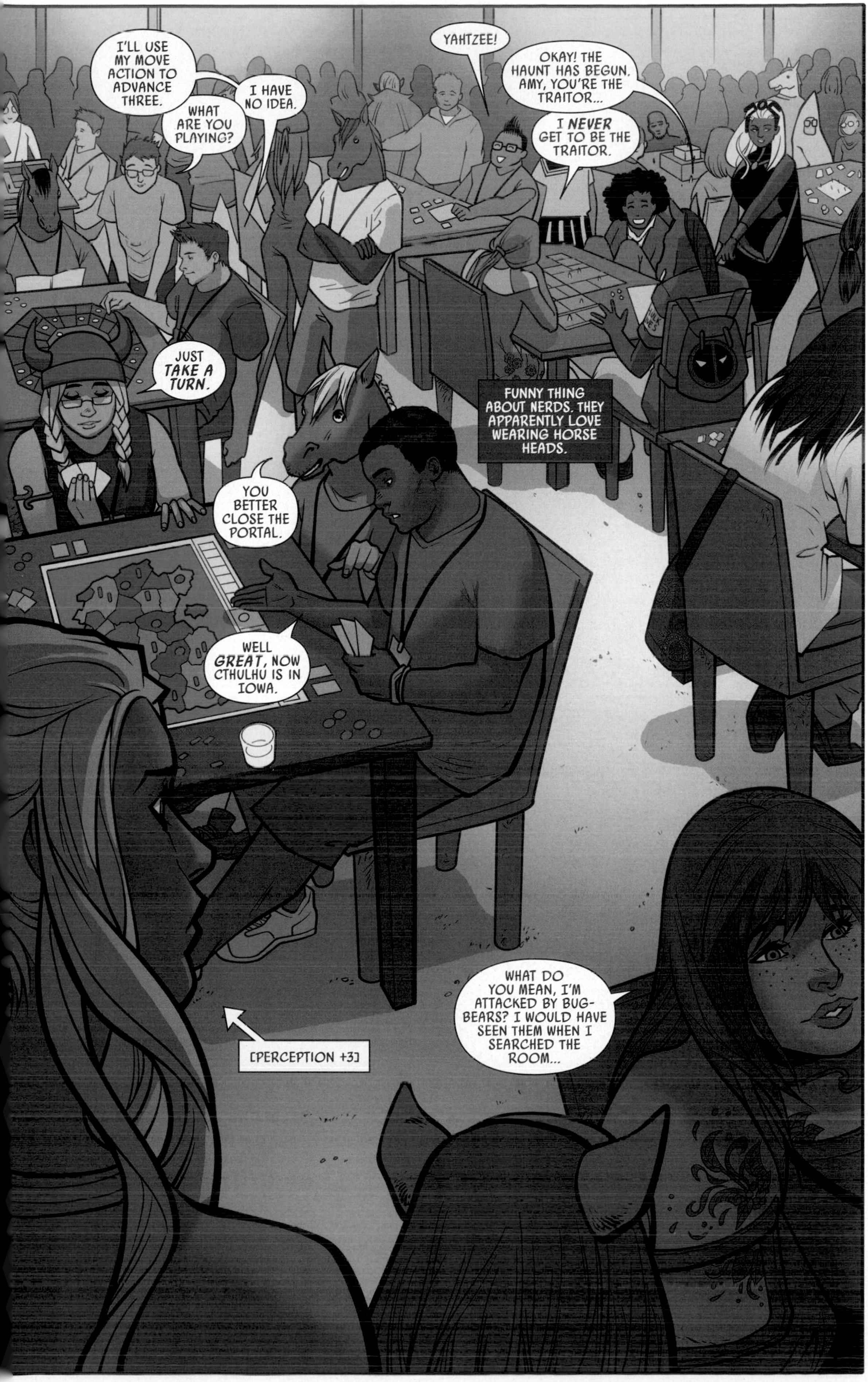
I'LL USE MY MOVE ACTION TO ADVANCE THREE.
WHAT ARE YOU PLAYING?
I HAVE NO IDEA.
YAHTZEE!
OKAY! THE HAUNT HAS BEGUN. AMY, YOU'RE THE TRAITOR...
I NEVER GET TO BE THE TRAITOR.
JUST TAKE A TURN.
FUNNY THING ABOUT NERDS. THEY APPARENTLY LOVE WEARING HORSE HEADS.
YOU BETTER CLOSE THE PORTAL.
WELL GREAT, NOW CTHULHU IS IN IOWA.
WHAT DO YOU MEAN, I'M ATTACKED BY BUG-BEARS? I WOULD HAVE SEEN THEM WHEN I SEARCHED THE ROOM...
[PERCEPTION +3]

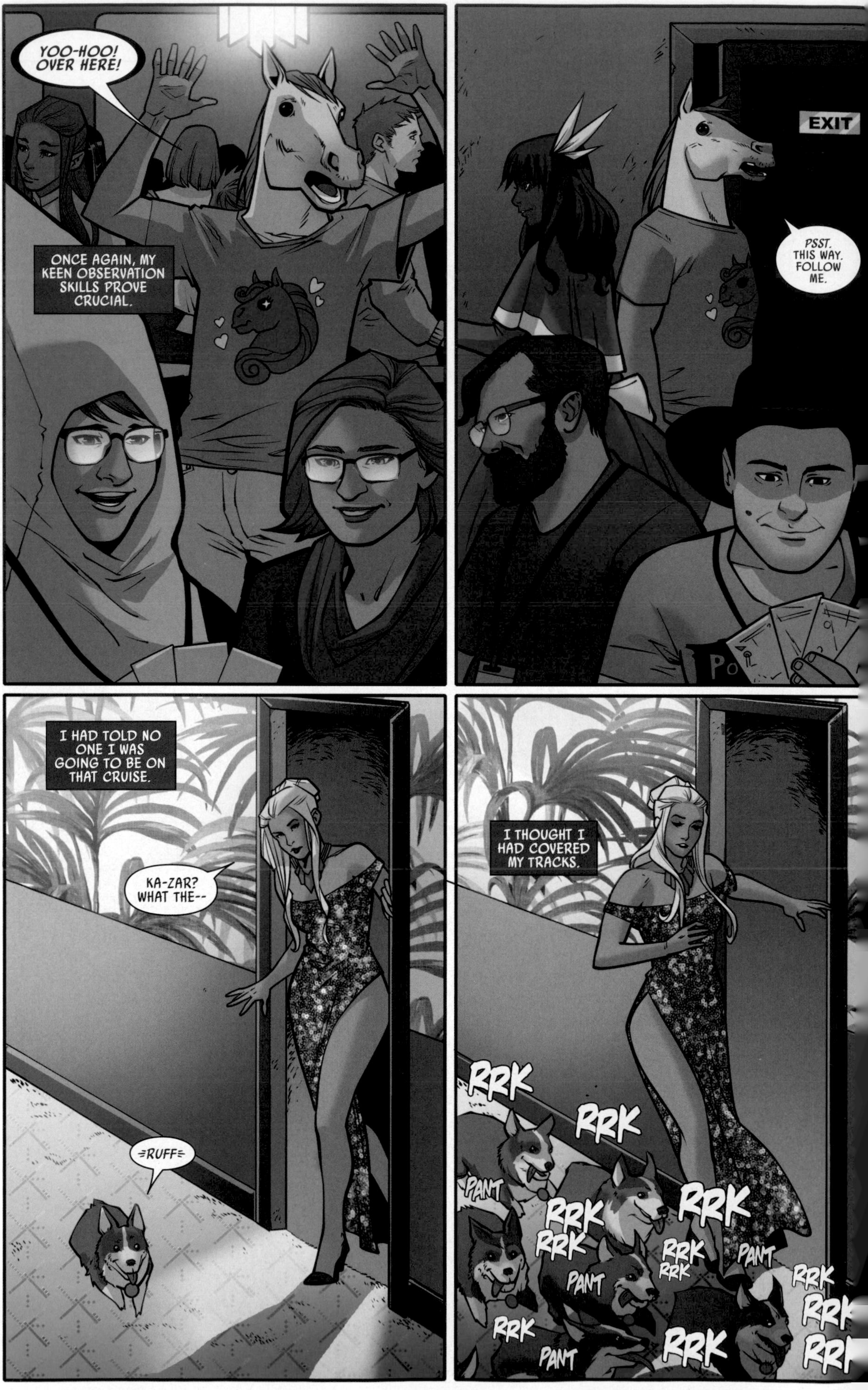

YOO-HOO! OVER HERE!
ONCE AGAIN, MY KEEN OBSERVATION SKILLS PROVE CRUCIAL.
EXIT
PSST. THIS WAY. FOLLOW ME.
I HAD TOLD NO ONE I WAS GOING TO BE ON THAT CRUISE.
KA-ZAR? WHAT THE--
RUFF
I THOUGHT I HAD COVERED MY TRACKS.
RRK
RRK
PANT
RRK RRK
RRK
RRK RRK
PANT
PANT
RRK
RRK
PANT
RRK

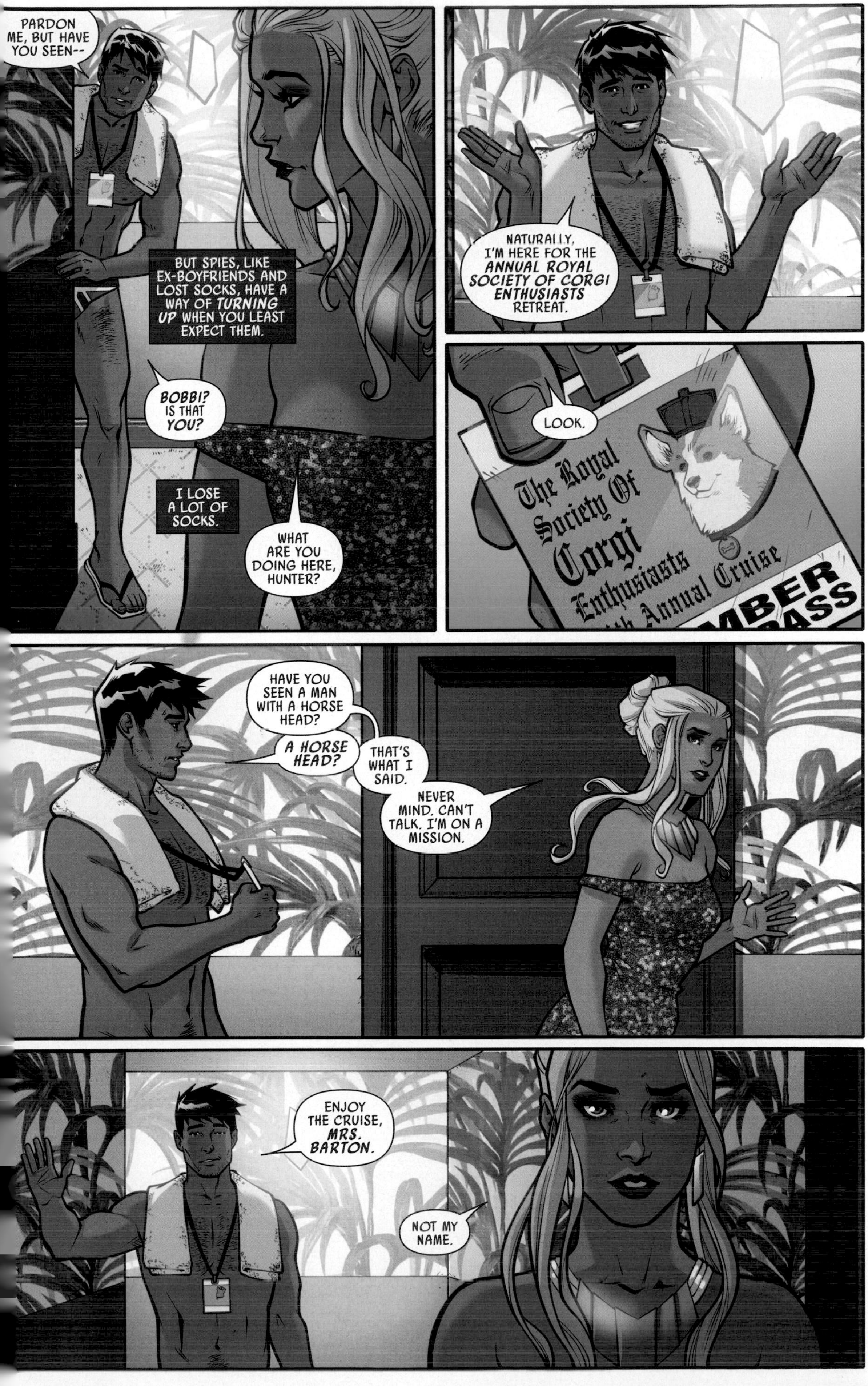
PARDON ME, BUT HAVE YOU SEEN--
BUT SPIES, LIKE EX-BOYFRIENDS AND LOST SOCKS, HAVE A WAY OF *TURNING UP* WHEN YOU LEAST EXPECT THEM.
BOBBI? IS THAT *YOU?*
I LOSE A LOT OF SOCKS.
WHAT ARE YOU DOING HERE, HUNTER?
NATURALLY, I'M HERE FOR THE *ANNUAL ROYAL SOCIETY OF CORGI ENTHUSIASTS* RETREAT.
LOOK.
The Royal Society Of Corgi Enthusiasts
Annual Cruise
MBER
PASS
HAVE YOU SEEN A MAN WITH A HORSE HEAD?
A HORSE HEAD?
THAT'S WHAT I SAID.
NEVER MIND. CAN'T TALK. I'M ON A MISSION.
ENJOY THE CRUISE, *MRS. BARTON.*
NOT MY NAME.

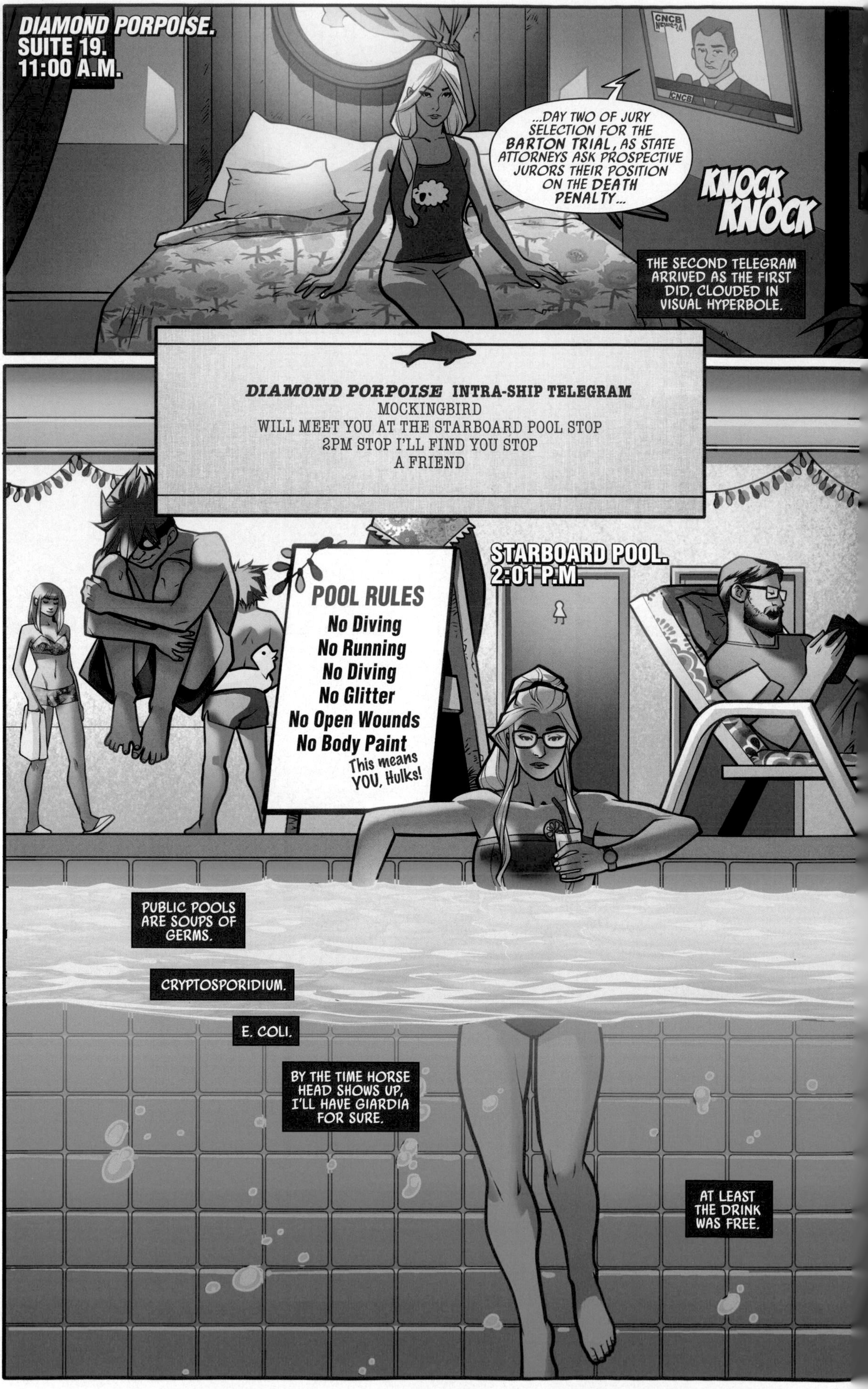
DIAMOND PORPOISE. SUITE 19. 11:00 A.M.
CNCB NEWS24
CNCB
...DAY TWO OF JURY SELECTION FOR THE BARTON TRIAL, AS STATE ATTORNEYS ASK PROSPECTIVE JURORS THEIR POSITION ON THE DEATH PENALTY...
KNOCK KNOCK
THE SECOND TELEGRAM ARRIVED AS THE FIRST DID, CLOUDED IN VISUAL HYPERBOLE.
DIAMOND PORPOISE INTRA-SHIP TELEGRAM
MOCKINGBIRD
WILL MEET YOU AT THE STARBOARD POOL STOP
2PM STOP I'LL FIND YOU STOP
A FRIEND
STARBOARD POOL. 2:01 P.M.
POOL RULES
No Diving
No Running
No Diving
No Glitter
No Open Wounds
No Body Paint
This means YOU, Hulks!
PUBLIC POOLS ARE SOUPS OF GERMS.
CRYPTOSPORIDIUM.
E. COLI.
BY THE TIME HORSE HEAD SHOWS UP, I'LL HAVE GIARDIA FOR SURE.
AT LEAST THE DRINK WAS FREE.

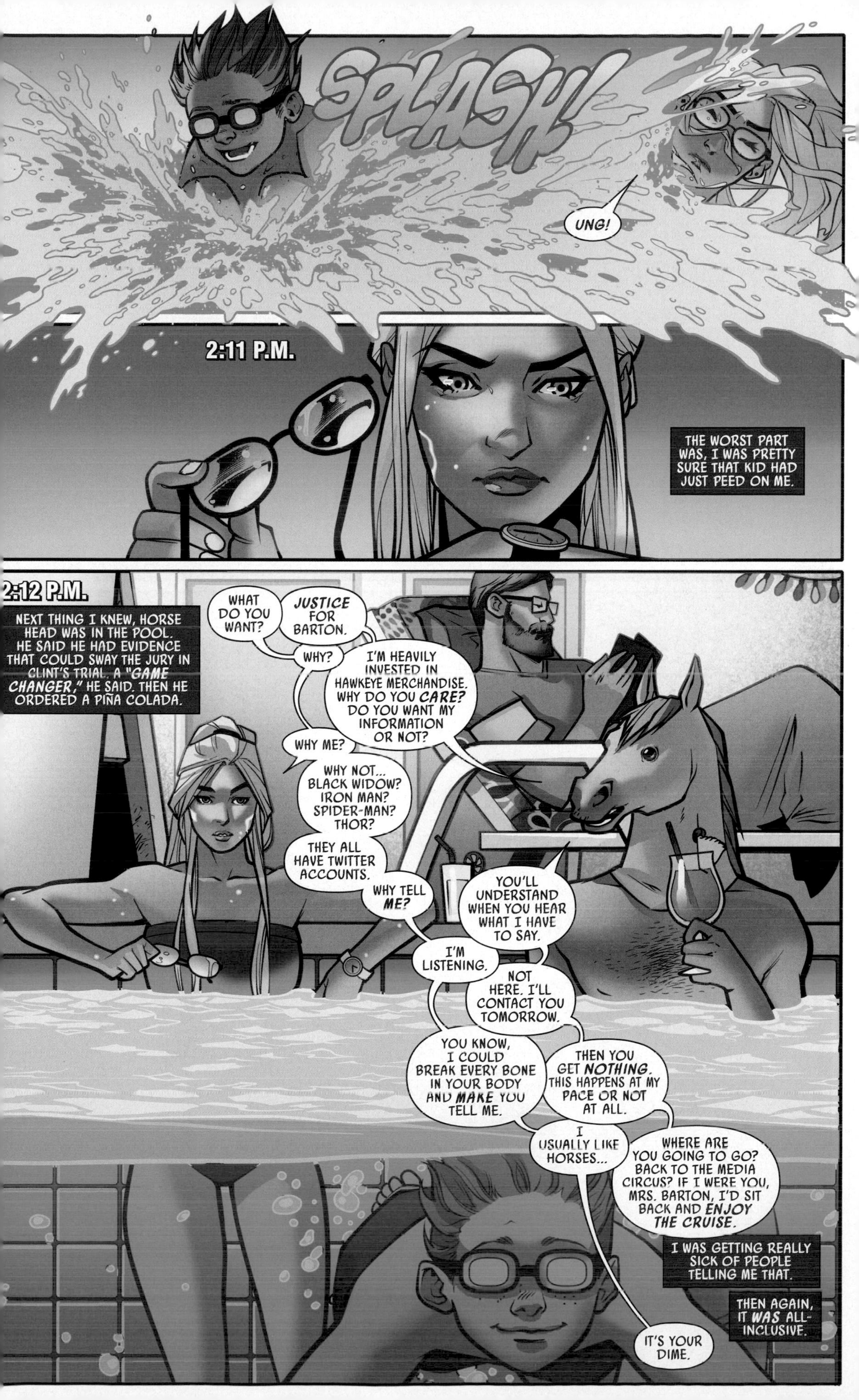
SPLASH!
UNG!
2:11 P.M.
THE WORST PART WAS, I WAS PRETTY SURE THAT KID HAD JUST PEED ON ME.
2:12 P.M.
NEXT THING I KNEW, HORSE HEAD WAS IN THE POOL. HE SAID HE HAD EVIDENCE THAT COULD SWAY THE JURY IN CLINT'S TRIAL. A "GAME CHANGER," HE SAID. THEN HE ORDERED A PIÑA COLADA.
WHAT DO YOU WANT?
JUSTICE FOR BARTON.
WHY?
I'M HEAVILY INVESTED IN HAWKEYE MERCHANDISE. WHY DO YOU CARE? DO YOU WANT MY INFORMATION OR NOT?
WHY ME?
WHY NOT... BLACK WIDOW? IRON MAN? SPIDER-MAN? THOR?
THEY ALL HAVE TWITTER ACCOUNTS.
WHY TELL ME?
YOU'LL UNDERSTAND WHEN YOU HEAR WHAT I HAVE TO SAY.
I'M LISTENING.
NOT HERE. I'LL CONTACT YOU TOMORROW.
YOU KNOW, I COULD BREAK EVERY BONE IN YOUR BODY AND MAKE YOU TELL ME.
THEN YOU GET NOTHING. THIS HAPPENS AT MY PACE OR NOT AT ALL.
I USUALLY LIKE HORSES...
WHERE ARE YOU GOING TO GO? BACK TO THE MEDIA CIRCUS? IF I WERE YOU, MRS. BARTON, I'D SIT BACK AND ENJOY THE CRUISE.
I WAS GETTING REALLY SICK OF PEOPLE TELLING ME THAT.
THEN AGAIN, IT WAS ALL-INCLUSIVE.
IT'S YOUR DIME.

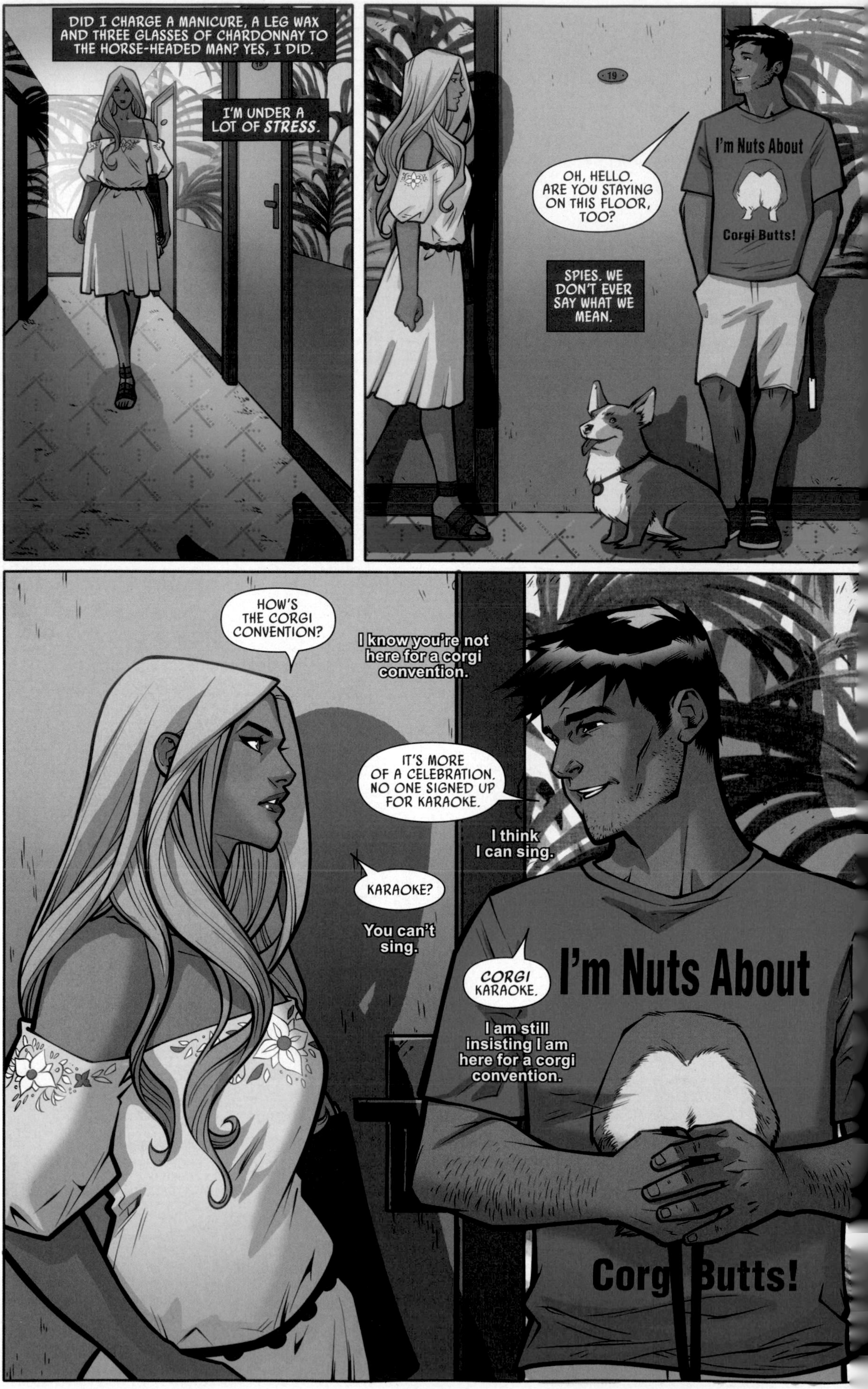
DID I CHARGE A MANICURE, A LEG WAX AND THREE GLASSES OF CHARDONNAY TO THE HORSE-HEADED MAN? YES, I DID.
I'M UNDER A LOT OF STRESS.
19
OH, HELLO. ARE YOU STAYING ON THIS FLOOR, TOO?
I'm Nuts About Corgi Butts!
SPIES. WE DON'T EVER SAY WHAT WE MEAN.
HOW'S THE CORGI CONVENTION?
I know you're not here for a corgi convention.
IT'S MORE OF A CELEBRATION. NO ONE SIGNED UP FOR KARAOKE.
I think I can sing.
KARAOKE?
You can't sing.
CORGI KARAOKE.
I am still insisting I am here for a corgi convention.
I'm Nuts About
Corg Butts!

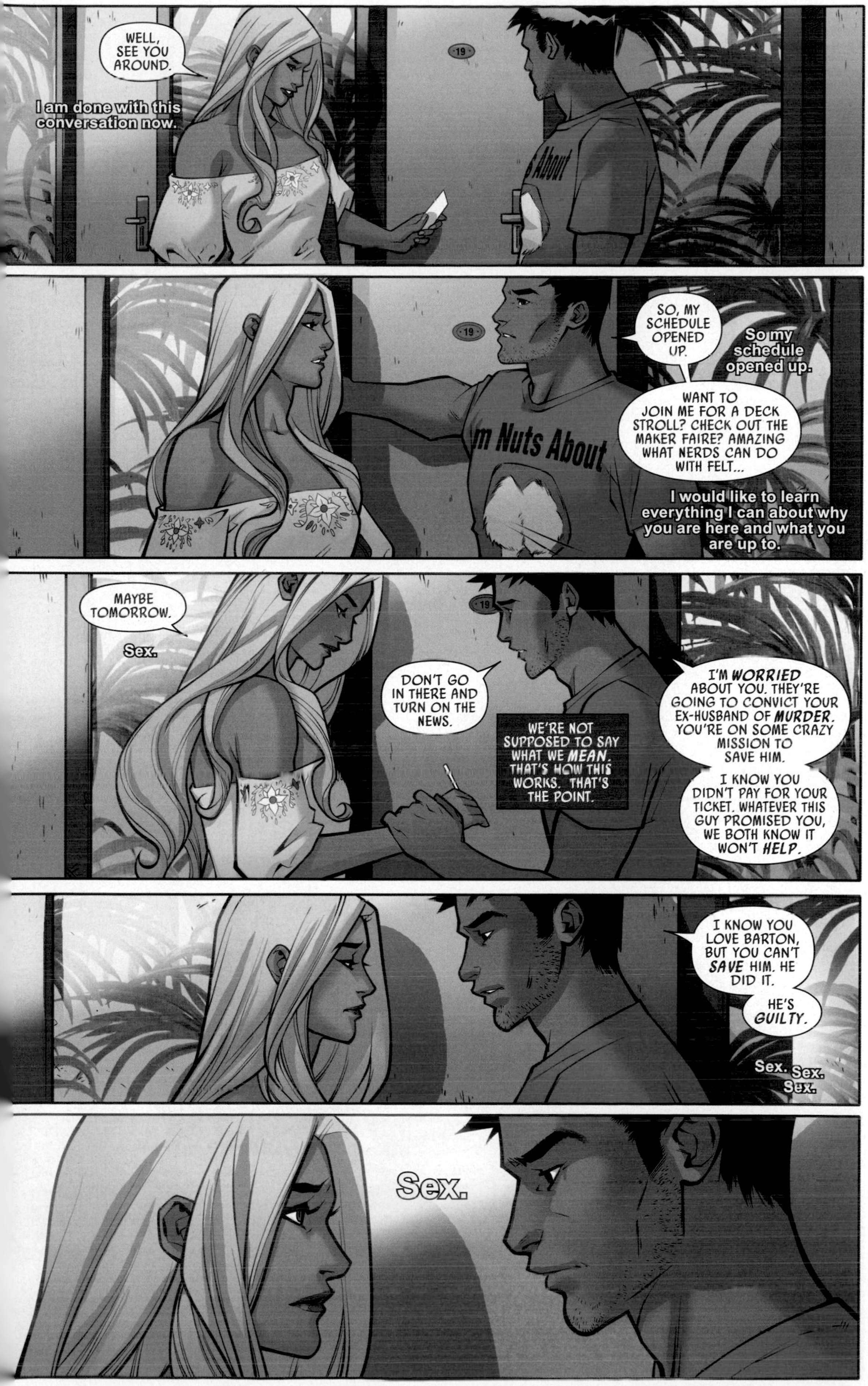
WELL, SEE YOU AROUND.
I am done with this conversation now.
So, my schedule opened up.
So my schedule opened up.
Want to join me for a deck stroll? Check out the maker faire? Amazing what nerds can do with felt...
I would like to learn everything I can about why you are here and what you are up to.
Maybe tomorrow.
Sex.
Don't go in there and turn on the news.
We're not supposed to say what we mean. That's how this works. That's the point.
I'm worried about you. They're going to convict your ex-husband of murder. You're on some crazy mission to save him.
I know you didn't pay for your ticket. Whatever this guy promised you, we both know it won't help.
I know you love Barton, but you can't save him. He did it.
He's guilty.
Sex. Sex. Sex.
Sex.

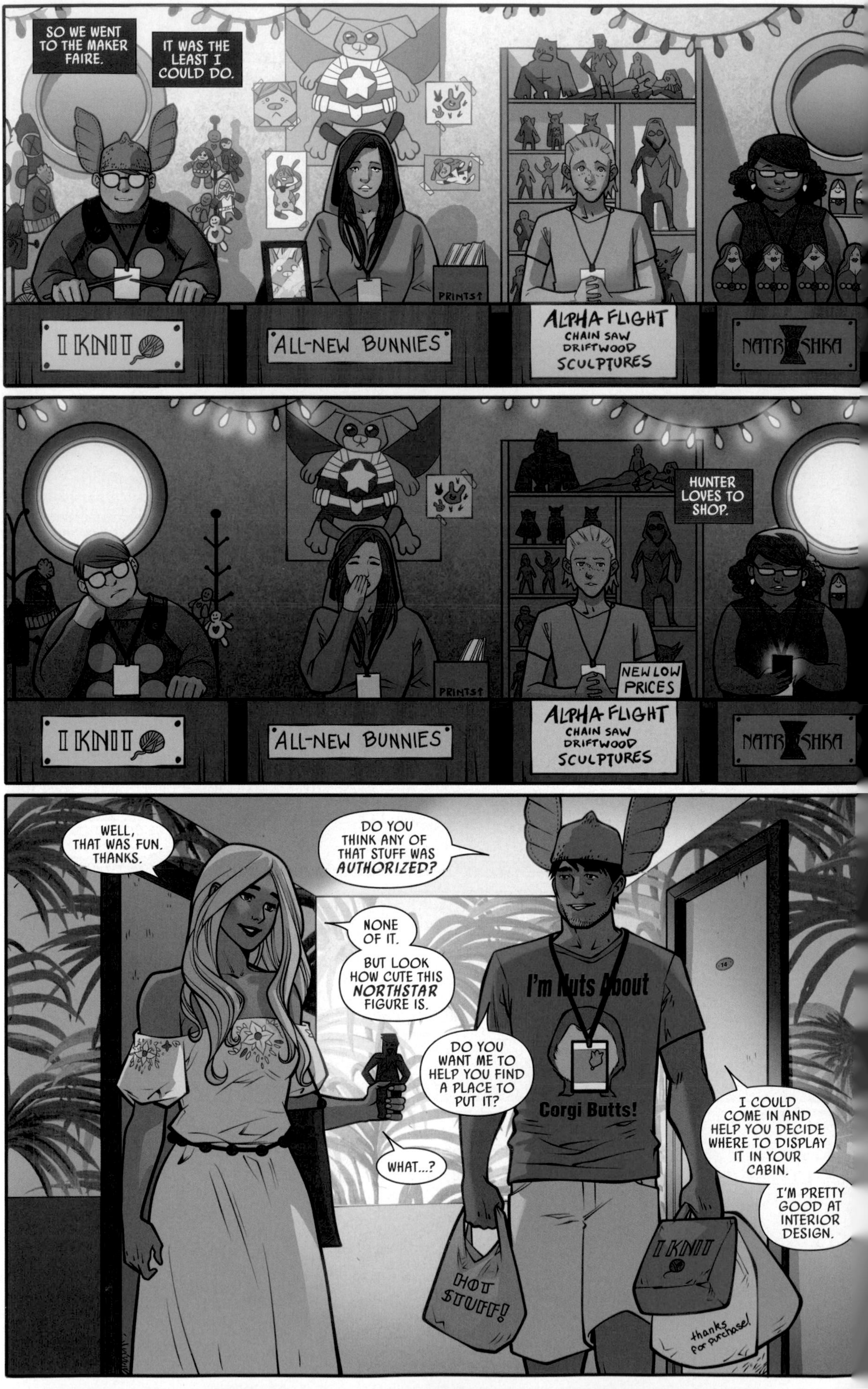

SO WE WENT TO THE MAKER FAIRE.
IT WAS THE LEAST I COULD DO.
I KNIT
ALL-NEW BUNNIES
PRINTS
ALPHA FLIGHT CHAIN SAW DRIFTWOOD SCULPTURES
NATRYOSHKA
HUNTER LOVES TO SHOP.
NEW LOW PRICES
I KNIT
ALL-NEW BUNNIES
PRINTS
ALPHA FLIGHT CHAIN SAW DRIFTWOOD SCULPTURES
NATRYOSHKA
WELL, THAT WAS FUN. THANKS.
DO YOU THINK ANY OF THAT STUFF WAS *AUTHORIZED?*
NONE OF IT.
BUT LOOK HOW CUTE THIS *NORTHSTAR* FIGURE IS.
I'm Nuts About Corgi Butts!
DO YOU WANT ME TO HELP YOU FIND A PLACE TO PUT IT?
WHAT...?
I COULD COME IN AND HELP YOU DECIDE WHERE TO DISPLAY IT IN YOUR CABIN.
I'M PRETTY GOOD AT INTERIOR DESIGN.
HOT STUFF!
I KNIT
thanks for purchase!

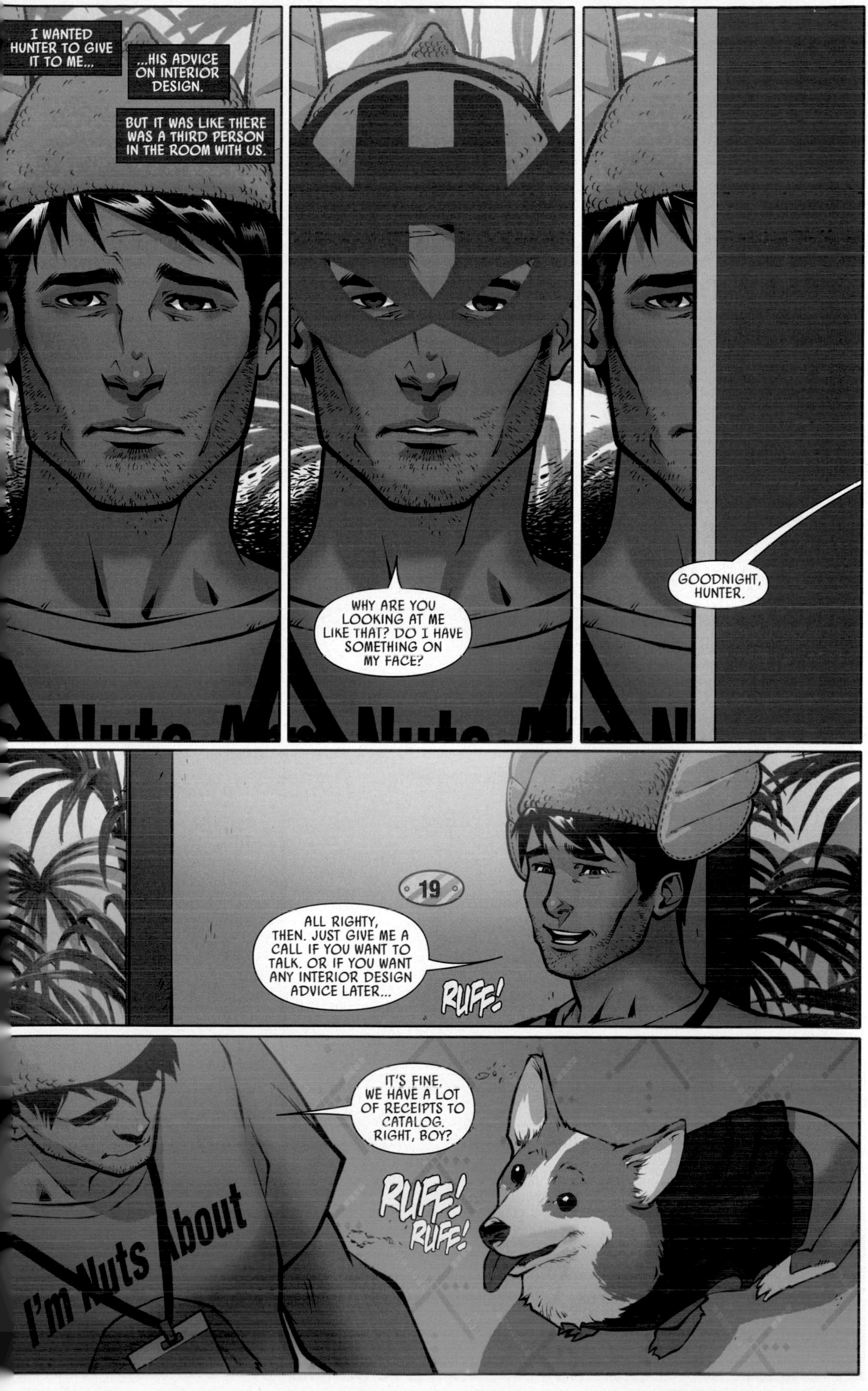
I WANTED HUNTER TO GIVE IT TO ME...
...HIS ADVICE ON INTERIOR DESIGN.
BUT IT WAS LIKE THERE WAS A THIRD PERSON IN THE ROOM WITH US.
WHY ARE YOU LOOKING AT ME LIKE THAT? DO I HAVE SOMETHING ON MY FACE?
GOODNIGHT, HUNTER.
19
ALL RIGHTY, THEN. JUST GIVE ME A CALL IF YOU WANT TO TALK. OR IF YOU WANT ANY INTERIOR DESIGN ADVICE LATER...
RUFF!
IT'S FINE, WE HAVE A LOT OF RECEIPTS TO CATALOG. RIGHT, BOY?
RUFF! RUFF!
I'm Nuts About

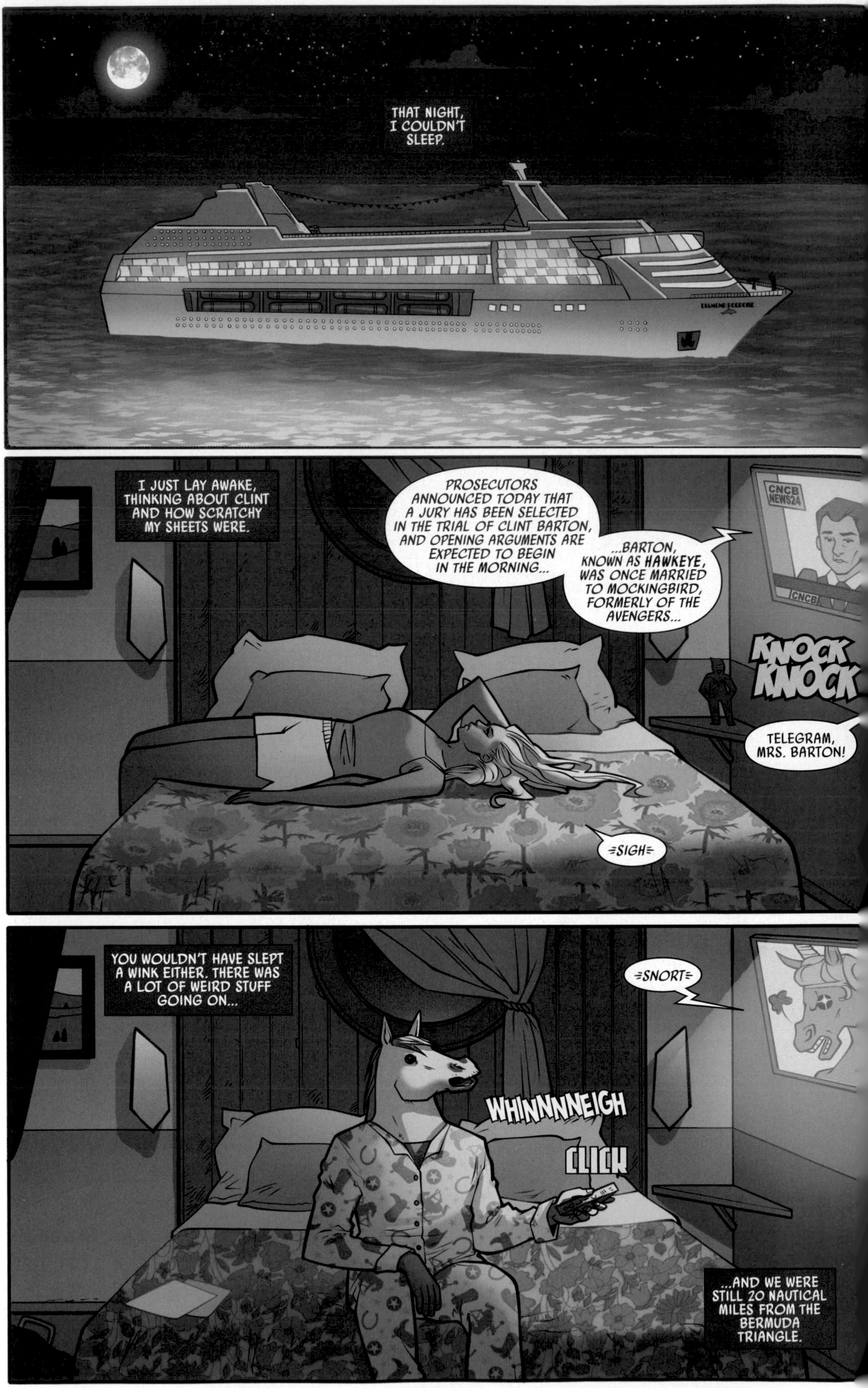
THAT NIGHT, I COULDN'T SLEEP.
I JUST LAY AWAKE, THINKING ABOUT CLINT AND HOW SCRATCHY MY SHEETS WERE.
PROSECUTORS ANNOUNCED TODAY THAT A JURY HAS BEEN SELECTED IN THE TRIAL OF CLINT BARTON, AND OPENING ARGUMENTS ARE EXPECTED TO BEGIN IN THE MORNING...
...BARTON, KNOWN AS HAWKEYE, WAS ONCE MARRIED TO MOCKINGBIRD, FORMERLY OF THE AVENGERS...
CNCB NEWS24
KNOCK KNOCK
TELEGRAM, MRS. BARTON!
SIGH
YOU WOULDN'T HAVE SLEPT A WINK EITHER. THERE WAS A LOT OF WEIRD STUFF GOING ON...
SNORT
WHINNNNEIGH
CLICK
...AND WE WERE STILL 20 NAUTICAL MILES FROM THE BERMUDA TRIANGLE.

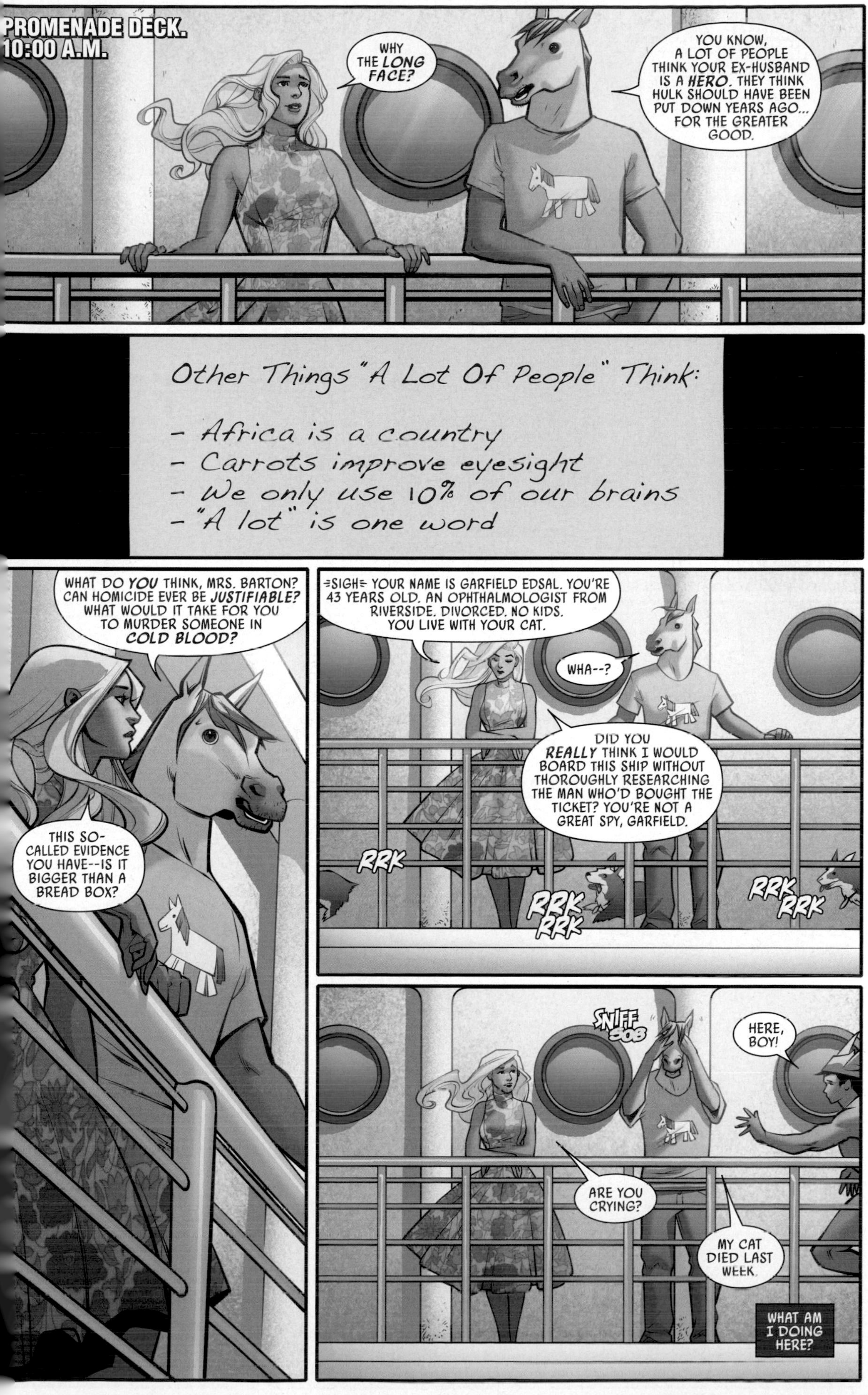
PROMENADE DECK. 10:00 A.M.
WHY THE LONG FACE?
YOU KNOW, A LOT OF PEOPLE THINK YOUR EX-HUSBAND IS A HERO. THEY THINK HULK SHOULD HAVE BEEN PUT DOWN YEARS AGO... FOR THE GREATER GOOD.
Other Things "A Lot Of People" Think:
- Africa is a country
- Carrots improve eyesight
- We only use 10% of our brains
- "A lot" is one word
WHAT DO YOU THINK, MRS. BARTON? CAN HOMICIDE EVER BE JUSTIFIABLE? WHAT WOULD IT TAKE FOR YOU TO MURDER SOMEONE IN COLD BLOOD?
THIS SO-CALLED EVIDENCE YOU HAVE--IS IT BIGGER THAN A BREAD BOX?
=SIGH= YOUR NAME IS GARFIELD EDSAL. YOU'RE 43 YEARS OLD. AN OPHTHALMOLOGIST FROM RIVERSIDE. DIVORCED. NO KIDS. YOU LIVE WITH YOUR CAT.
WHA--?
DID YOU REALLY THINK I WOULD BOARD THIS SHIP WITHOUT THOROUGHLY RESEARCHING THE MAN WHO'D BOUGHT THE TICKET? YOU'RE NOT A GREAT SPY, GARFIELD.
RRK
RRK RRK
RRK RRK
SNIFF SOB
HERE, BOY!
ARE YOU CRYING?
MY CAT DIED LAST WEEK.
WHAT AM I DOING HERE?

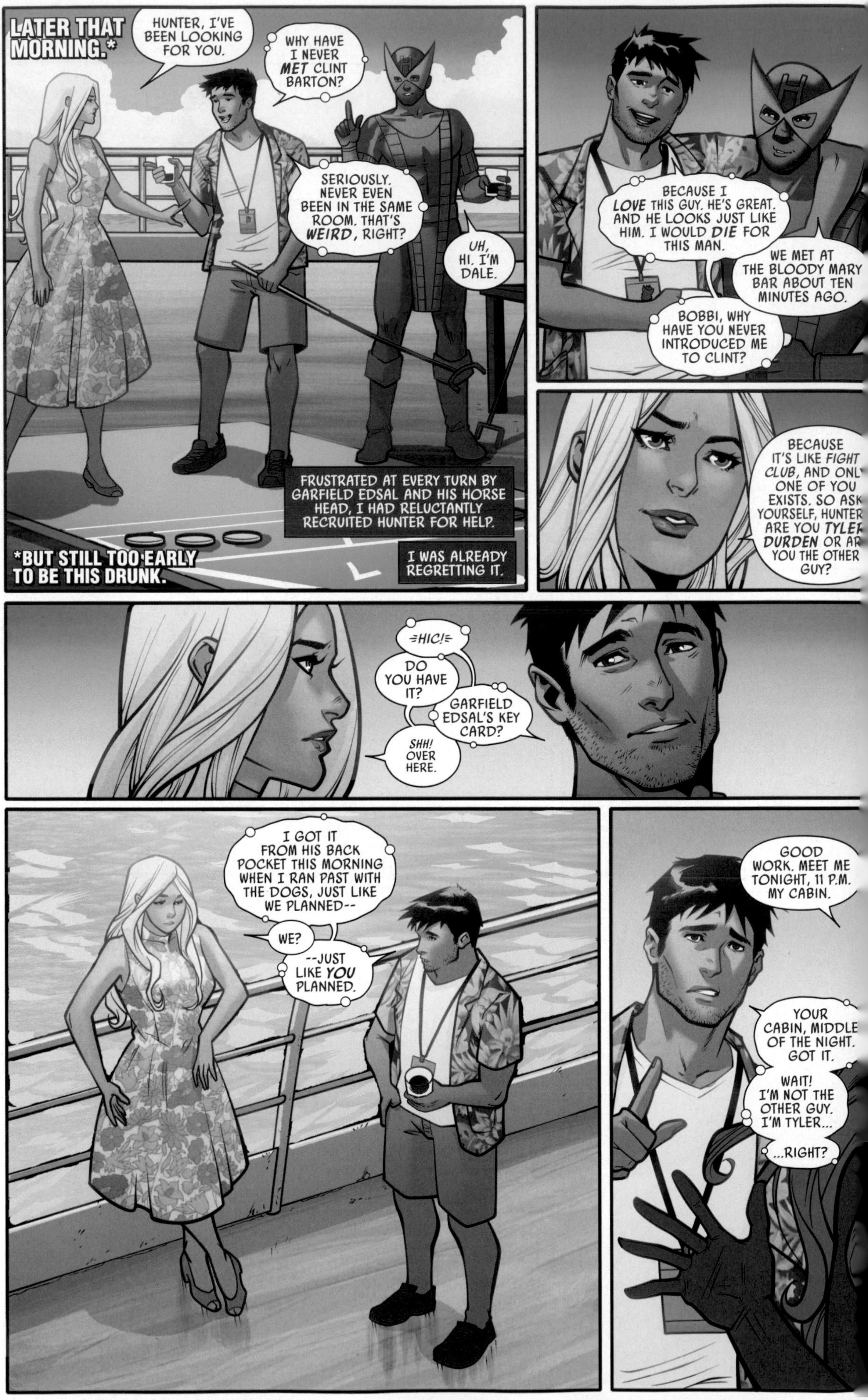
LATER THAT MORNING.*
HUNTER, I'VE BEEN LOOKING FOR YOU.
WHY HAVE I NEVER MET CLINT BARTON?
SERIOUSLY. NEVER EVEN BEEN IN THE SAME ROOM. THAT'S WEIRD, RIGHT?
UH, HI. I'M DALE.
FRUSTRATED AT EVERY TURN BY GARFIELD EDSAL AND HIS HORSE HEAD, I HAD RELUCTANTLY RECRUITED HUNTER FOR HELP.
I WAS ALREADY REGRETTING IT.
*BUT STILL TOO EARLY TO BE THIS DRUNK.
BECAUSE I LOVE THIS GUY. HE'S GREAT. AND HE LOOKS JUST LIKE HIM. I WOULD DIE FOR THIS MAN.
WE MET AT THE BLOODY MARY BAR ABOUT TEN MINUTES AGO.
BOBBI, WHY HAVE YOU NEVER INTRODUCED ME TO CLINT?
BECAUSE IT'S LIKE FIGHT CLUB, AND ONLY ONE OF YOU EXISTS. SO ASK YOURSELF, HUNTER. ARE YOU TYLER DURDEN OR ARE YOU THE OTHER GUY?
HIC!
DO YOU HAVE IT?
GARFIELD EDSAL'S KEY CARD?
SHH! OVER HERE.
I GOT IT FROM HIS BACK POCKET THIS MORNING WHEN I RAN PAST WITH THE DOGS, JUST LIKE WE PLANNED--
WE?
--JUST LIKE YOU PLANNED.
GOOD WORK. MEET ME TONIGHT, 11 P.M. MY CABIN.
YOUR CABIN, MIDDLE OF THE NIGHT. GOT IT.
WAIT! I'M NOT THE OTHER GUY. I'M TYLER...
...RIGHT?

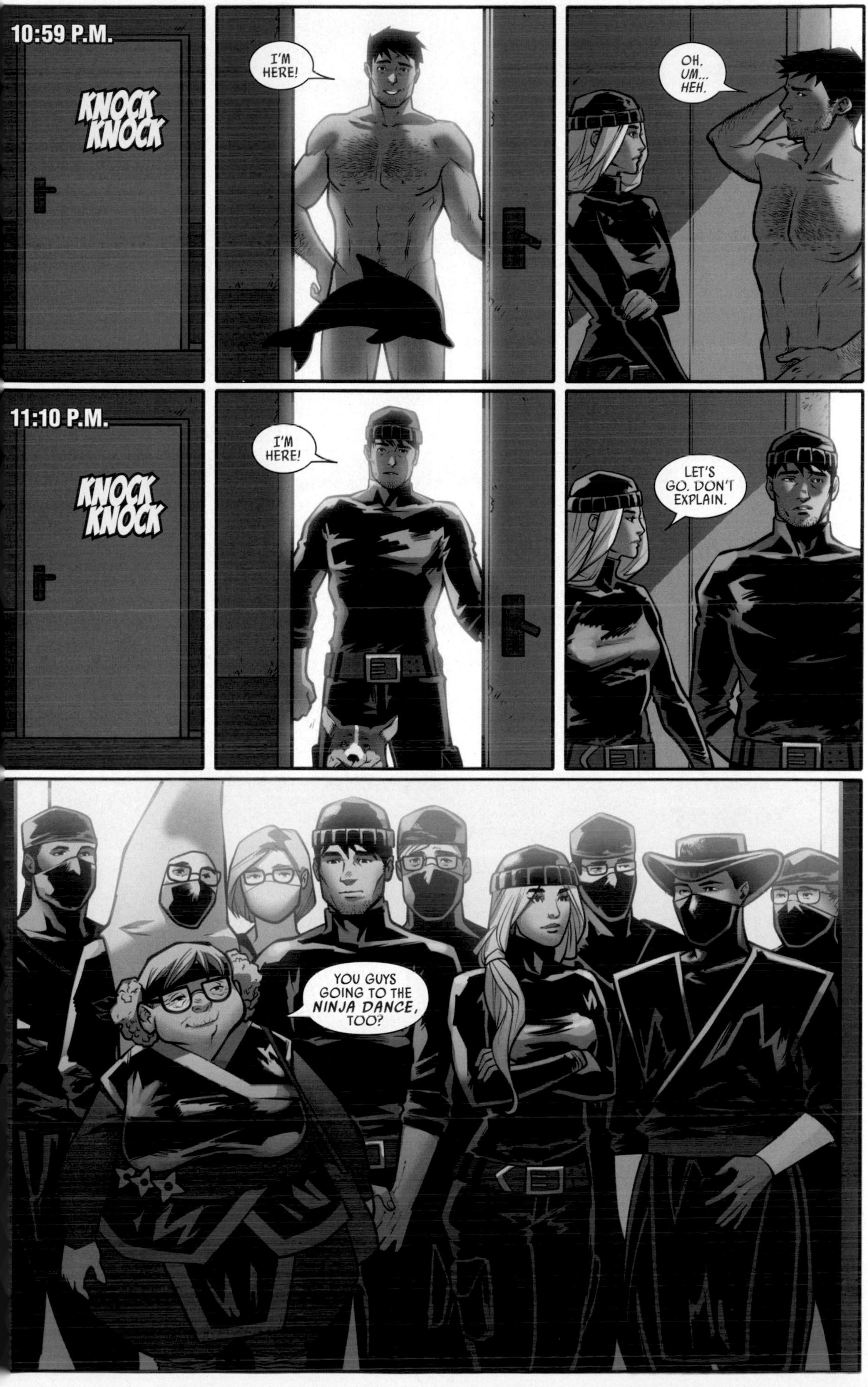
10:59 P.M.
KNOCK KNOCK
I'M HERE!
OH. UM... HEH.
11:10 P.M.
KNOCK KNOCK
I'M HERE!
LET'S GO. DON'T EXPLAIN.
YOU GUYS GOING TO THE NINJA DANCE, TOO?

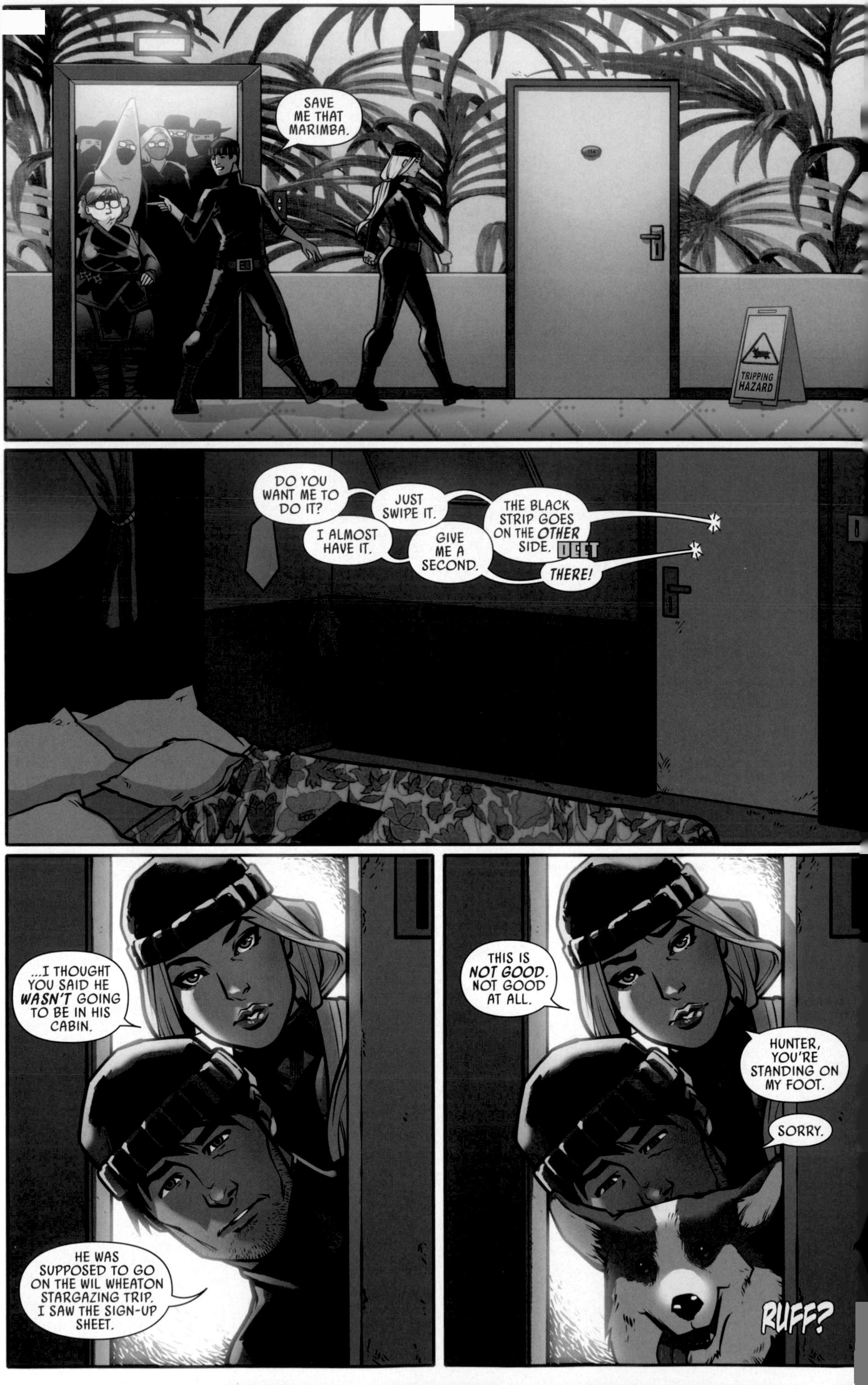
SAVE ME THAT MARIMBA.
TRIPPING HAZARD
DO YOU WANT ME TO DO IT?
I ALMOST HAVE IT.
JUST SWIPE IT.
GIVE ME A SECOND.
THE BLACK STRIP GOES ON THE OTHER SIDE.
DEET
THERE!
...I THOUGHT YOU SAID HE WASN'T GOING TO BE IN HIS CABIN.
HE WAS SUPPOSED TO GO ON THE WIL WHEATON STARGAZING TRIP. I SAW THE SIGN-UP SHEET.
THIS IS NOT GOOD. NOT GOOD AT ALL.
HUNTER, YOU'RE STANDING ON MY FOOT.
SORRY.
RUFF?

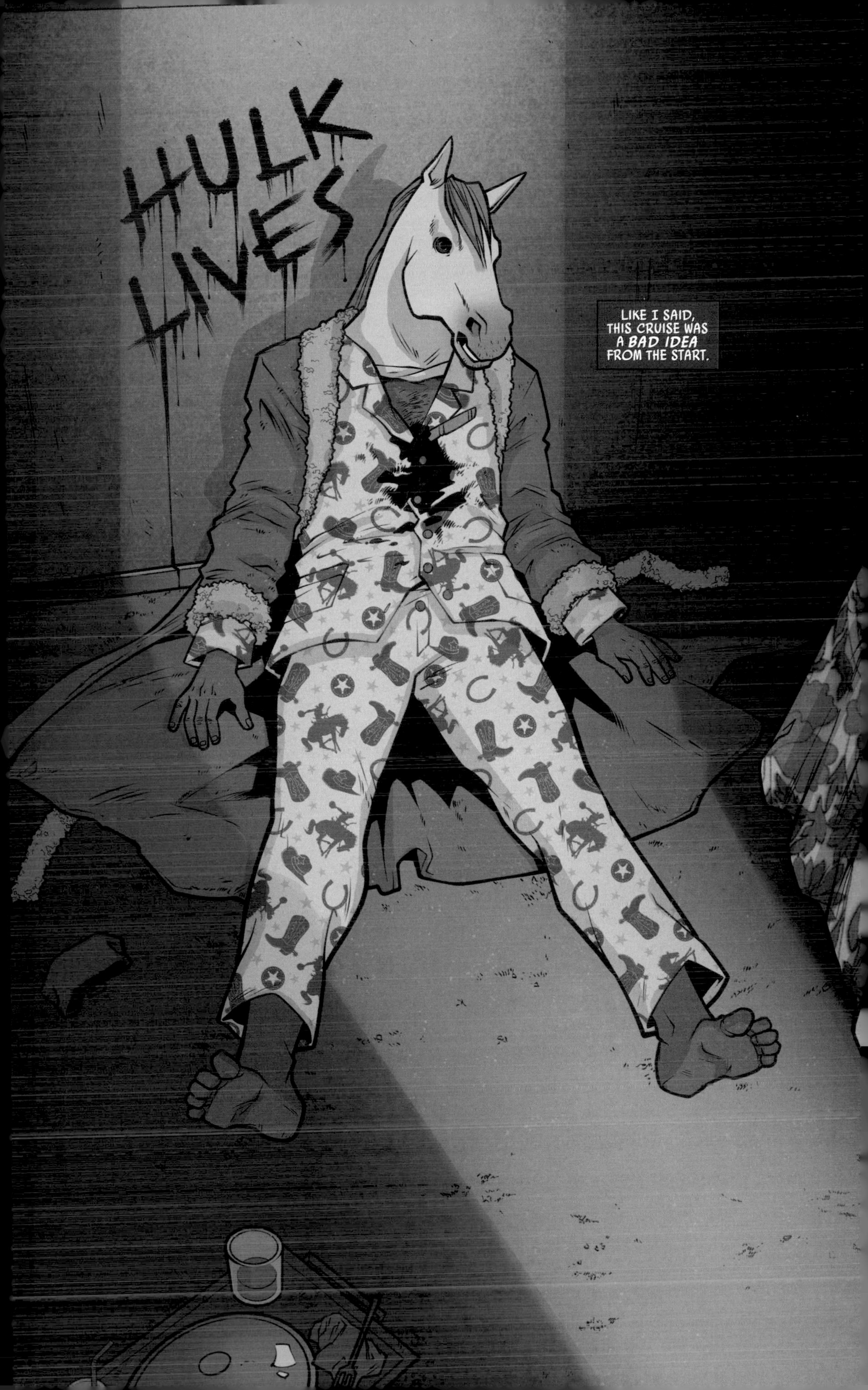
HULK LIVES
LIKE I SAID, THIS CRUISE WAS A *BAD IDEA* FROM THE START.

DE-STRESS WITH THESE DAILY YOGA POSES

BY BOBBI MORSE

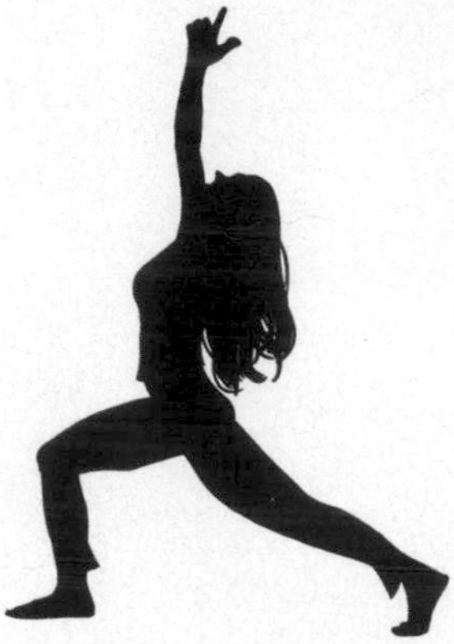

CHARLIE'S ANGEL

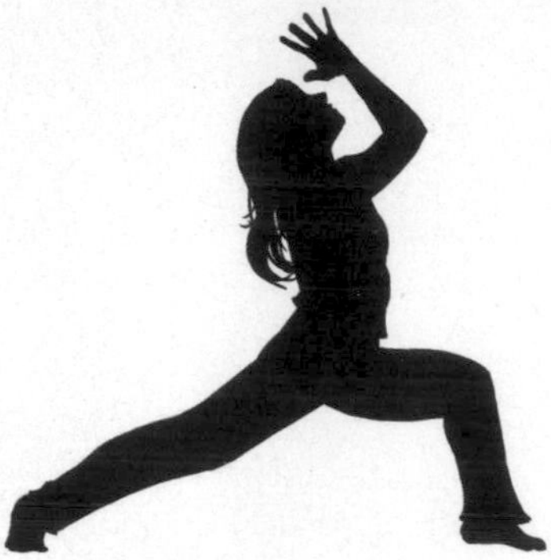

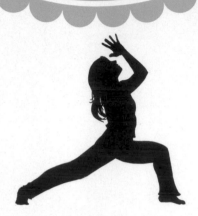

MY EX-HUSBAND IS ON TRIAL FOR MURDER

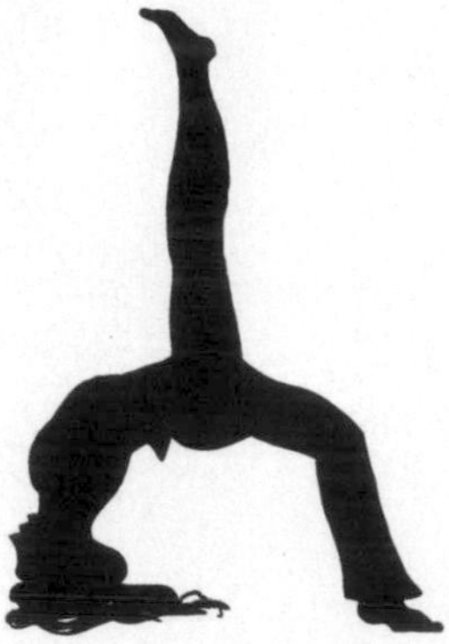

UPSIDE DOWN MARTINI

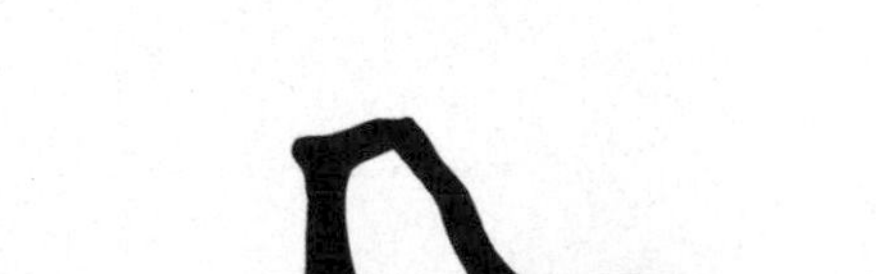

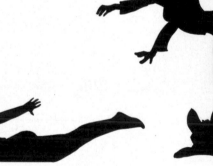

DIAMOND PORPOISE

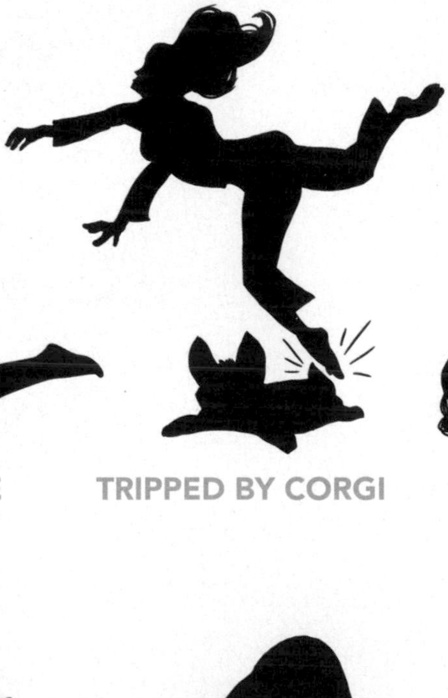

TRIPPED BY CORGI

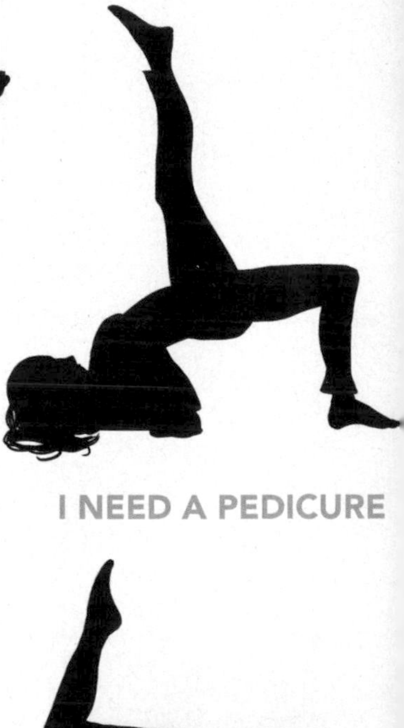

I NEED A PEDICURE

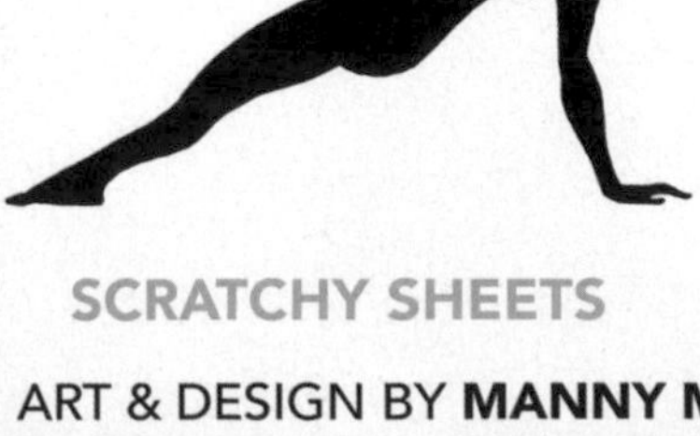

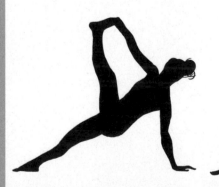

SCRATCHY SHEETS

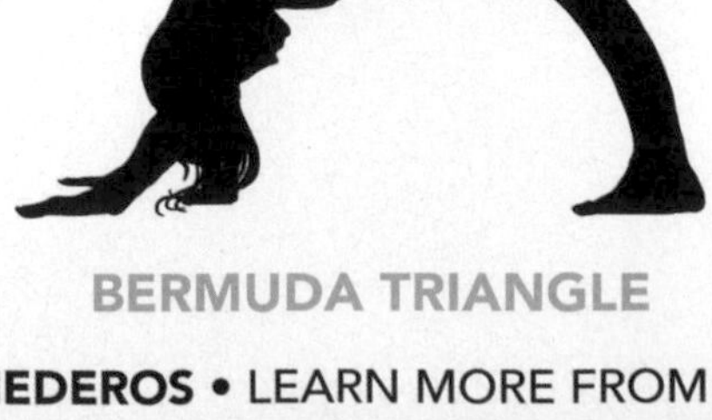

BERMUDA TRIANGLE

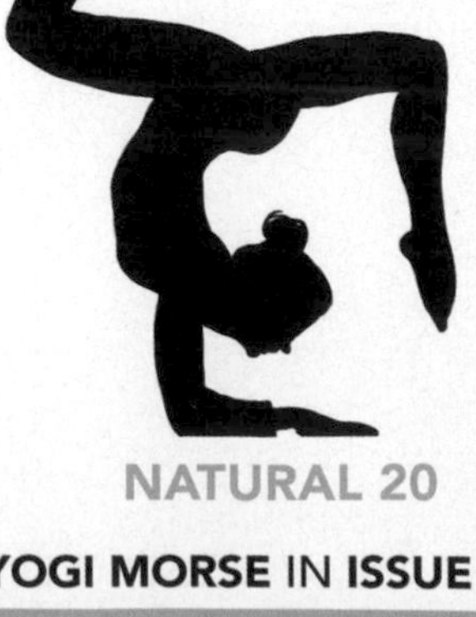

NATURAL 20

ART & DESIGN BY **MANNY MEDEROS** • LEARN MORE FROM **YOGI MORSE** IN **ISSUE #7**

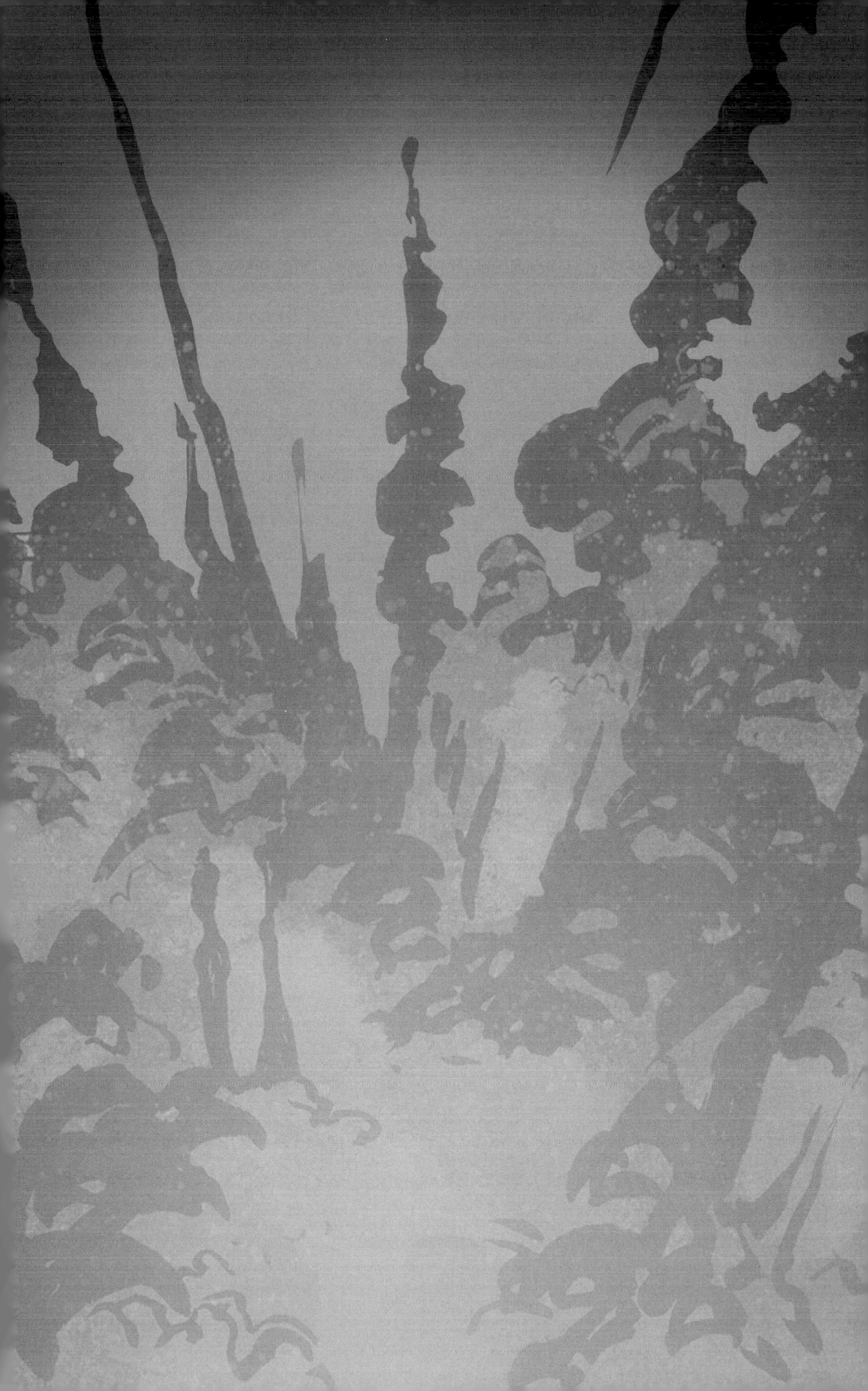

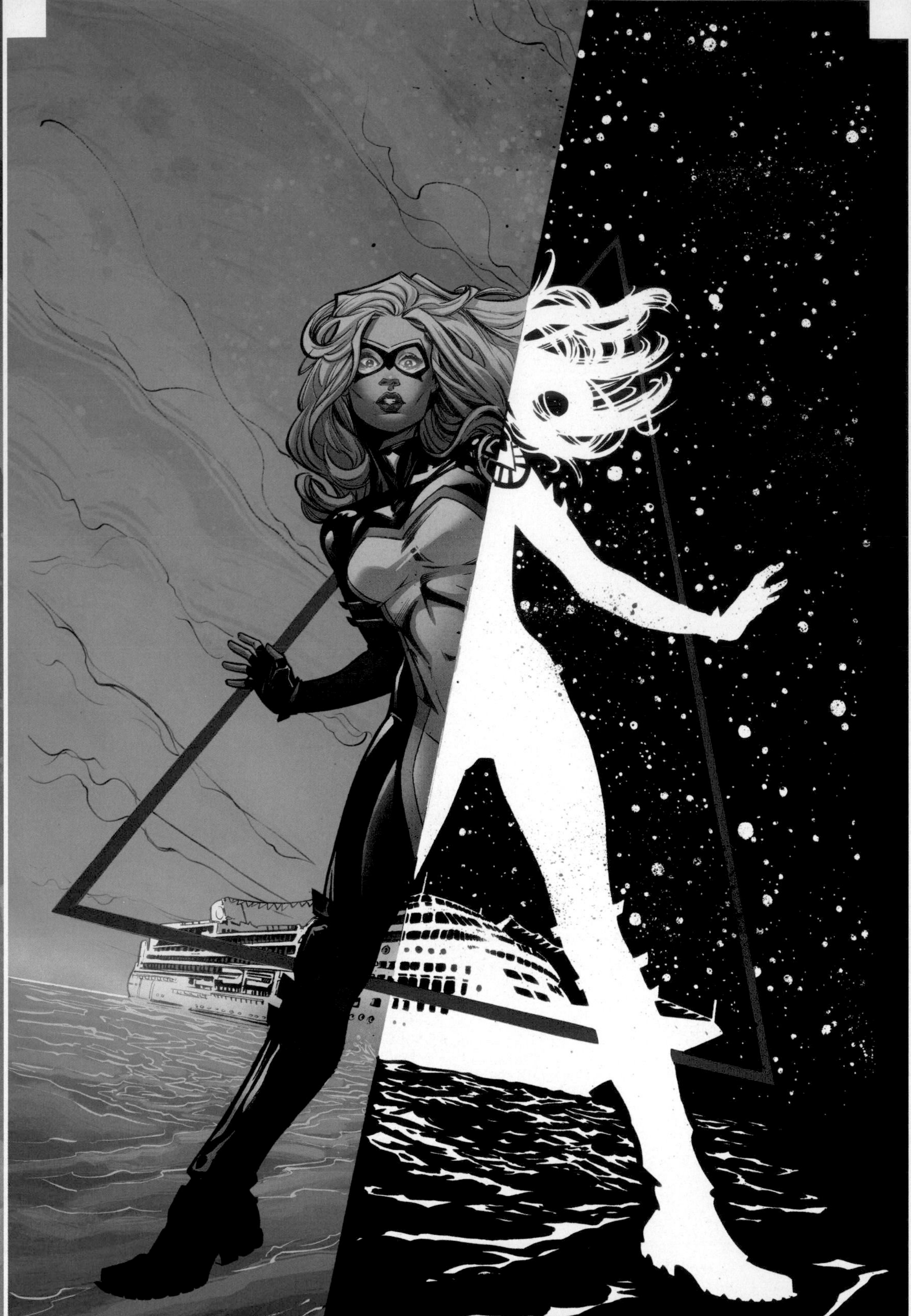

7

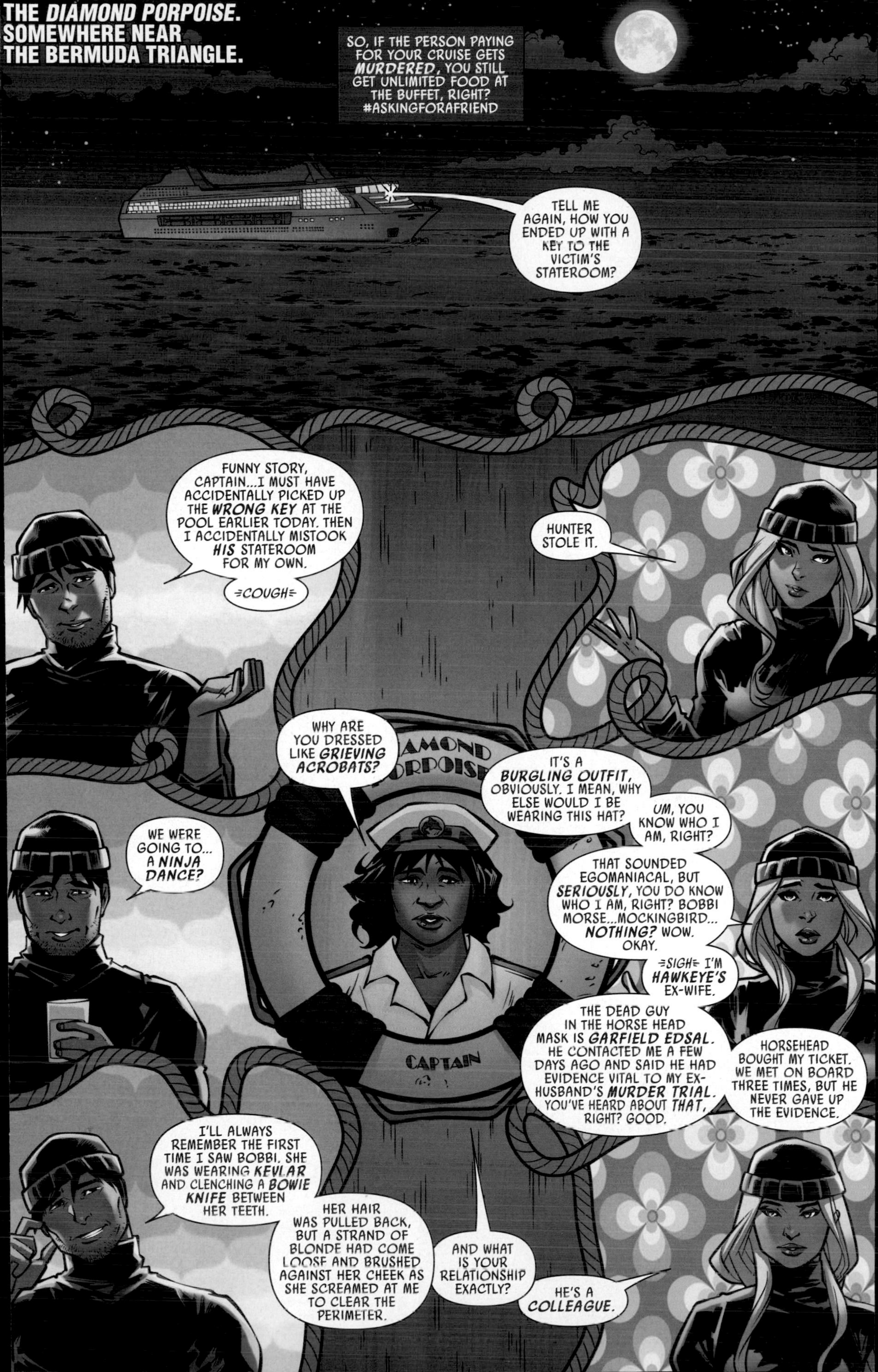
THE DIAMOND PORPOISE. SOMEWHERE NEAR THE BERMUDA TRIANGLE.
SO, IF THE PERSON PAYING FOR YOUR CRUISE GETS MURDERED, YOU STILL GET UNLIMITED FOOD AT THE BUFFET, RIGHT? #ASKINGFORAFRIEND
TELL ME AGAIN, HOW YOU ENDED UP WITH A KEY TO THE VICTIM'S STATEROOM?
FUNNY STORY, CAPTAIN...I MUST HAVE ACCIDENTALLY PICKED UP THE WRONG KEY AT THE POOL EARLIER TODAY. THEN I ACCIDENTALLY MISTOOK HIS STATEROOM FOR MY OWN.
=COUGH=
HUNTER STOLE IT.
WHY ARE YOU DRESSED LIKE GRIEVING ACROBATS?
DIAMOND PORPOISE
IT'S A BURGLING OUTFIT, OBVIOUSLY. I MEAN, WHY ELSE WOULD I BE WEARING THIS HAT?
WE WERE GOING TO... A NINJA DANCE?
UM, YOU KNOW WHO I AM, RIGHT?
THAT SOUNDED EGOMANIACAL, BUT SERIOUSLY, YOU DO KNOW WHO I AM, RIGHT? BOBBI MORSE...MOCKINGBIRD... NOTHING? WOW. OKAY.
=SIGH= I'M HAWKEYE'S EX-WIFE.
THE DEAD GUY IN THE HORSE HEAD MASK IS GARFIELD EDSAL. HE CONTACTED ME A FEW DAYS AGO AND SAID HE HAD EVIDENCE VITAL TO MY EX-HUSBAND'S MURDER TRIAL. YOU'VE HEARD ABOUT THAT, RIGHT? GOOD.
HORSEHEAD BOUGHT MY TICKET. WE MET ON BOARD THREE TIMES, BUT HE NEVER GAVE UP THE EVIDENCE.
CAPTAIN
I'LL ALWAYS REMEMBER THE FIRST TIME I SAW BOBBI. SHE WAS WEARING KEVLAR AND CLENCHING A BOWIE KNIFE BETWEEN HER TEETH.
HER HAIR WAS PULLED BACK, BUT A STRAND OF BLONDE HAD COME LOOSE AND BRUSHED AGAINST HER CHEEK AS SHE SCREAMED AT ME TO CLEAR THE PERIMETER.
AND WHAT IS YOUR RELATIONSHIP EXACTLY?
HE'S A COLLEAGUE.

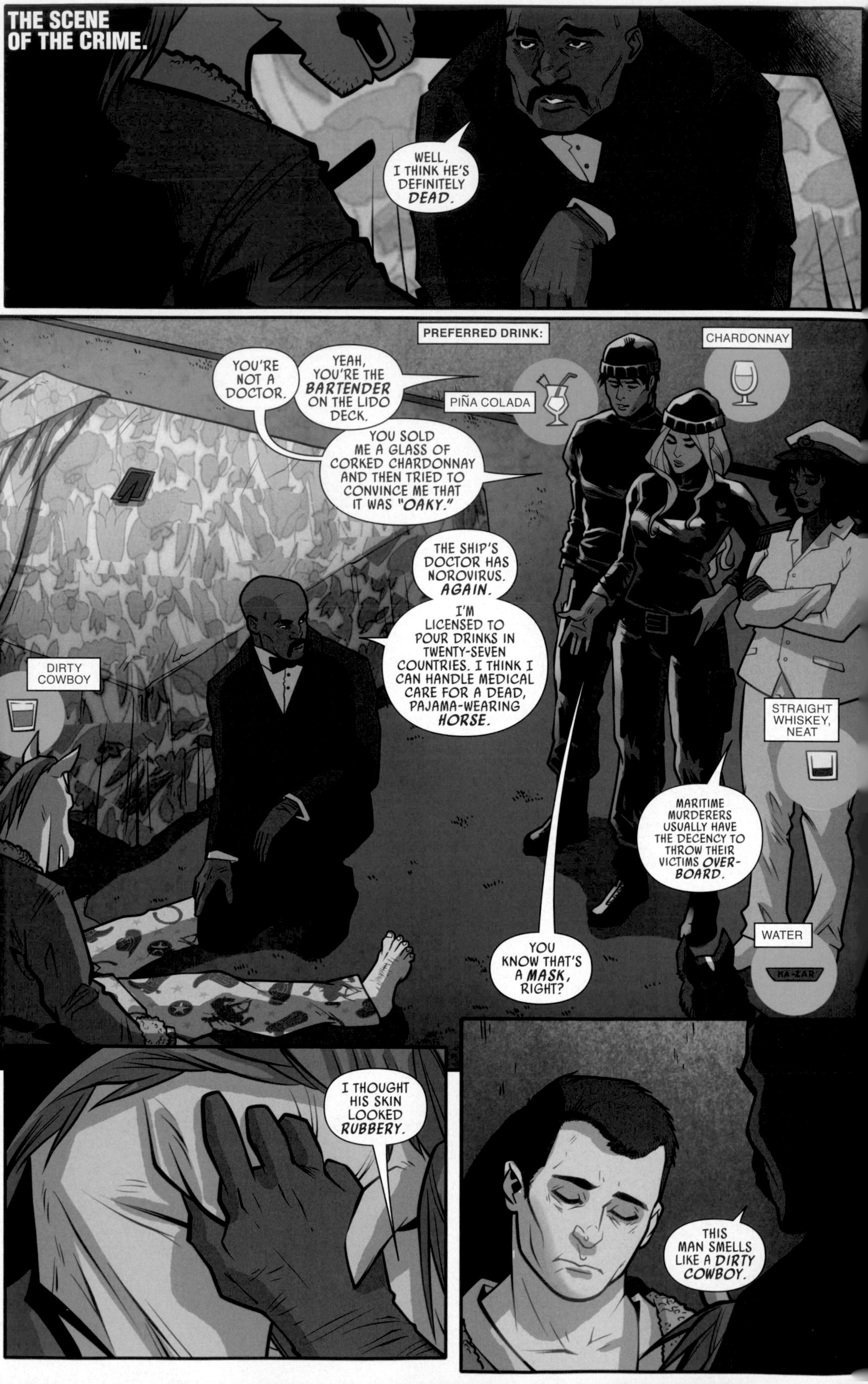
THE SCENE OF THE CRIME.
WELL, I THINK HE'S DEFINITELY DEAD.
PREFERRED DRINK:
YOU'RE NOT A DOCTOR.
YEAH, YOU'RE THE BARTENDER ON THE LIDO DECK.
YOU SOLD ME A GLASS OF CORKED CHARDONNAY AND THEN TRIED TO CONVINCE ME THAT IT WAS "OAKY."
PIÑA COLADA
CHARDONNAY
THE SHIP'S DOCTOR HAS NOROVIRUS. AGAIN.
I'M LICENSED TO POUR DRINKS IN TWENTY-SEVEN COUNTRIES. I THINK I CAN HANDLE MEDICAL CARE FOR A DEAD, PAJAMA-WEARING HORSE.
DIRTY COWBOY
STRAIGHT WHISKEY, NEAT
MARITIME MURDERERS USUALLY HAVE THE DECENCY TO THROW THEIR VICTIMS OVER-BOARD.
WATER
KA-ZAR
YOU KNOW THAT'S A MASK, RIGHT?
I THOUGHT HIS SKIN LOOKED RUBBERY.
THIS MAN SMELLS LIKE A DIRTY COWBOY.

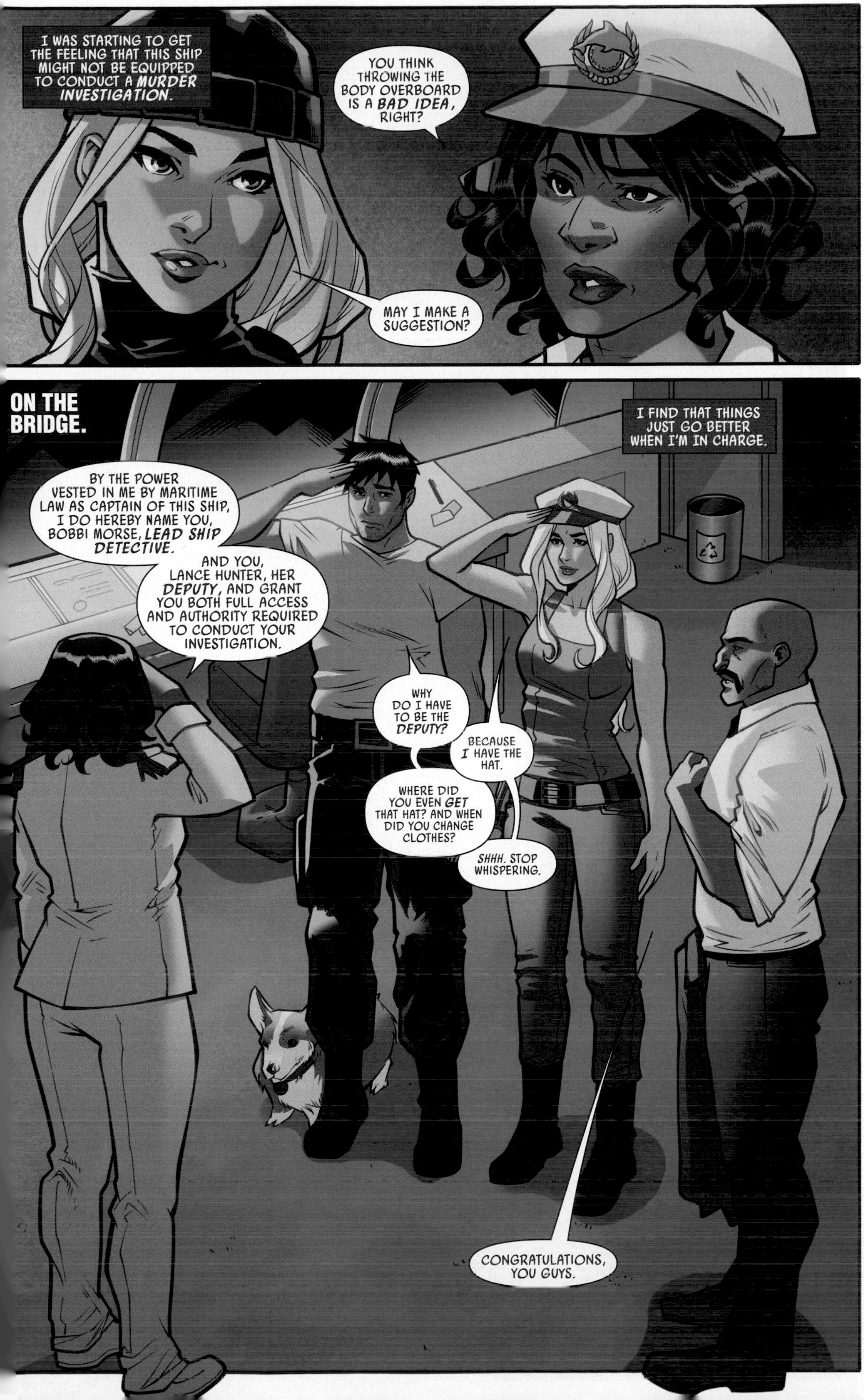
I WAS STARTING TO GET THE FEELING THAT THIS SHIP MIGHT NOT BE EQUIPPED TO CONDUCT A MURDER INVESTIGATION.
YOU THINK THROWING THE BODY OVERBOARD IS A BAD IDEA, RIGHT?
MAY I MAKE A SUGGESTION?
ON THE BRIDGE.
I FIND THAT THINGS JUST GO BETTER WHEN I'M IN CHARGE.
BY THE POWER VESTED IN ME BY MARITIME LAW AS CAPTAIN OF THIS SHIP, I DO HEREBY NAME YOU, BOBBI MORSE, LEAD SHIP DETECTIVE.
AND YOU, LANCE HUNTER, HER DEPUTY, AND GRANT YOU BOTH FULL ACCESS AND AUTHORITY REQUIRED TO CONDUCT YOUR INVESTIGATION.
WHY DO I HAVE TO BE THE DEPUTY?
BECAUSE I HAVE THE HAT.
WHERE DID YOU EVEN GET THAT HAT? AND WHEN DID YOU CHANGE CLOTHES?
SHHH. STOP WHISPERING.
CONGRATULATIONS, YOU GUYS.

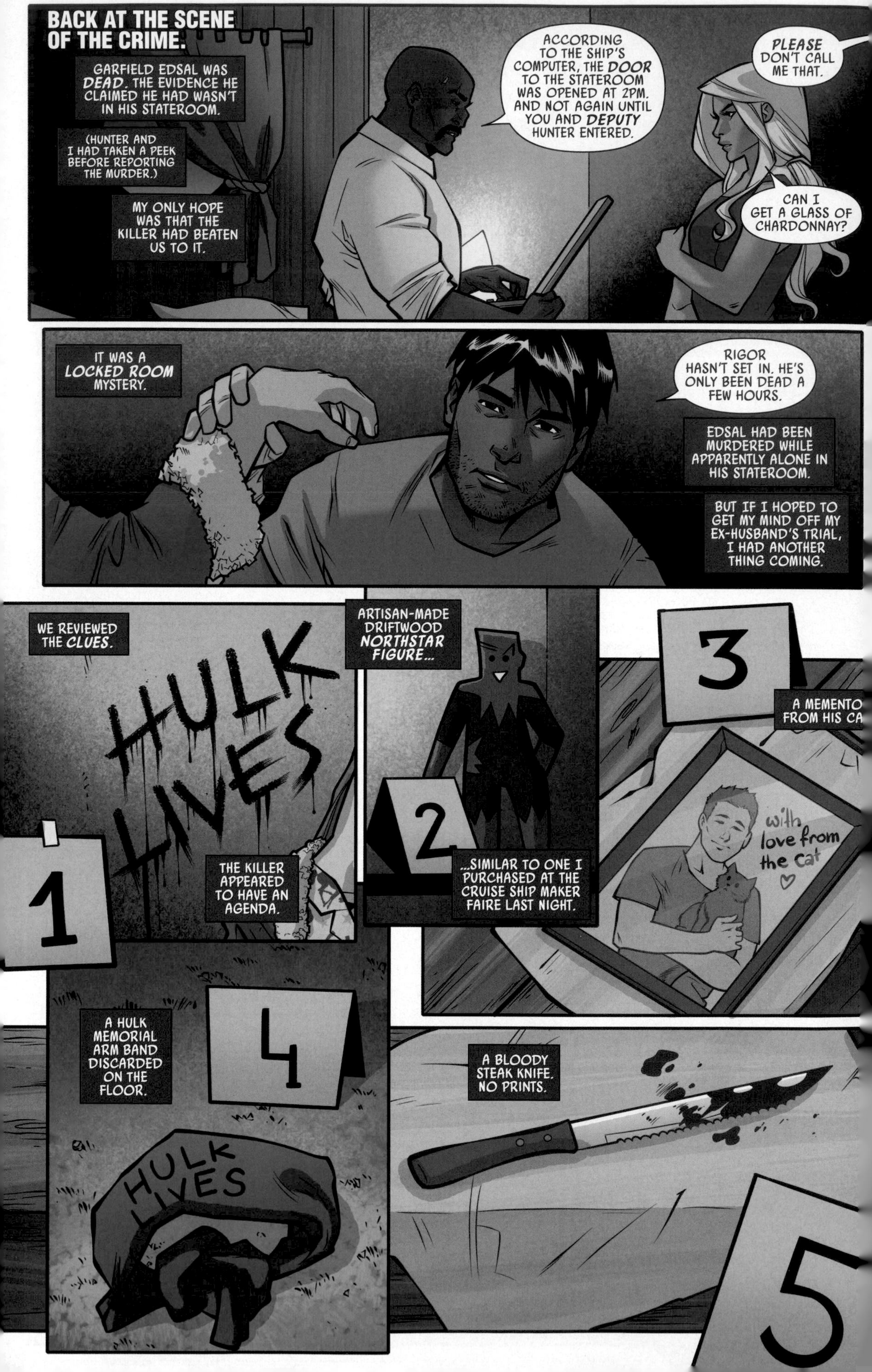
BACK AT THE SCENE OF THE CRIME.
GARFIELD EDSAL WAS DEAD. THE EVIDENCE HE CLAIMED HE HAD WASN'T IN HIS STATEROOM.
(HUNTER AND I HAD TAKEN A PEEK BEFORE REPORTING THE MURDER.)
MY ONLY HOPE WAS THAT THE KILLER HAD BEATEN US TO IT.
ACCORDING TO THE SHIP'S COMPUTER, THE DOOR TO THE STATEROOM WAS OPENED AT 2PM. AND NOT AGAIN UNTIL YOU AND DEPUTY HUNTER ENTERED.
PLEASE DON'T CALL ME THAT.
CAN I GET A GLASS OF CHARDONNAY?
IT WAS A LOCKED ROOM MYSTERY.
RIGOR HASN'T SET IN. HE'S ONLY BEEN DEAD A FEW HOURS.
EDSAL HAD BEEN MURDERED WHILE APPARENTLY ALONE IN HIS STATEROOM.
BUT IF I HOPED TO GET MY MIND OFF MY EX-HUSBAND'S TRIAL, I HAD ANOTHER THING COMING.
WE REVIEWED THE CLUES.
HULK LIVES
1
THE KILLER APPEARED TO HAVE AN AGENDA.
ARTISAN-MADE DRIFTWOOD NORTHSTAR FIGURE...
2
...SIMILAR TO ONE I PURCHASED AT THE CRUISE SHIP MAKER FAIRE LAST NIGHT.
3
A MEMENTO FROM HIS CA
with love from the cat
A HULK MEMORIAL ARM BAND DISCARDED ON THE FLOOR.
4
HULK LIVES
A BLOODY STEAK KNIFE. NO PRINTS.
5

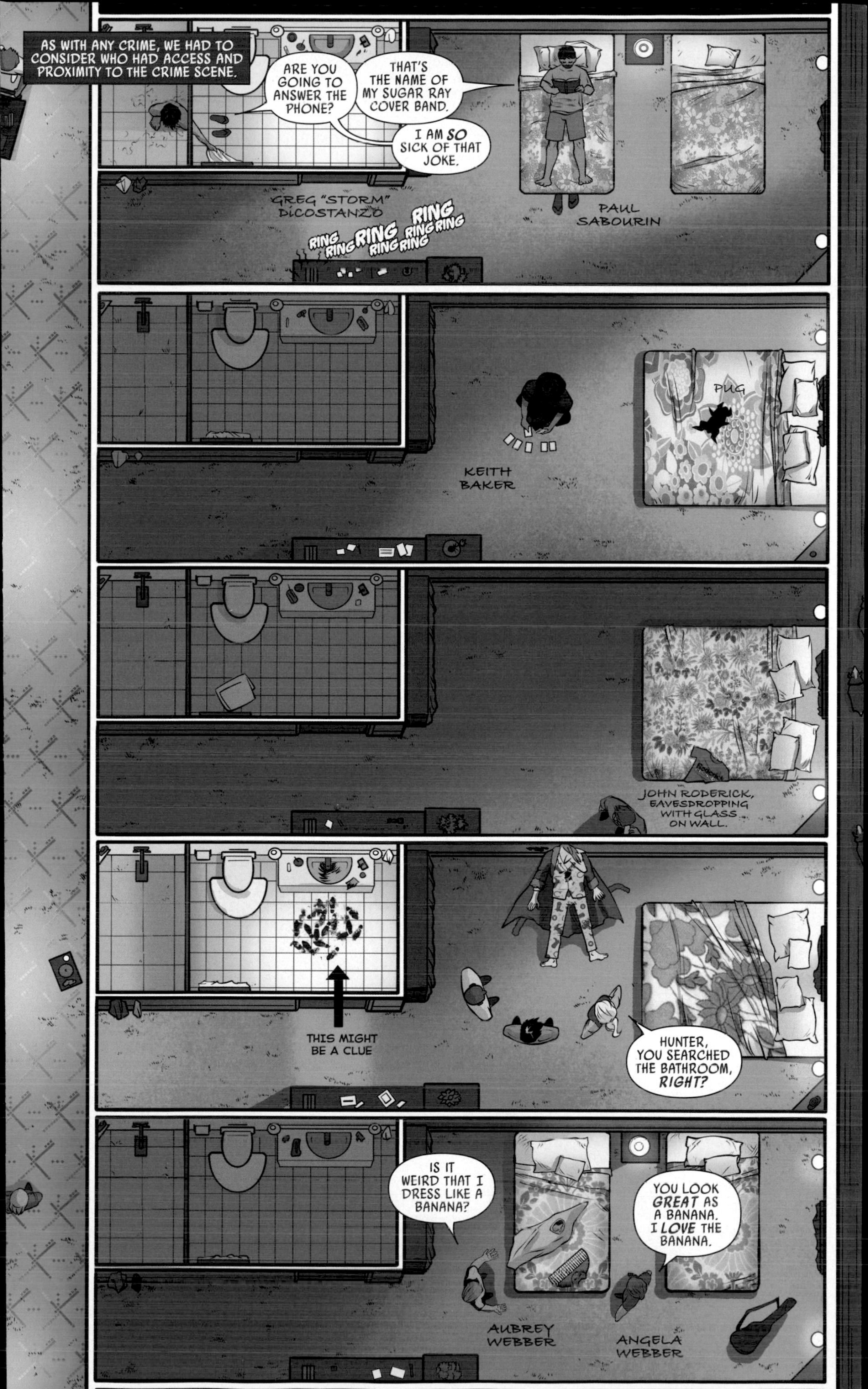
AS WITH ANY CRIME, WE HAD TO CONSIDER WHO HAD ACCESS AND PROXIMITY TO THE CRIME SCENE.
ARE YOU GOING TO ANSWER THE PHONE?
THAT'S THE NAME OF MY SUGAR RAY COVER BAND.
I AM SO SICK OF THAT JOKE.
GREG "STORM" DICOSTANZO
PAUL SABOURIN
RING RING RING RING RING RING RING RING
PUG
KEITH BAKER
JOHN RODERICK, EAVESDROPPING WITH GLASS ON WALL.
THIS MIGHT BE A CLUE
HUNTER, YOU SEARCHED THE BATHROOM, RIGHT?
IS IT WEIRD THAT I DRESS LIKE A BANANA?
YOU LOOK GREAT AS A BANANA. I LOVE THE BANANA.
AUBREY WEBBER
ANGELA WEBBER

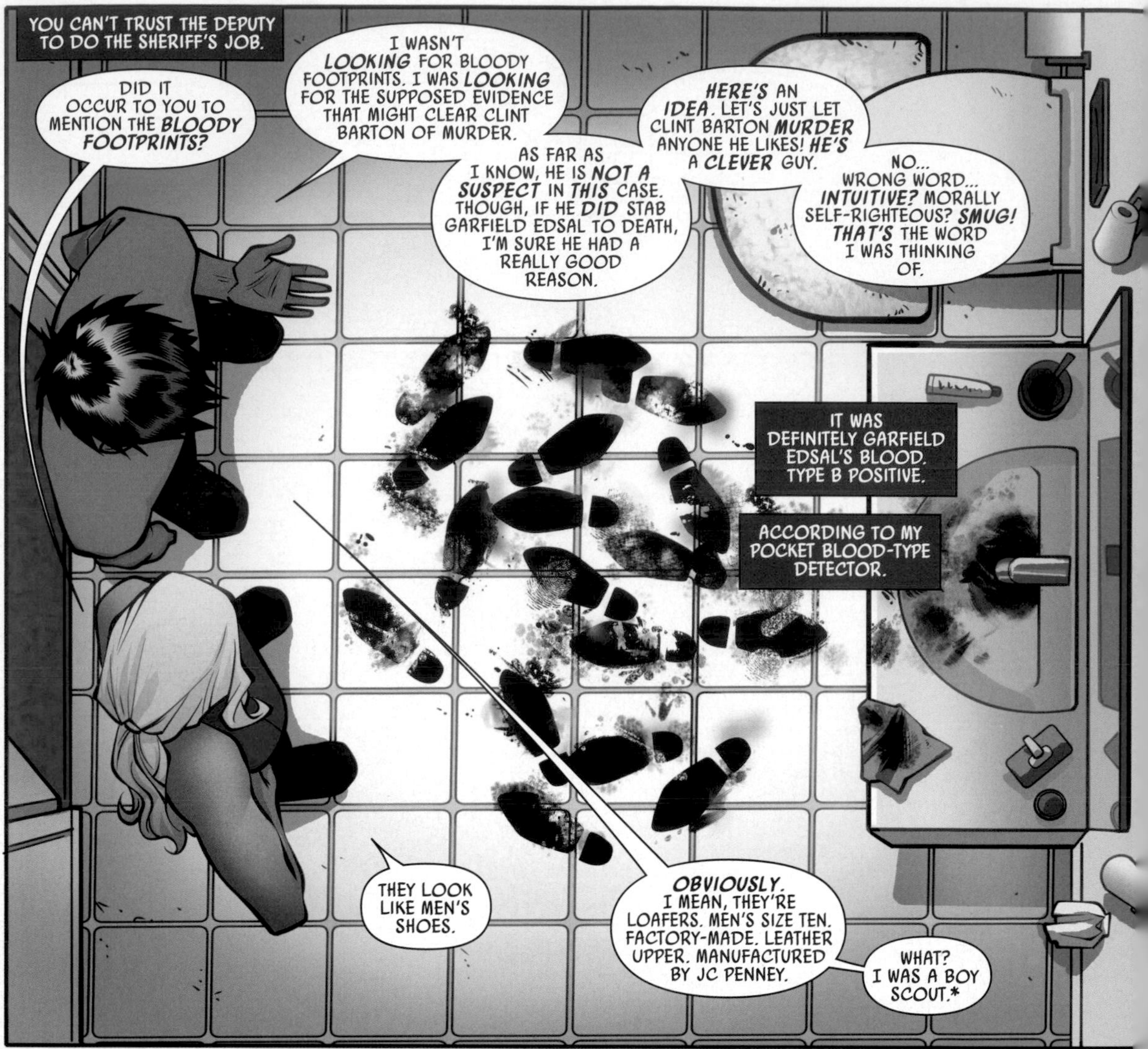
YOU CAN'T TRUST THE DEPUTY TO DO THE SHERIFF'S JOB.
DID IT OCCUR TO YOU TO MENTION THE BLOODY FOOTPRINTS?
I WASN'T LOOKING FOR BLOODY FOOTPRINTS. I WAS LOOKING FOR THE SUPPOSED EVIDENCE THAT MIGHT CLEAR CLINT BARTON OF MURDER.
AS FAR AS I KNOW, HE IS NOT A SUSPECT IN THIS CASE. THOUGH, IF HE DID STAB GARFIELD EDSAL TO DEATH, I'M SURE HE HAD A REALLY GOOD REASON.
HERE'S AN IDEA. LET'S JUST LET CLINT BARTON MURDER ANYONE HE LIKES! HE'S A CLEVER GUY.
NO... WRONG WORD... INTUITIVE? MORALLY SELF-RIGHTEOUS? SMUG! THAT'S THE WORD I WAS THINKING OF.
IT WAS DEFINITELY GARFIELD EDSAL'S BLOOD. TYPE B POSITIVE.
ACCORDING TO MY POCKET BLOOD-TYPE DETECTOR.
THEY LOOK LIKE MEN'S SHOES.
OBVIOUSLY. I MEAN, THEY'RE LOAFERS. MEN'S SIZE TEN. FACTORY-MADE. LEATHER UPPER. MANUFACTURED BY JC PENNEY.
WHAT? I WAS A BOY SCOUT.*

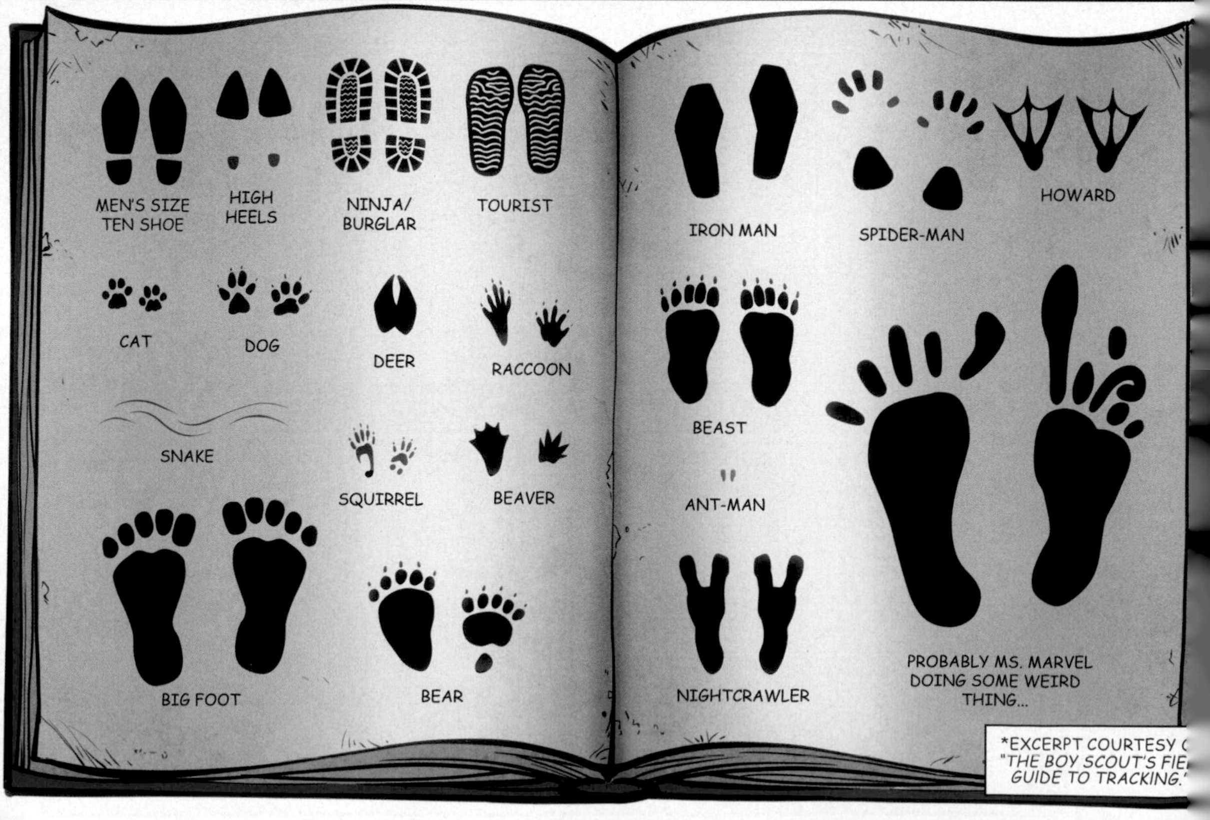
MEN'S SIZE TEN SHOE
HIGH HEELS
NINJA/ BURGLAR
TOURIST
IRON MAN
SPIDER-MAN
HOWARD
CAT
DOG
DEER
RACCOON
BEAST
SNAKE
SQUIRREL
BEAVER
ANT-MAN
BIG FOOT
BEAR
NIGHTCRAWLER
PROBABLY MS. MARVEL DOING SOME WEIRD THING...
*EXCERPT COURTESY O
"THE BOY SCOUT'S FIE
GUIDE TO TRACKING."

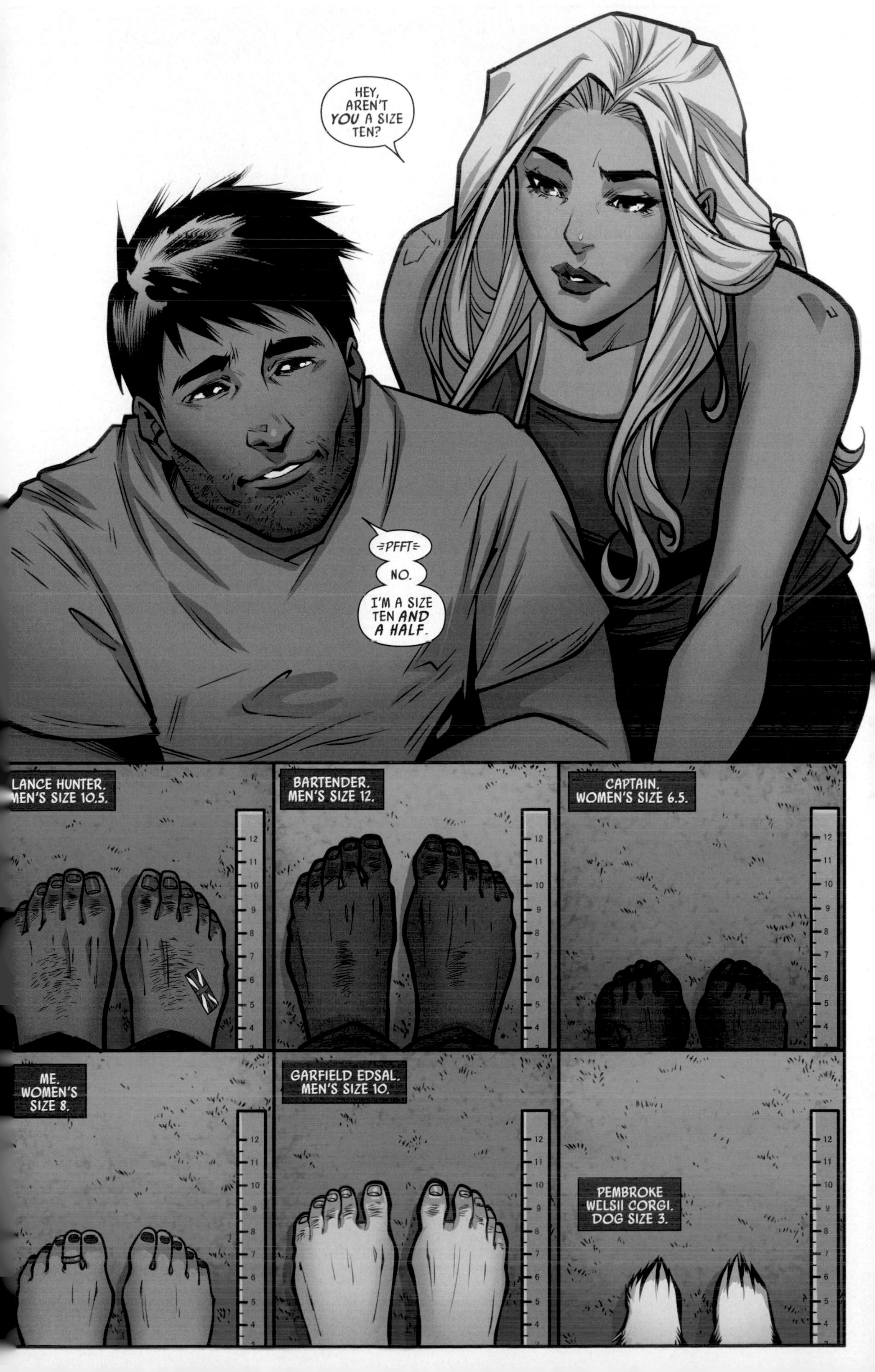
HEY, AREN'T YOU A SIZE TEN?
PFFT
NO.
I'M A SIZE TEN AND A HALF.
LANCE HUNTER. MEN'S SIZE 10.5.
BARTENDER. MEN'S SIZE 12.
CAPTAIN. WOMEN'S SIZE 6.5.
ME. WOMEN'S SIZE 8.
GARFIELD EDSAL. MEN'S SIZE 10.
PEMBROKE WELSH CORGI. DOG SIZE 3.

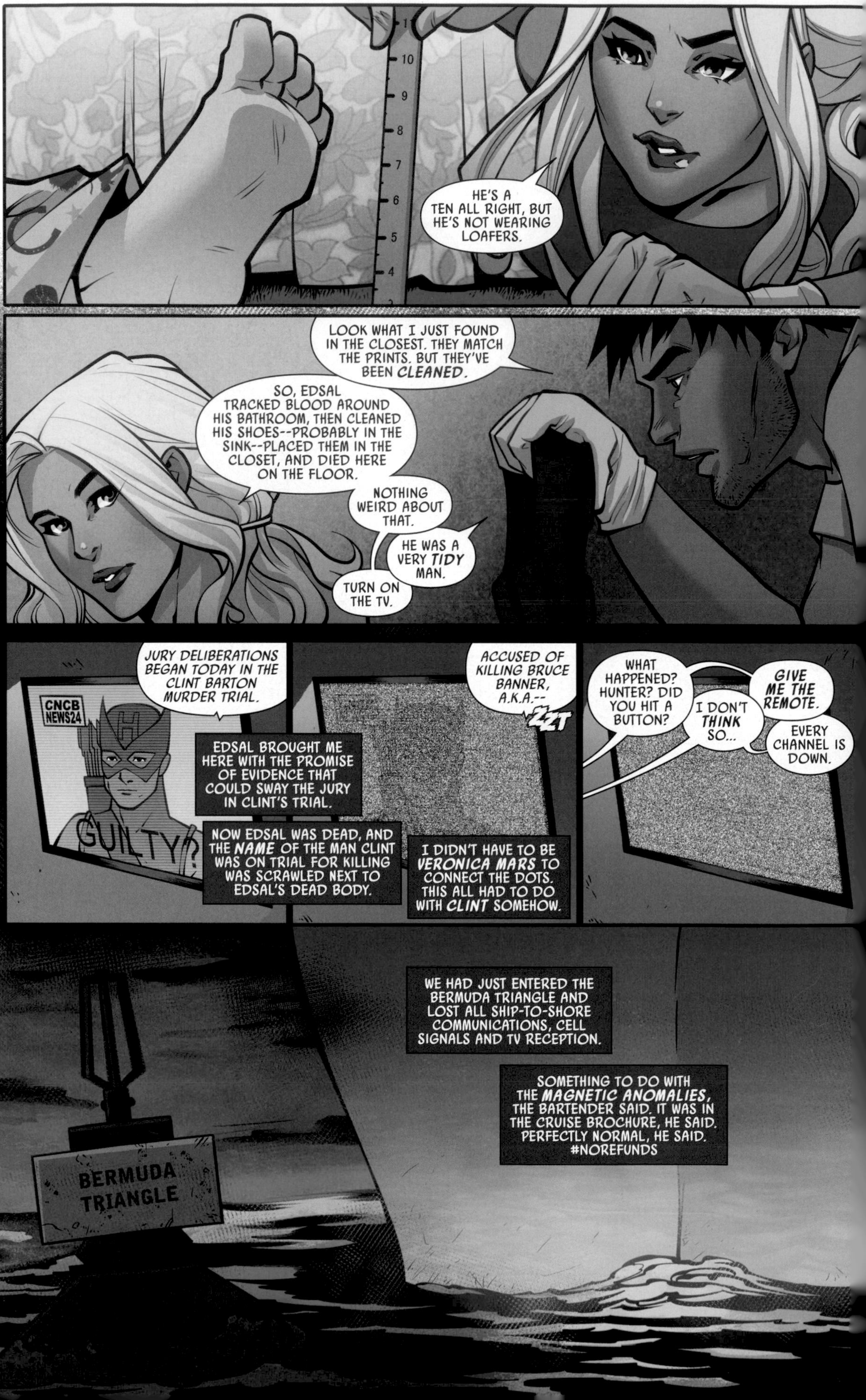

HE'S A TEN ALL RIGHT, BUT HE'S NOT WEARING LOAFERS.
LOOK WHAT I JUST FOUND IN THE CLOSEST. THEY MATCH THE PRINTS. BUT THEY'VE BEEN CLEANED.
SO, EDSAL TRACKED BLOOD AROUND HIS BATHROOM, THEN CLEANED HIS SHOES--PROBABLY IN THE SINK--PLACED THEM IN THE CLOSET, AND DIED HERE ON THE FLOOR.
NOTHING WEIRD ABOUT THAT.
HE WAS A VERY TIDY MAN.
TURN ON THE TV.
JURY DELIBERATIONS BEGAN TODAY IN THE CLINT BARTON MURDER TRIAL.
CNCB NEWS24
GUILTY?
EDSAL BROUGHT ME HERE WITH THE PROMISE OF EVIDENCE THAT COULD SWAY THE JURY IN CLINT'S TRIAL.
NOW EDSAL WAS DEAD, AND THE NAME OF THE MAN CLINT WAS ON TRIAL FOR KILLING WAS SCRAWLED NEXT TO EDSAL'S DEAD BODY.
ACCUSED OF KILLING BRUCE BANNER, A.K.A.--
ZZT
I DIDN'T HAVE TO BE VERONICA MARS TO CONNECT THE DOTS. THIS ALL HAD TO DO WITH CLINT SOMEHOW.
WHAT HAPPENED? HUNTER? DID YOU HIT A BUTTON?
I DON'T THINK SO...
GIVE ME THE REMOTE.
EVERY CHANNEL IS DOWN.
WE HAD JUST ENTERED THE BERMUDA TRIANGLE AND LOST ALL SHIP-TO-SHORE COMMUNICATIONS, CELL SIGNALS AND TV RECEPTION.
SOMETHING TO DO WITH THE MAGNETIC ANOMALIES, THE BARTENDER SAID. IT WAS IN THE CRUISE BROCHURE, HE SAID. PERFECTLY NORMAL, HE SAID. #NOREFUNDS
BERMUDA TRIANGLE

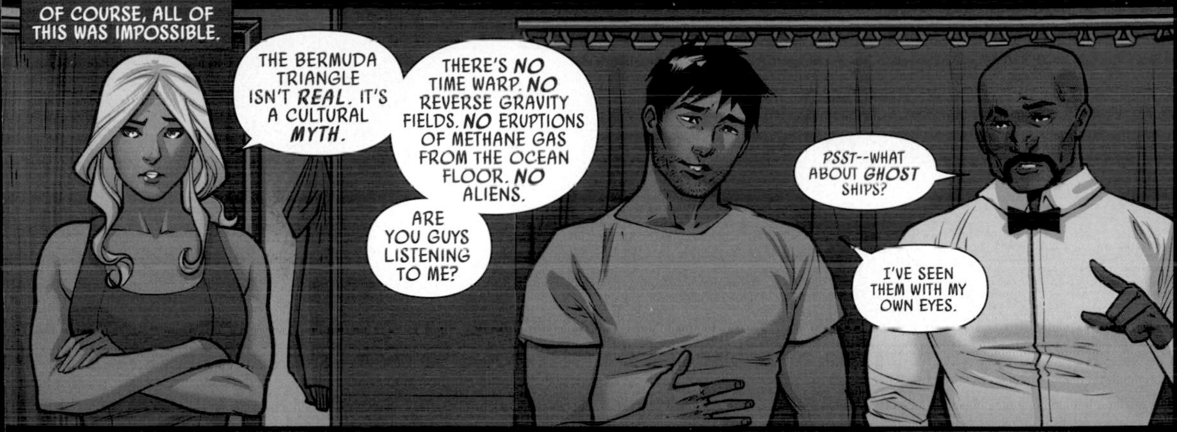
OF COURSE, ALL OF THIS WAS IMPOSSIBLE.
THE BERMUDA TRIANGLE ISN'T REAL. IT'S A CULTURAL MYTH.
THERE'S NO TIME WARP. NO REVERSE GRAVITY FIELDS. NO ERUPTIONS OF METHANE GAS FROM THE OCEAN FLOOR. NO ALIENS.
ARE YOU GUYS LISTENING TO ME?
PSST--WHAT ABOUT GHOST SHIPS?
I'VE SEEN THEM WITH MY OWN EYES.

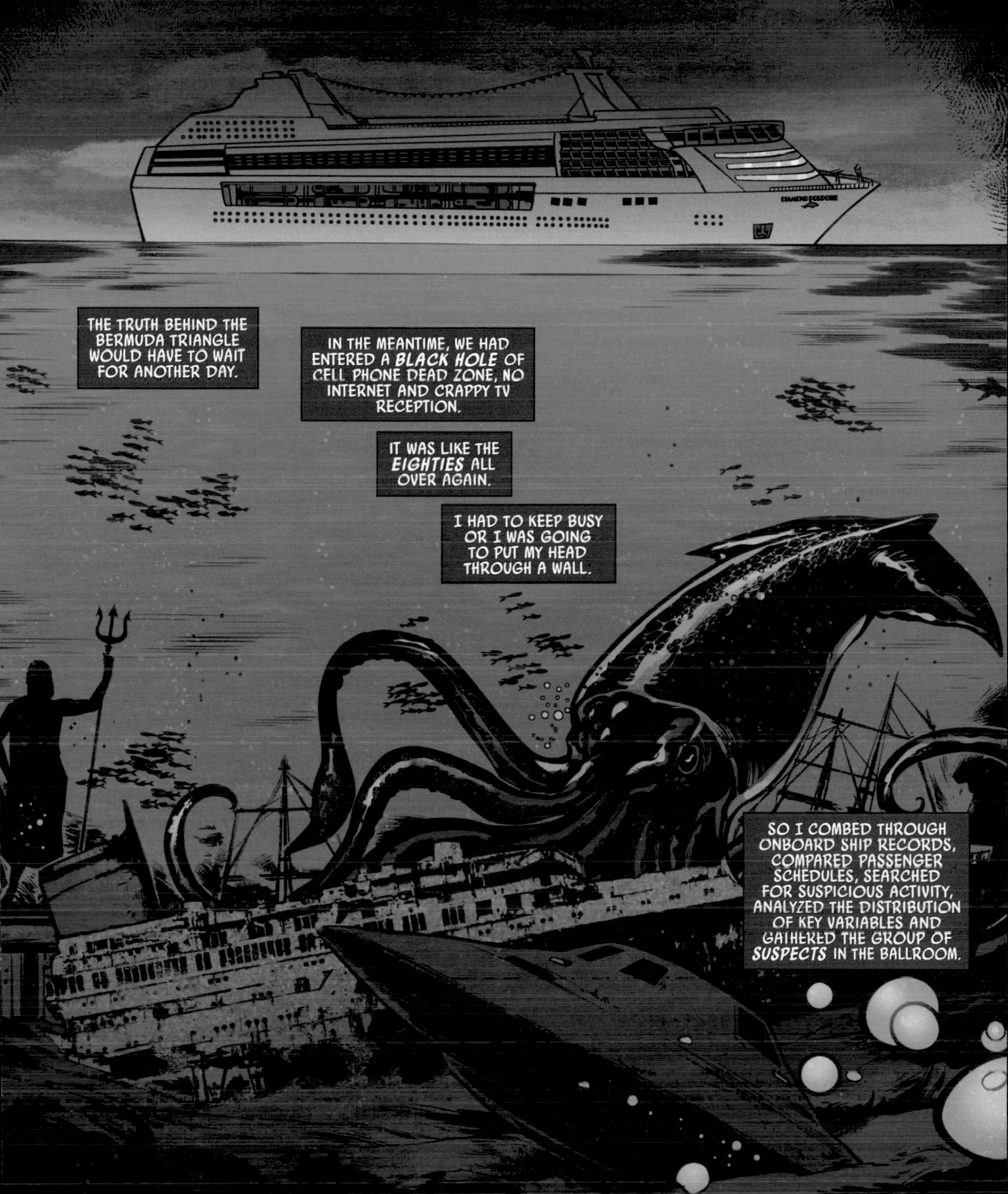
THE TRUTH BEHIND THE BERMUDA TRIANGLE WOULD HAVE TO WAIT FOR ANOTHER DAY.
IN THE MEANTIME, WE HAD ENTERED A BLACK HOLE OF CELL PHONE DEAD ZONE, NO INTERNET AND CRAPPY TV RECEPTION.
IT WAS LIKE THE EIGHTIES ALL OVER AGAIN.
I HAD TO KEEP BUSY OR I WAS GOING TO PUT MY HEAD THROUGH A WALL.
SO I COMBED THROUGH ONBOARD SHIP RECORDS, COMPARED PASSENGER SCHEDULES, SEARCHED FOR SUSPICIOUS ACTIVITY, ANALYZED THE DISTRIBUTION OF KEY VARIABLES AND GATHERED THE GROUP OF SUSPECTS IN THE BALLROOM.

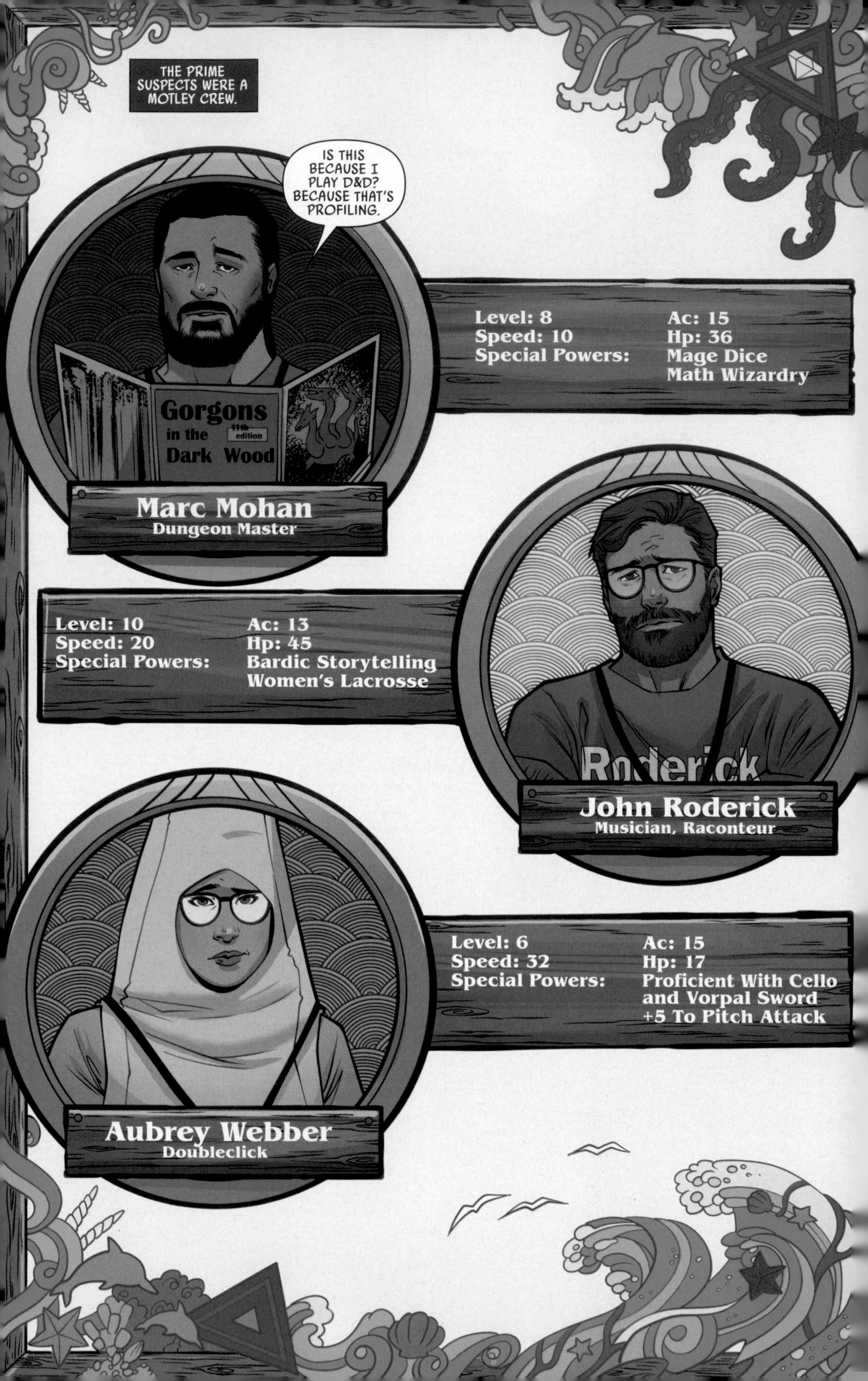
THE PRIME SUSPECTS WERE A MOTLEY CREW.
IS THIS BECAUSE I PLAY D&D? BECAUSE THAT'S PROFILING.
Gorgons in the Dark Wood 11th edition
Marc Mohan
Dungeon Master
Level: 8
Speed: 10
Special Powers:
Ac: 15
Hp: 36
Mage Dice
Math Wizardry
Roderick
John Roderick
Musician, Raconteur
Level: 10
Speed: 20
Special Powers:
Ac: 13
Hp: 45
Bardic Storytelling
Women's Lacrosse
Aubrey Webber
Doubleclick
Level: 6
Speed: 32
Special Powers:
Ac: 15
Hp: 17
Proficient With Cello
and Vorpal Sword
+5 To Pitch Attack

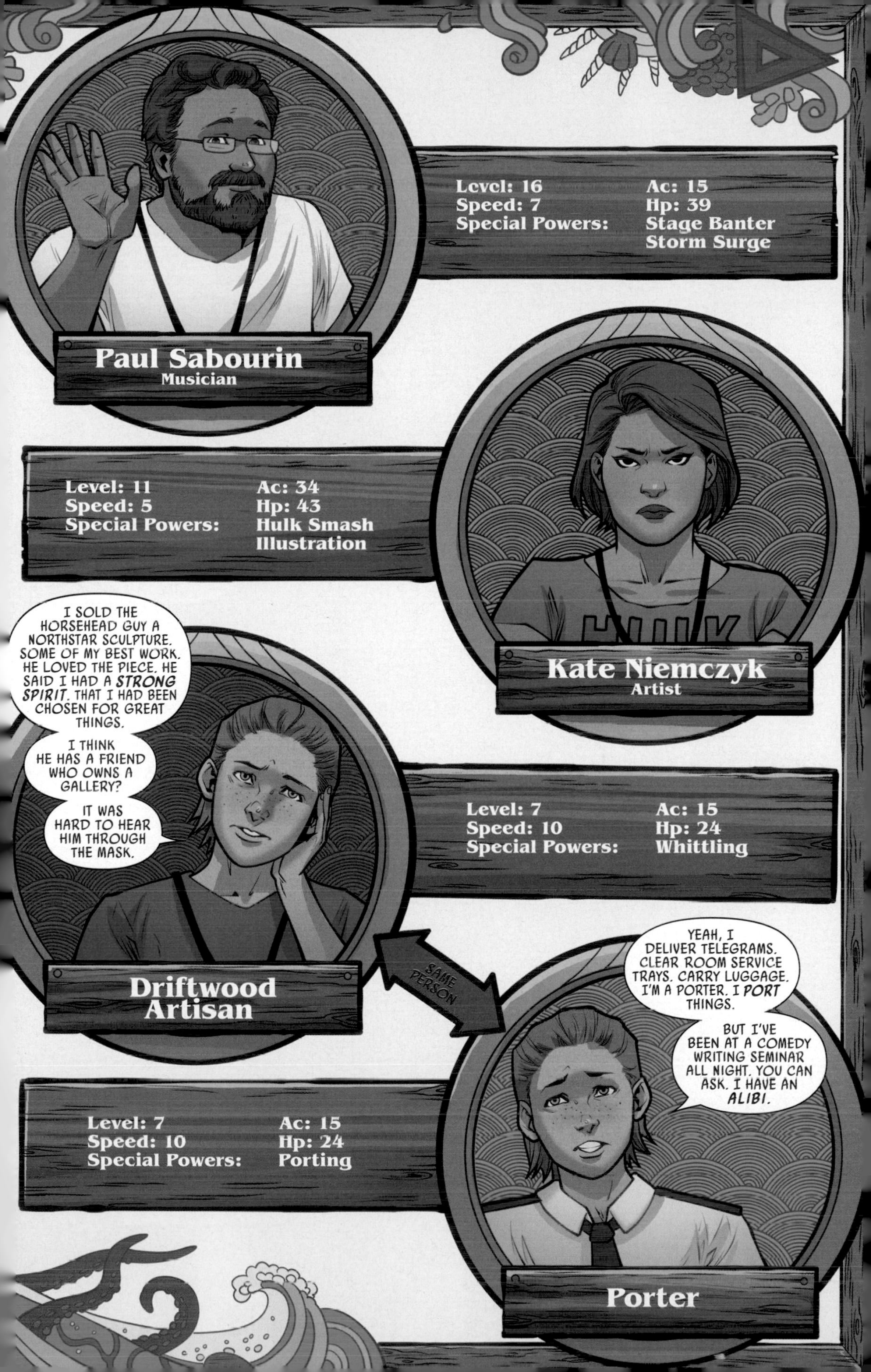

Level: 16
Speed: 7
Special Powers:
Ac: 15
Hp: 39
Stage Banter
Storm Surge
Paul Sabourin
Musician
Level: 11
Speed: 5
Special Powers:
Ac: 34
Hp: 43
Hulk Smash
Illustration
Kate Niemczyk
Artist
I SOLD THE HORSEHEAD GUY A NORTHSTAR SCULPTURE. SOME OF MY BEST WORK. HE LOVED THE PIECE. HE SAID I HAD A STRONG SPIRIT. THAT I HAD BEEN CHOSEN FOR GREAT THINGS.
I THINK HE HAS A FRIEND WHO OWNS A GALLERY?
IT WAS HARD TO HEAR HIM THROUGH THE MASK.
Level: 7
Speed: 10
Special Powers:
Ac: 15
Hp: 24
Whittling
Driftwood Artisan
SAME PERSON
YEAH, I DELIVER TELEGRAMS. CLEAR ROOM SERVICE TRAYS. CARRY LUGGAGE. I'M A PORTER. I PORT THINGS.
BUT I'VE BEEN AT A COMEDY WRITING SEMINAR ALL NIGHT. YOU CAN ASK. I HAVE AN ALIBI.
Level: 7
Speed: 10
Special Powers:
Ac: 15
Hp: 24
Porting
Porter

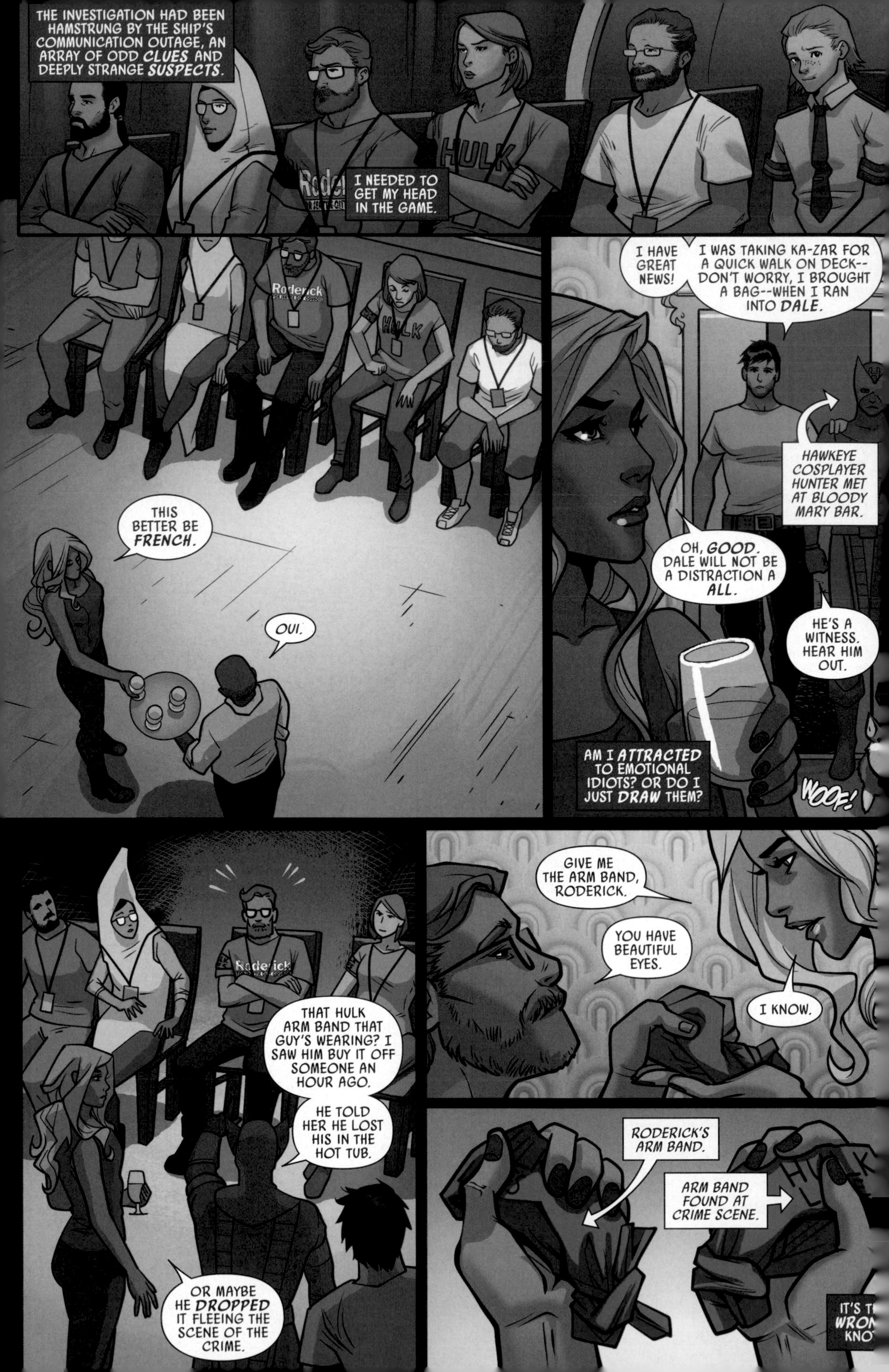
THE INVESTIGATION HAD BEEN HAMSTRUNG BY THE SHIP'S COMMUNICATION OUTAGE, AN ARRAY OF ODD CLUES AND DEEPLY STRANGE SUSPECTS.
I NEEDED TO GET MY HEAD IN THE GAME.
THIS BETTER BE FRENCH.
OUI.
I HAVE GREAT NEWS!
I WAS TAKING KA-ZAR FOR A QUICK WALK ON DECK--DON'T WORRY, I BROUGHT A BAG--WHEN I RAN INTO DALE.
HAWKEYE COSPLAYER HUNTER MET AT BLOODY MARY BAR.
OH, GOOD. DALE WILL NOT BE A DISTRACTION A ALL.
HE'S A WITNESS. HEAR HIM OUT.
AM I ATTRACTED TO EMOTIONAL IDIOTS? OR DO I JUST DRAW THEM?
WOOF!
THAT HULK ARM BAND THAT GUY'S WEARING? I SAW HIM BUY IT OFF SOMEONE AN HOUR AGO.
HE TOLD HER HE LOST HIS IN THE HOT TUB.
OR MAYBE HE DROPPED IT FLEEING THE SCENE OF THE CRIME.
GIVE ME THE ARM BAND, RODERICK.
YOU HAVE BEAUTIFUL EYES.
I KNOW.
RODERICK'S ARM BAND.
ARM BAND FOUND AT CRIME SCENE.

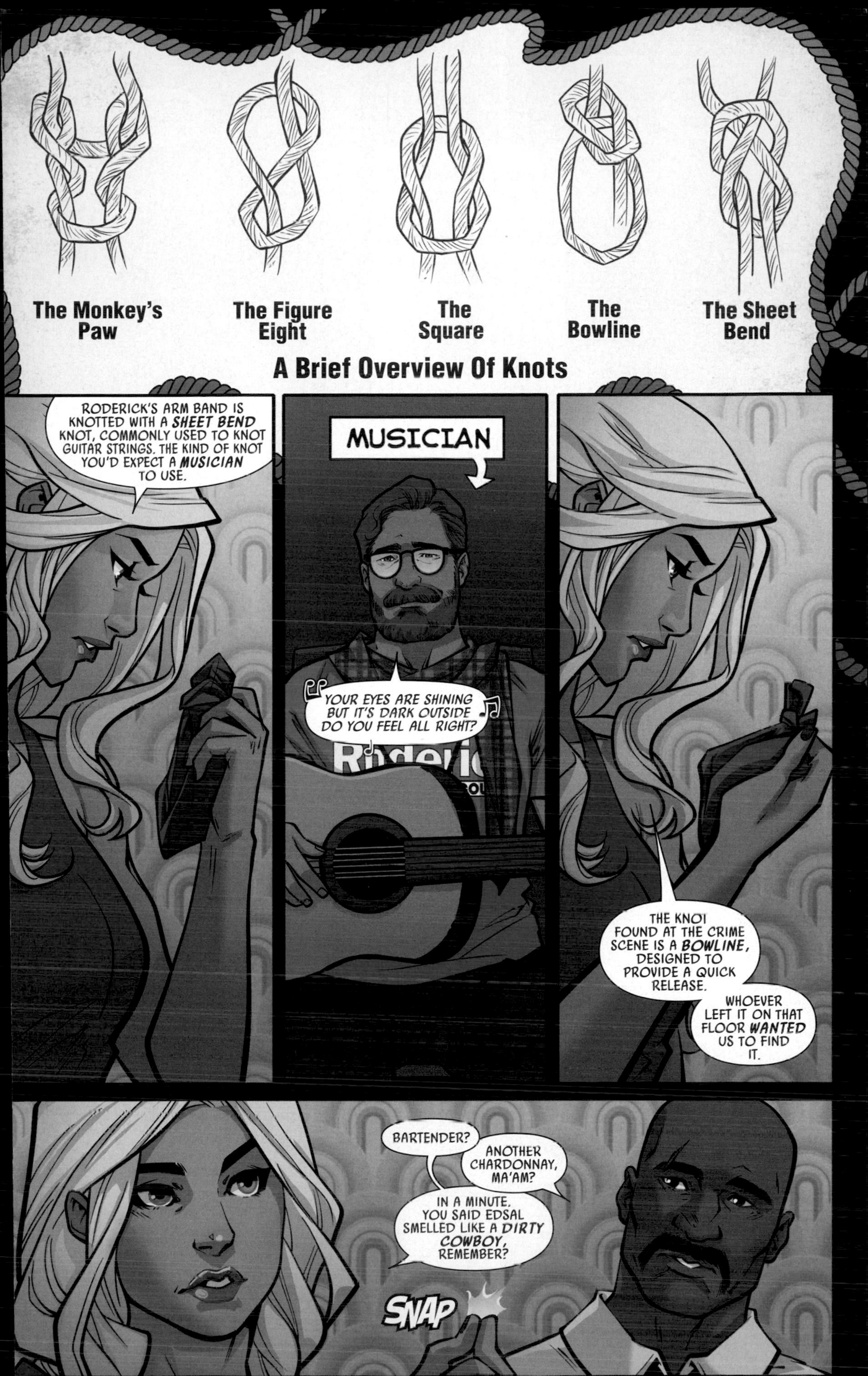
The Monkey's Paw
The Figure Eight
The Square
The Bowline
The Sheet Bend
A Brief Overview Of Knots
RODERICK'S ARM BAND IS KNOTTED WITH A SHEET BEND KNOT, COMMONLY USED TO KNOT GUITAR STRINGS. THE KIND OF KNOT YOU'D EXPECT A MUSICIAN TO USE.
MUSICIAN
YOUR EYES ARE SHINING BUT IT'S DARK OUTSIDE DO YOU FEEL ALL RIGHT?
THE KNOT FOUND AT THE CRIME SCENE IS A BOWLINE, DESIGNED TO PROVIDE A QUICK RELEASE.
WHOEVER LEFT IT ON THAT FLOOR WANTED US TO FIND IT.
BARTENDER?
ANOTHER CHARDONNAY, MA'AM?
IN A MINUTE. YOU SAID EDSAL SMELLED LIKE A DIRTY COWBOY, REMEMBER?
SNAP

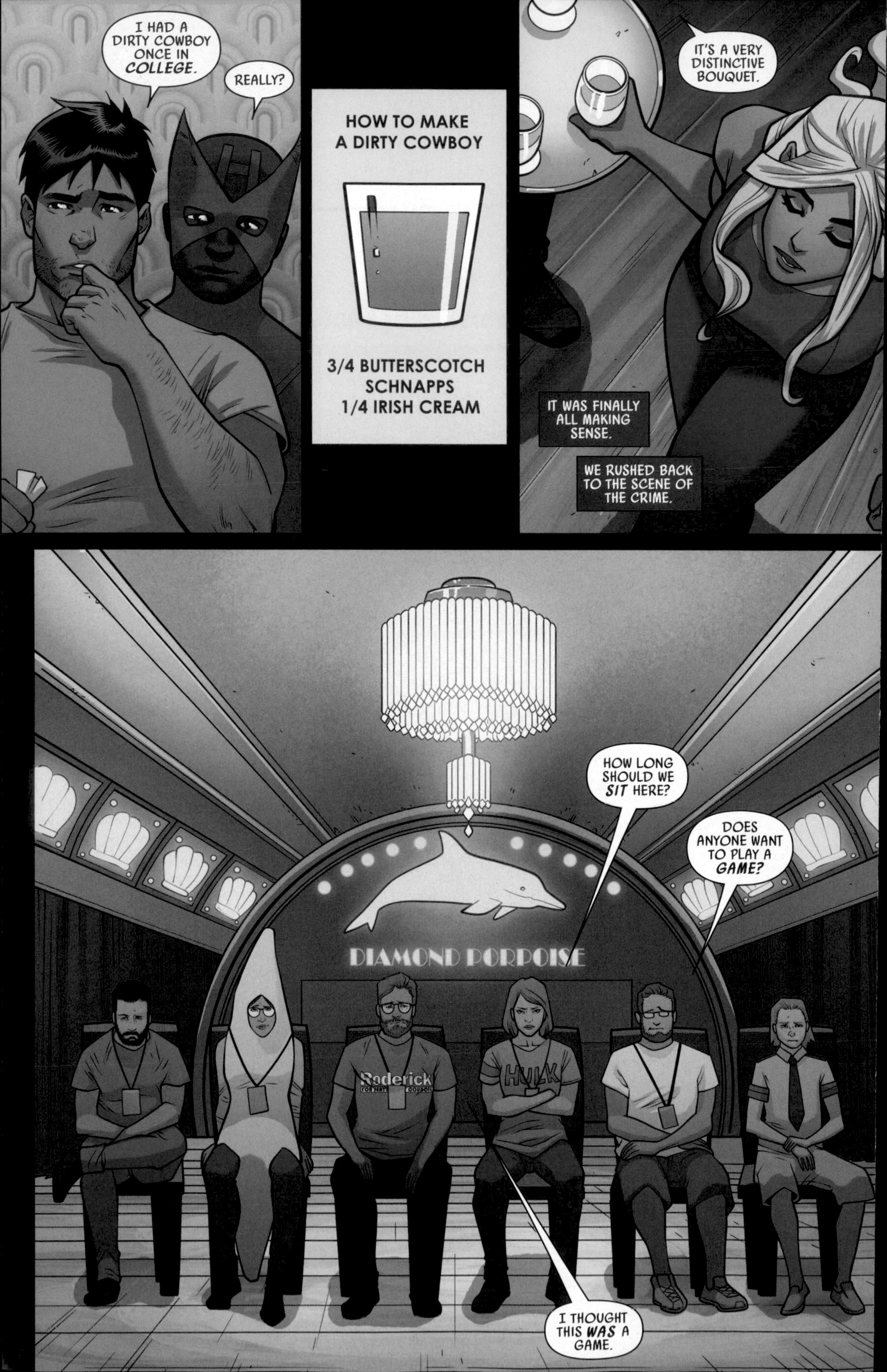
I HAD A DIRTY COWBOY ONCE IN COLLEGE.
REALLY?
HOW TO MAKE A DIRTY COWBOY
3/4 BUTTERSCOTCH SCHNAPPS
1/4 IRISH CREAM
IT'S A VERY DISTINCTIVE BOUQUET.
IT WAS FINALLY ALL MAKING SENSE.
WE RUSHED BACK TO THE SCENE OF THE CRIME.
DIAMOND PORPOISE
Roderick
HULK
HOW LONG SHOULD WE SIT HERE?
DOES ANYONE WANT TO PLAY A GAME?
I THOUGHT THIS WAS A GAME.

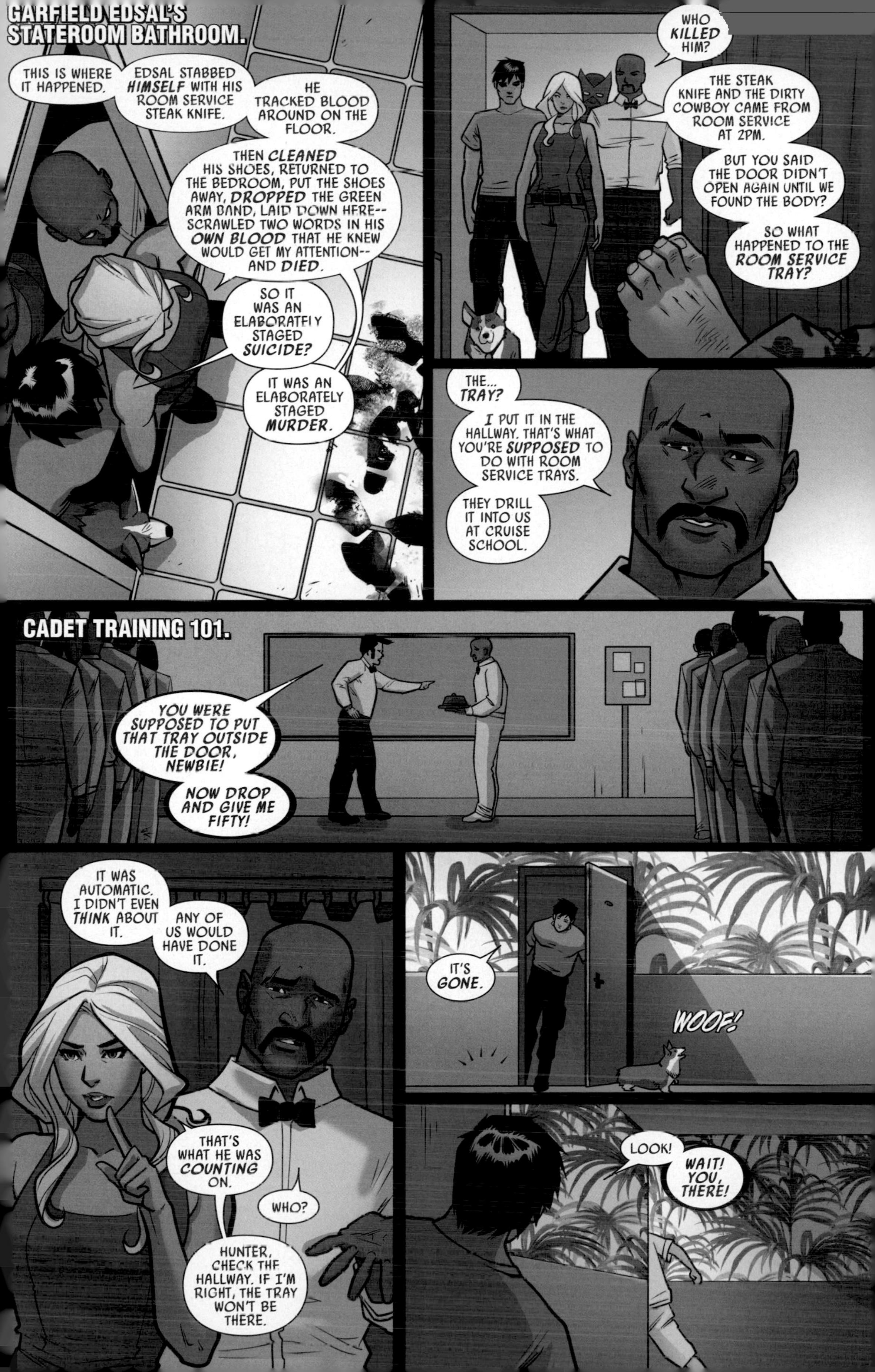
GARFIELD EDSAL'S STATEROOM BATHROOM.
THIS IS WHERE IT HAPPENED.
EDSAL STABBED HIMSELF WITH HIS ROOM SERVICE STEAK KNIFE.
HE TRACKED BLOOD AROUND ON THE FLOOR.
THEN CLEANED HIS SHOES, RETURNED TO THE BEDROOM, PUT THE SHOES AWAY, DROPPED THE GREEN ARM BAND, LAID DOWN HERE-- SCRAWLED TWO WORDS IN HIS OWN BLOOD THAT HE KNEW WOULD GET MY ATTENTION-- AND DIED.
SO IT WAS AN ELABORATELY STAGED SUICIDE?
IT WAS AN ELABORATELY STAGED MURDER.
WHO KILLED HIM?
THE STEAK KNIFE AND THE DIRTY COWBOY CAME FROM ROOM SERVICE AT 2PM.
BUT YOU SAID THE DOOR DIDN'T OPEN AGAIN UNTIL WE FOUND THE BODY?
SO WHAT HAPPENED TO THE ROOM SERVICE TRAY?
THE... TRAY?
I PUT IT IN THE HALLWAY. THAT'S WHAT YOU'RE SUPPOSED TO DO WITH ROOM SERVICE TRAYS.
THEY DRILL IT INTO US AT CRUISE SCHOOL.
CADET TRAINING 101.
YOU WERE SUPPOSED TO PUT THAT TRAY OUTSIDE THE DOOR, NEWBIE!
NOW DROP AND GIVE ME FIFTY!
IT WAS AUTOMATIC. I DIDN'T EVEN THINK ABOUT IT.
ANY OF US WOULD HAVE DONE IT.
THAT'S WHAT HE WAS COUNTING ON.
WHO?
HUNTER, CHECK THE HALLWAY. IF I'M RIGHT, THE TRAY WON'T BE THERE.
IT'S GONE.
WOOF!
LOOK!
WAIT! YOU, THERE!

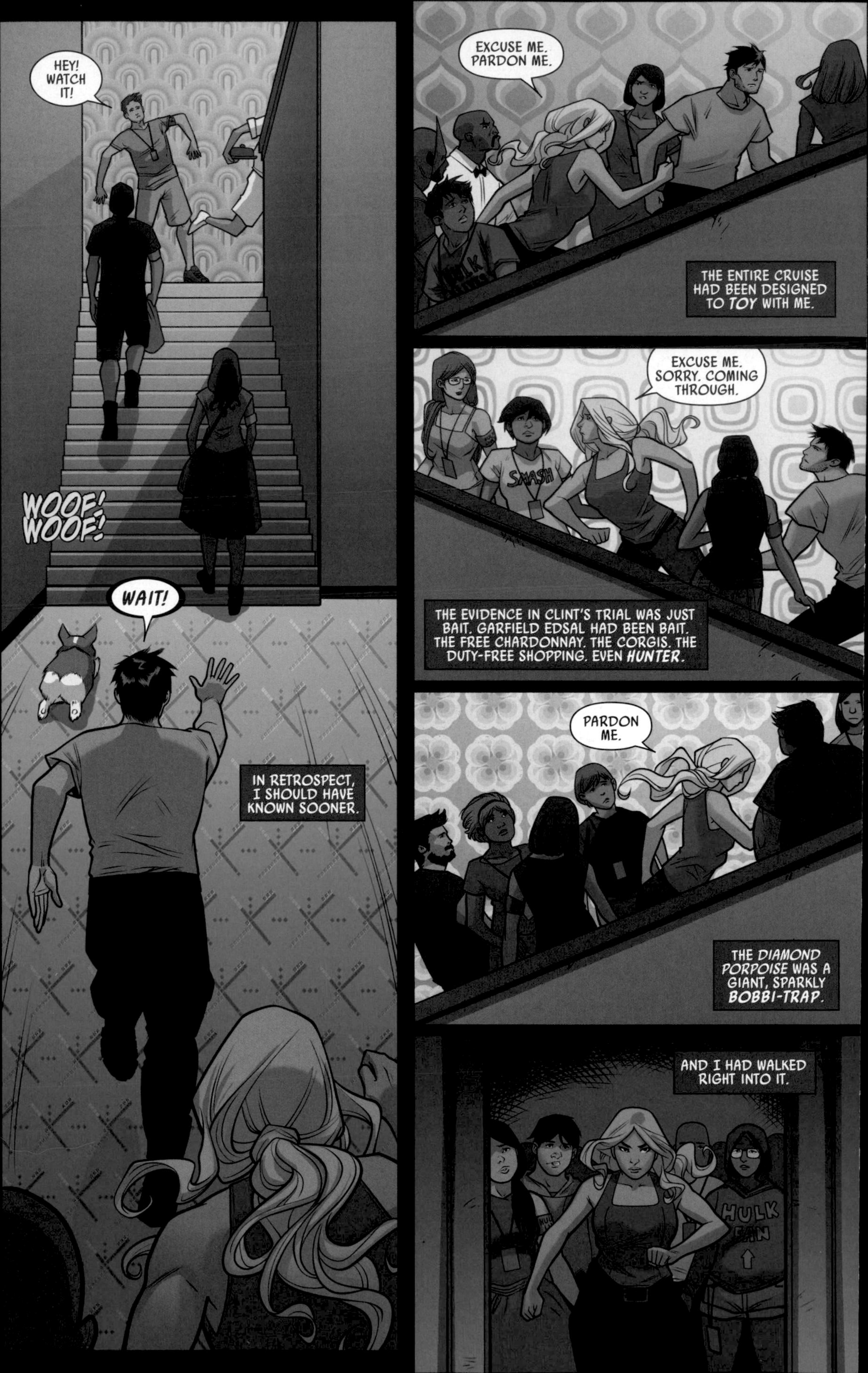
HEY! WATCH IT!
WOOF! WOOF!
WAIT!
IN RETROSPECT, I SHOULD HAVE KNOWN SOONER.
EXCUSE ME. PARDON ME.
THE ENTIRE CRUISE HAD BEEN DESIGNED TO TOY WITH ME.
EXCUSE ME. SORRY. COMING THROUGH.
SMASH
THE EVIDENCE IN CLINT'S TRIAL WAS JUST BAIT. GARFIELD EDSAL HAD BEEN BAIT. THE FREE CHARDONNAY. THE CORGIS. THE DUTY-FREE SHOPPING. EVEN HUNTER.
PARDON ME.
THE DIAMOND PORPOISE WAS A GIANT, SPARKLY BOBBI-TRAP.
AND I HAD WALKED RIGHT INTO IT.
HULK

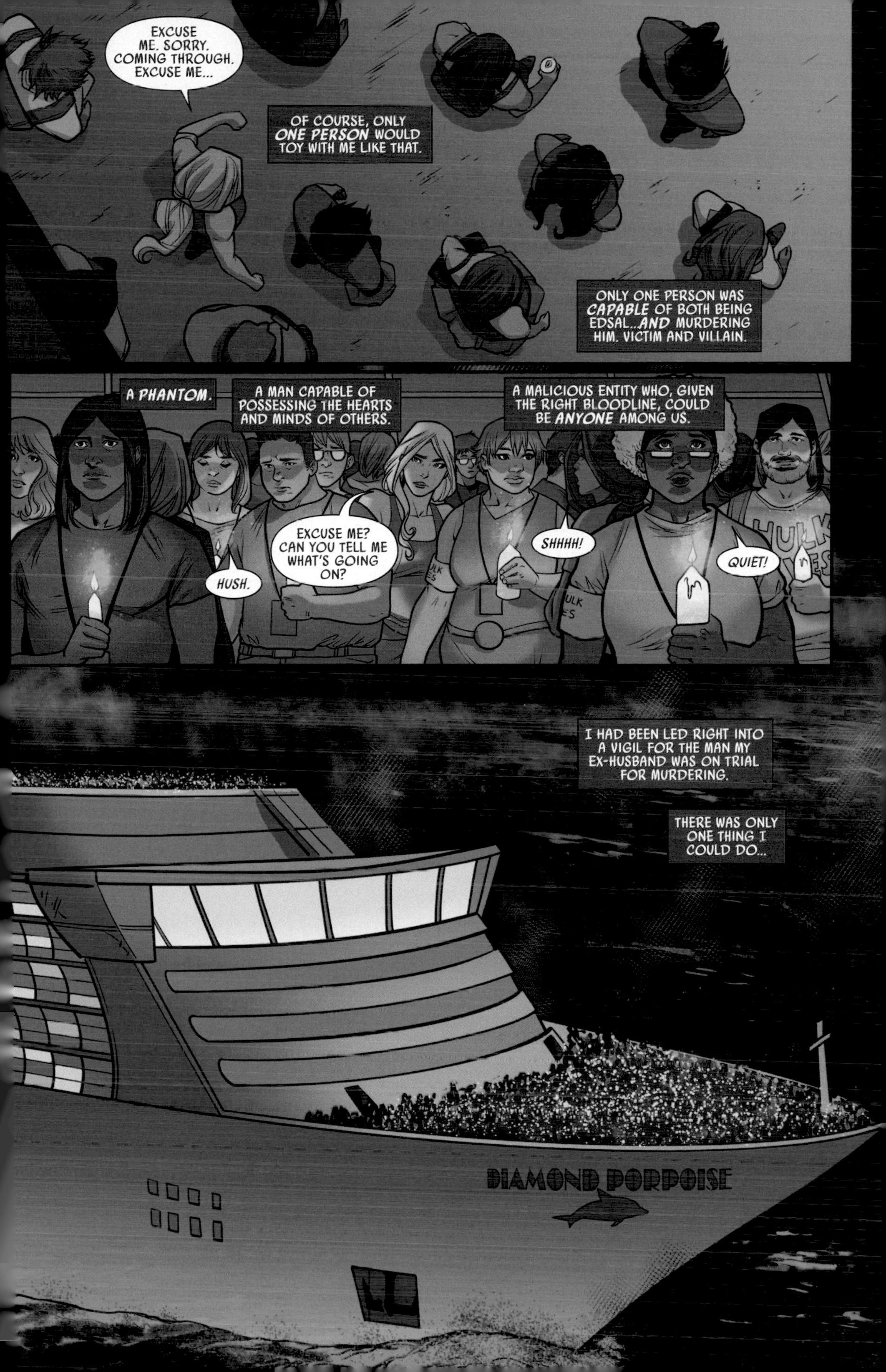
EXCUSE ME. SORRY. COMING THROUGH. EXCUSE ME...
OF COURSE, ONLY ONE PERSON WOULD TOY WITH ME LIKE THAT.
ONLY ONE PERSON WAS CAPABLE OF BOTH BEING EDSAL...AND MURDERING HIM. VICTIM AND VILLAIN.
A PHANTOM.
A MAN CAPABLE OF POSSESSING THE HEARTS AND MINDS OF OTHERS.
A MALICIOUS ENTITY WHO, GIVEN THE RIGHT BLOODLINE, COULD BE ANYONE AMONG US.
EXCUSE ME? CAN YOU TELL ME WHAT'S GOING ON?
HUSH.
SHHHH!
QUIET!
I HAD BEEN LED RIGHT INTO A VIGIL FOR THE MAN MY EX-HUSBAND WAS ON TRIAL FOR MURDERING.
THERE WAS ONLY ONE THING I COULD DO...
DIAMOND PORPOISE

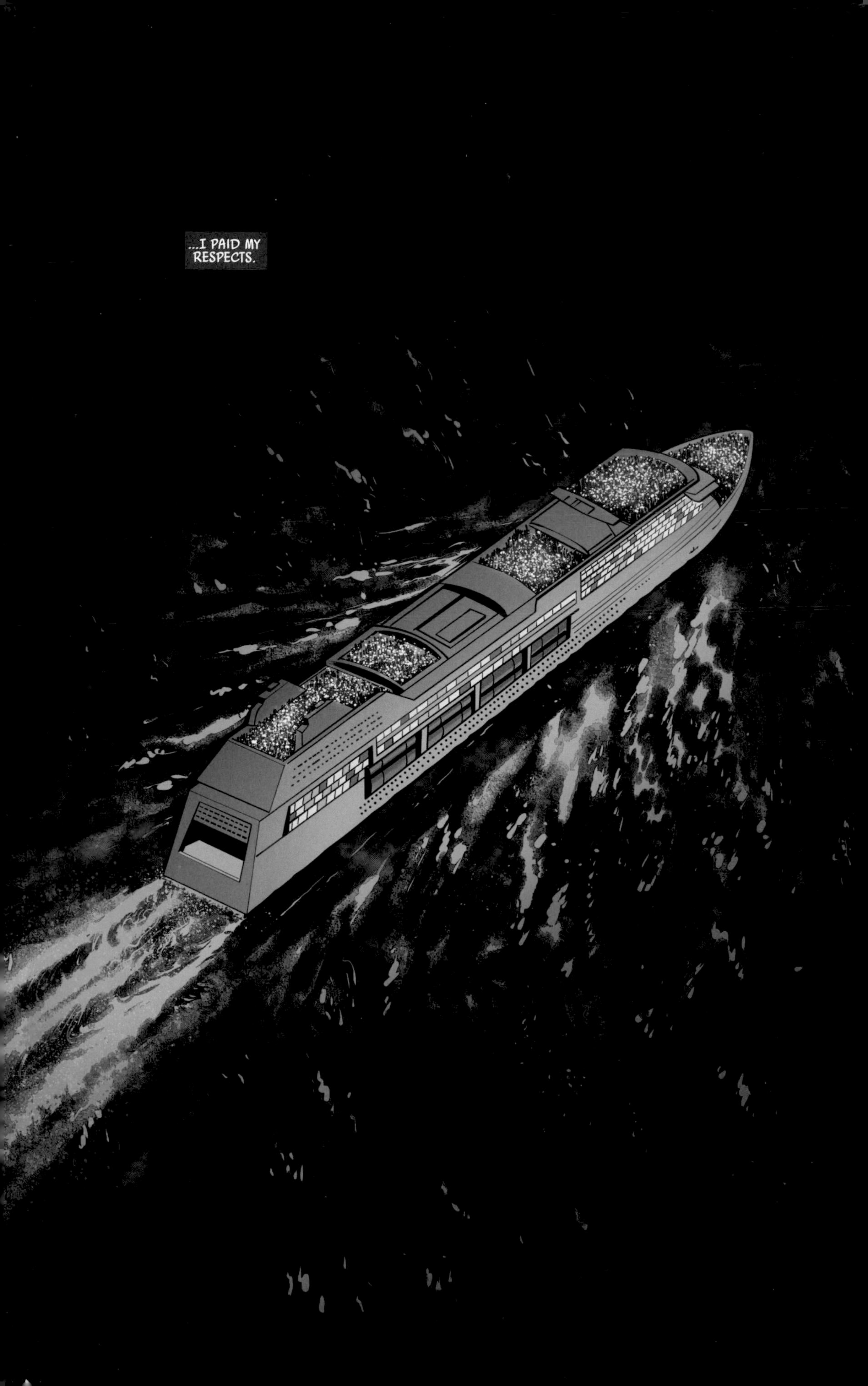
...I PAID MY
RESPECTS.

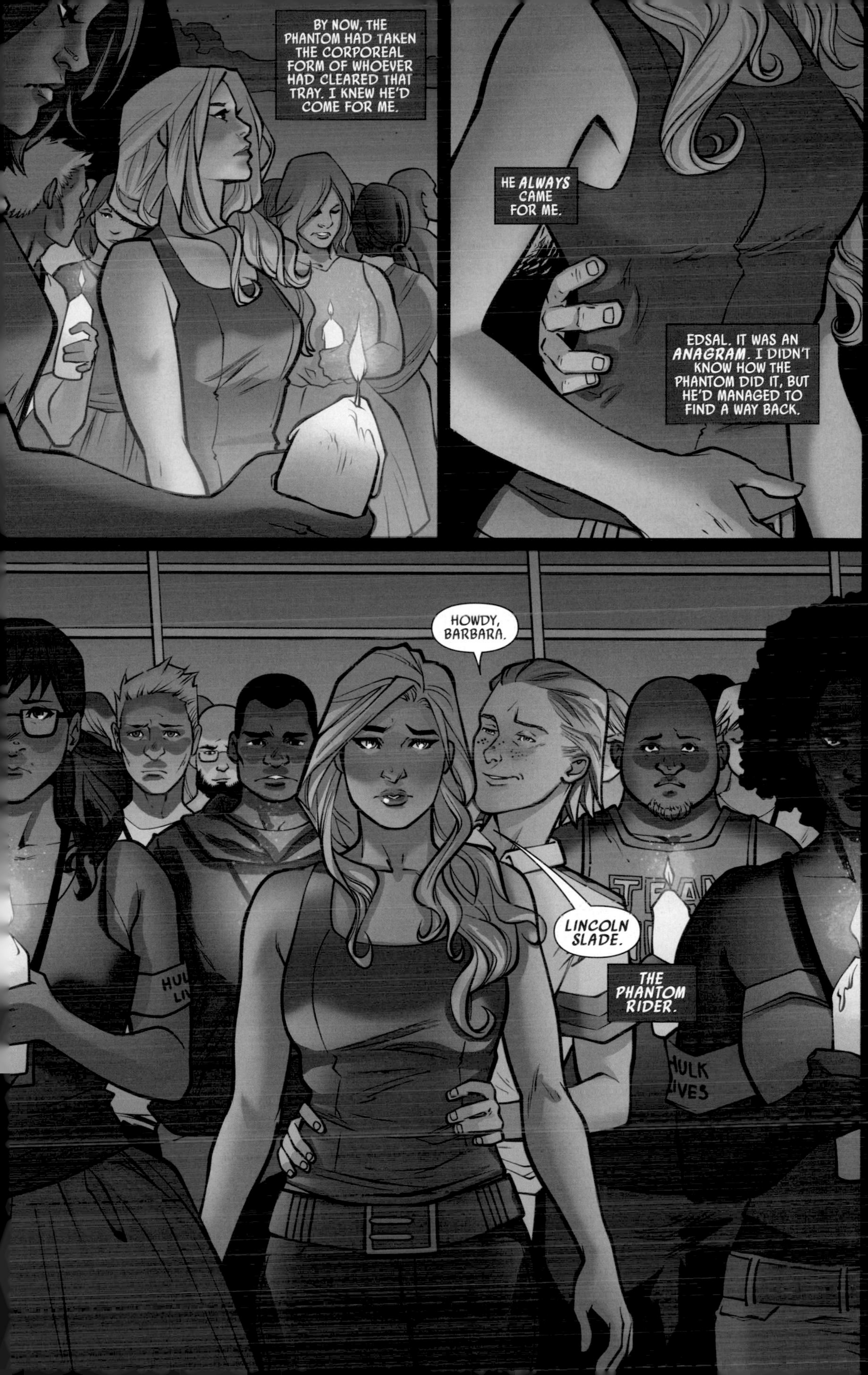
BY NOW, THE PHANTOM HAD TAKEN THE CORPOREAL FORM OF WHOEVER HAD CLEARED THAT TRAY. I KNEW HE'D COME FOR ME.
HE ALWAYS CAME FOR ME.
EDSAL. IT WAS AN ANAGRAM. I DIDN'T KNOW HOW THE PHANTOM DID IT, BUT HE'D MANAGED TO FIND A WAY BACK.
HOWDY, BARBARA.
LINCOLN SLADE.
THE PHANTOM RIDER.
HULK LIVES
HULK LIVES

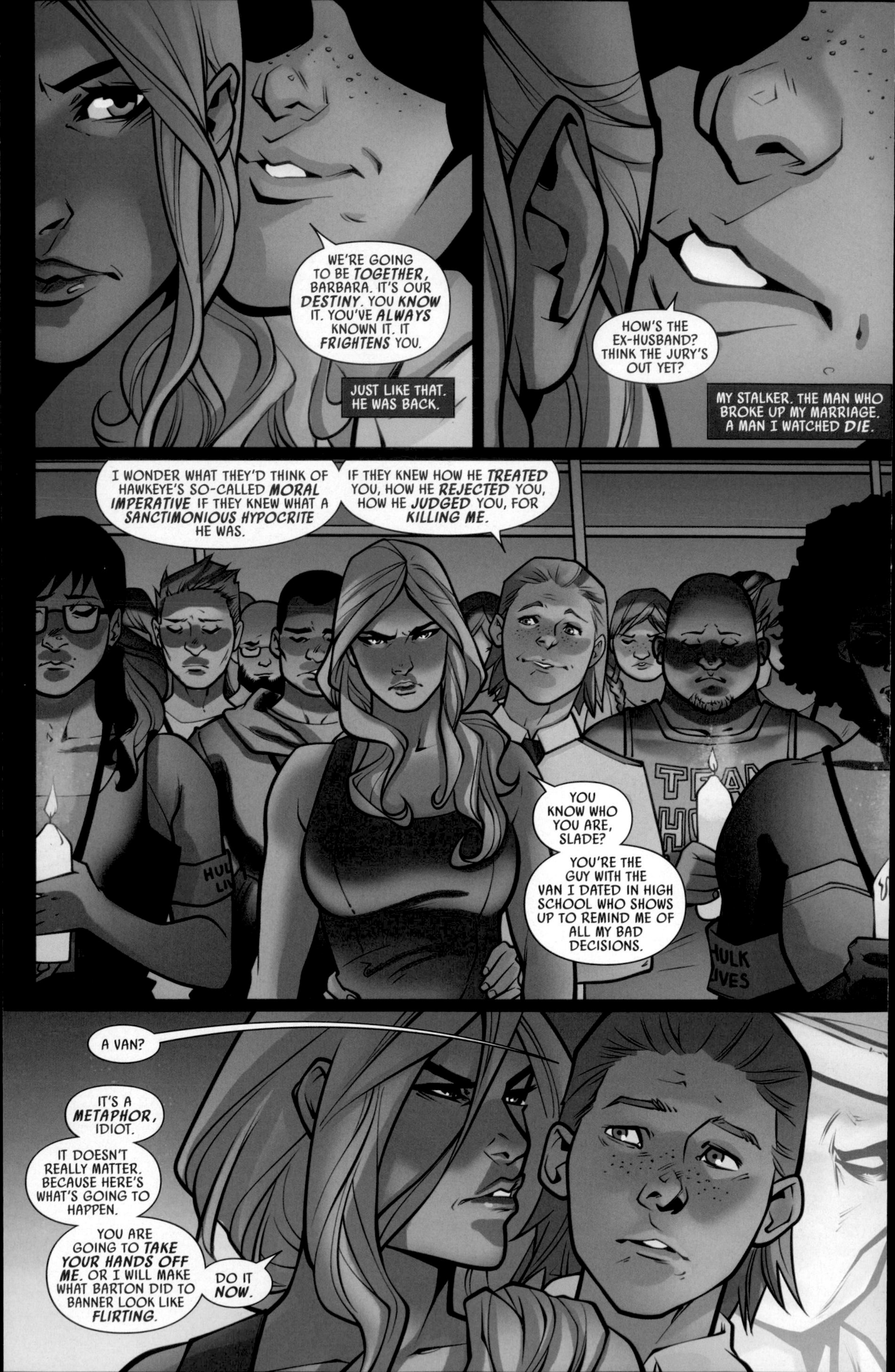

WE'RE GOING TO BE TOGETHER, BARBARA. IT'S OUR DESTINY. YOU KNOW IT. YOU'VE ALWAYS KNOWN IT. IT FRIGHTENS YOU.
JUST LIKE THAT. HE WAS BACK.
HOW'S THE EX-HUSBAND? THINK THE JURY'S OUT YET?
MY STALKER. THE MAN WHO BROKE UP MY MARRIAGE. A MAN I WATCHED DIE.
I WONDER WHAT THEY'D THINK OF HAWKEYE'S SO-CALLED MORAL IMPERATIVE IF THEY KNEW WHAT A SANCTIMONIOUS HYPOCRITE HE WAS.
IF THEY KNEW HOW HE TREATED YOU, HOW HE REJECTED YOU, HOW HE JUDGED YOU, FOR KILLING ME.
YOU KNOW WHO YOU ARE, SLADE?
YOU'RE THE GUY WITH THE VAN I DATED IN HIGH SCHOOL WHO SHOWS UP TO REMIND ME OF ALL MY BAD DECISIONS.
HULK LIVES
HULK LIVES
A VAN?
IT'S A METAPHOR, IDIOT.
IT DOESN'T REALLY MATTER. BECAUSE HERE'S WHAT'S GOING TO HAPPEN.
YOU ARE GOING TO TAKE YOUR HANDS OFF ME. OR I WILL MAKE WHAT BARTON DID TO BANNER LOOK LIKE FLIRTING.
DO IT NOW.

RESTRAINING ORDER

MB 2016 007

GRANTED
BY THE SUPREME COURT
Designed & Officiated by:
MANNY MEDEROS

APPLICANT NAME: BARBARA "BOBBI" MORSE

FILING ATTORNEY: MATT MURDOCK

ATTORNEY MAILING ADDRESS:

CITY: New York **STATE:** NY **ZIP:** 10020

NAME OF RESTRAINED:
LINCOLN SLADE, A.K.A. THE PHANTOM RIDER

OTHER ALIASES:
Ghost Rider, Night Rider, Son of the Spirits,
He Who Rides The Night Winds

KNOWN ASSOCIATES:
BANSHEE, his horse

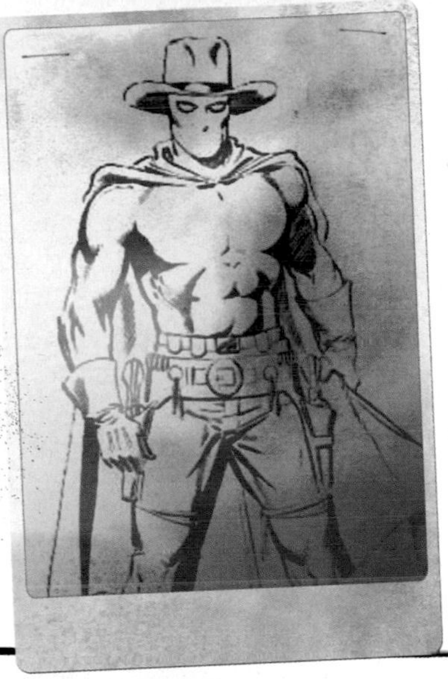

Attach photo of restrained to this page if available.

DESCRIPTION OF RESTRAINED PERSON:

Sex: [X] M [ ] F Height: 5' 11" Weight: 190 lbs. DOB: early 1800s

Hair Color: phosphorescent white Eye Color: phosphorescent white

Race: phosphorescent white Age: Technically dead

Mailing Address:

City: State: Texas? Zip:

Relationship to protected person:
Stalker ex-boyfriend

DESCRIPTION OF EVENT IN QUESTION:

Lincoln Slade broke up my marriage to Clint Barton and continues to harass me. While I briefly cohabited with Mr. Slade, it should be noted that this was during a difficult period of my marriage, and also I had traveled back in time and was trapped in the Old West. While I have clearly and emphatically expressed my lack of interest in Mr. Slade, to this day he continues to pursue my affections. I fear he may harm me or my ex-husband, Hawkeye.

EXT COURT APPEARANCE IS ON 10/19/16

MB 2016 007

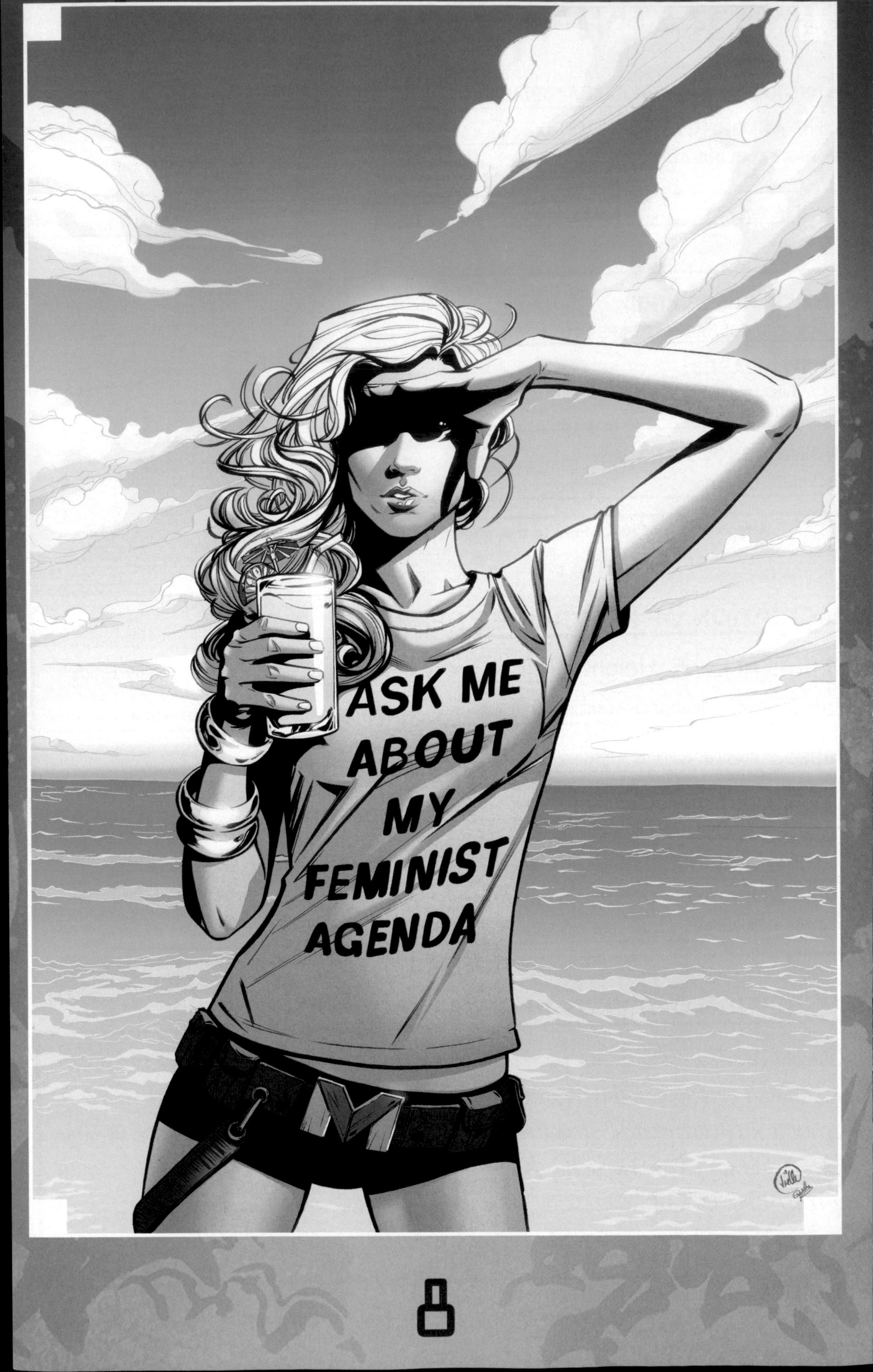
ASK ME ABOUT MY FEMINIST AGENDA

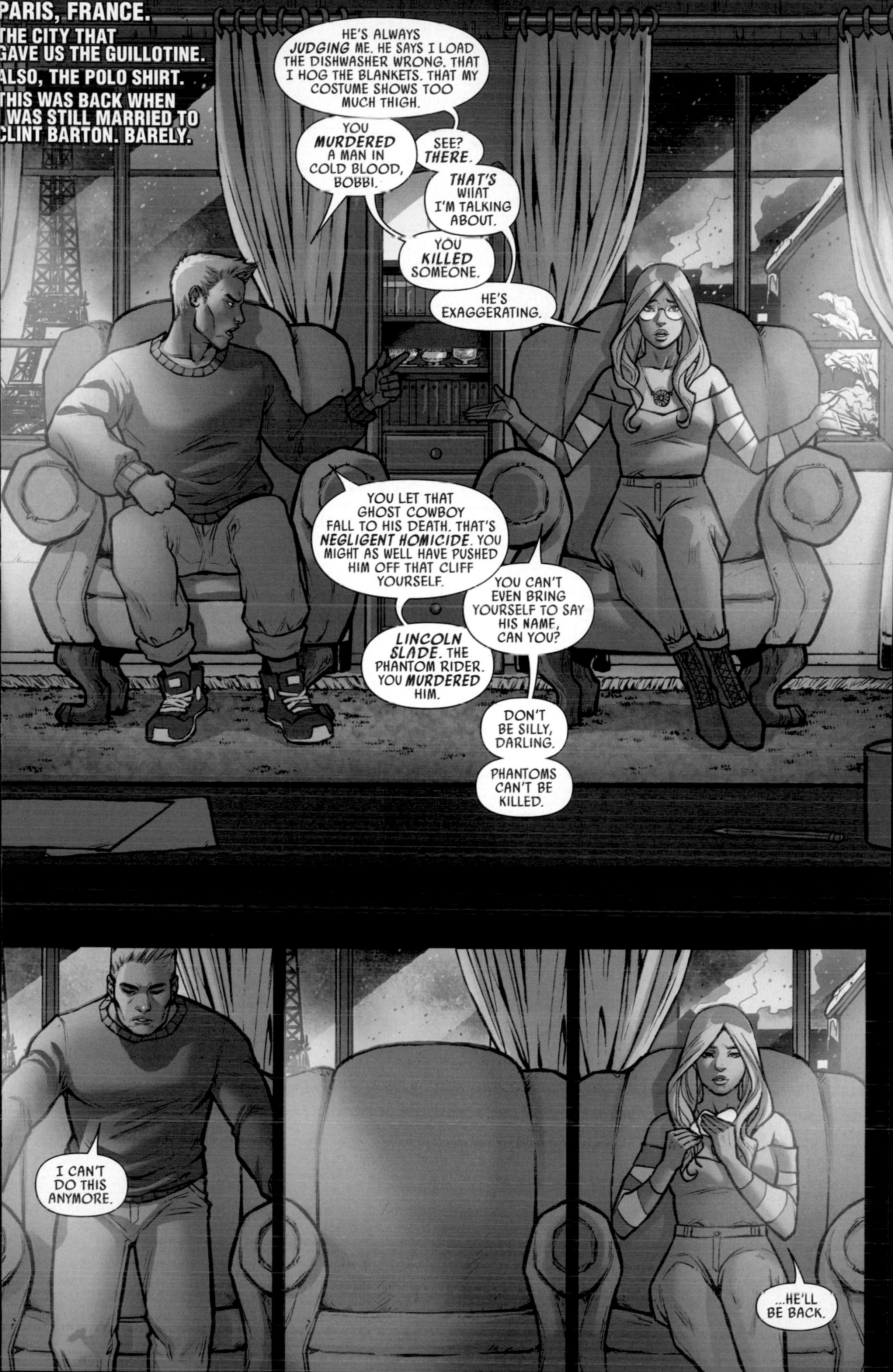
PARIS, FRANCE.
THE CITY THAT GAVE US THE GUILLOTINE.
ALSO, THE POLO SHIRT.
THIS WAS BACK WHEN I WAS STILL MARRIED TO CLINT BARTON. BARELY.
HE'S ALWAYS JUDGING ME. HE SAYS I LOAD THE DISHWASHER WRONG. THAT I HOG THE BLANKETS. THAT MY COSTUME SHOWS TOO MUCH THIGH.
YOU MURDERED A MAN IN COLD BLOOD, BOBBI.
SEE? THERE.
THAT'S WHAT I'M TALKING ABOUT.
YOU KILLED SOMEONE.
HE'S EXAGGERATING.
YOU LET THAT GHOST COWBOY FALL TO HIS DEATH. THAT'S NEGLIGENT HOMICIDE. YOU MIGHT AS WELL HAVE PUSHED HIM OFF THAT CLIFF YOURSELF.
YOU CAN'T EVEN BRING YOURSELF TO SAY HIS NAME, CAN YOU?
LINCOLN SLADE. THE PHANTOM RIDER. YOU MURDERED HIM.
DON'T BE SILLY, DARLING.
PHANTOMS CAN'T BE KILLED.
I CAN'T DO THIS ANYMORE.
...HE'LL BE BACK.

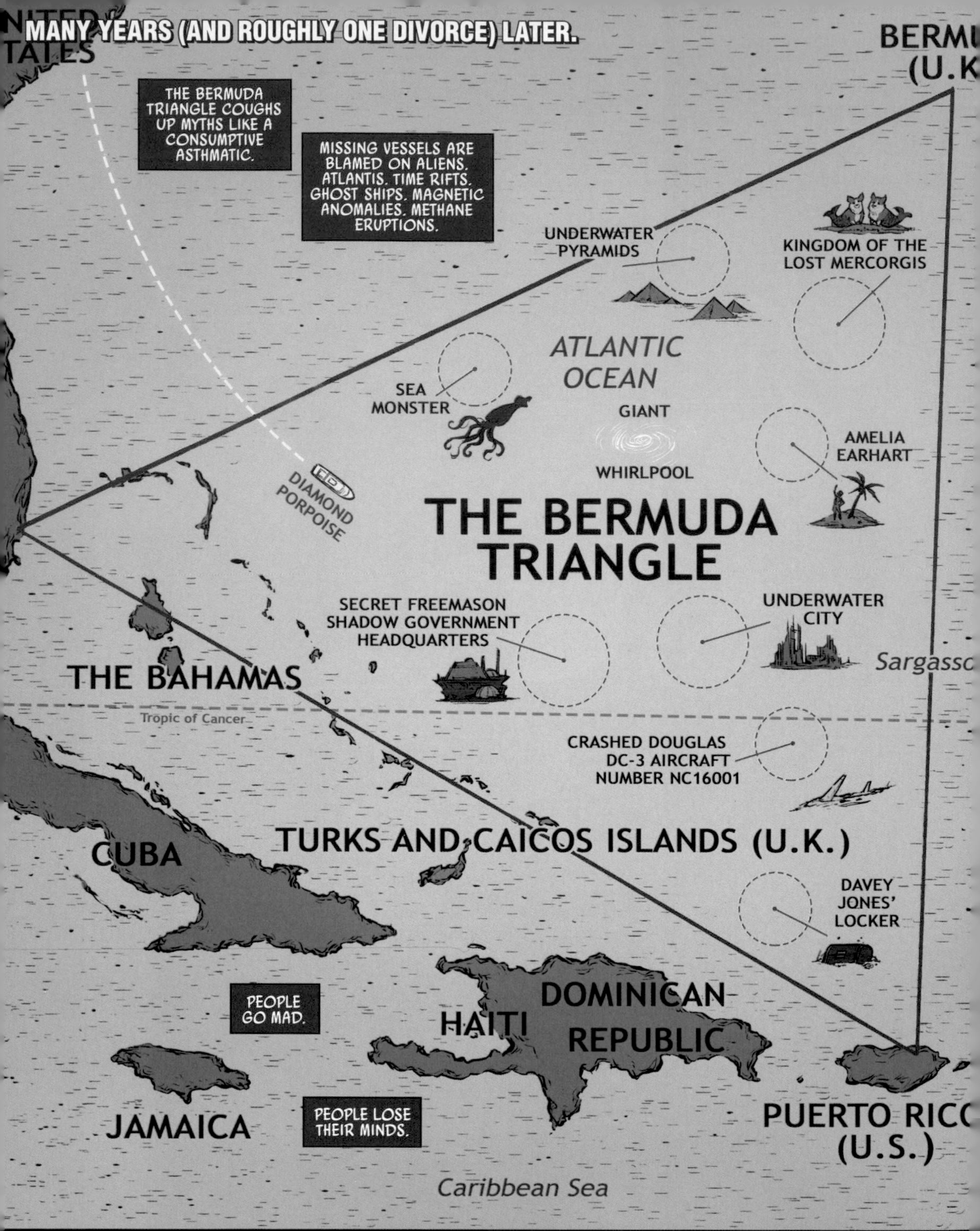
MANY YEARS (AND ROUGHLY ONE DIVORCE) LATER.
THE BERMUDA TRIANGLE COUGHS UP MYTHS LIKE A CONSUMPTIVE ASTHMATIC.
MISSING VESSELS ARE BLAMED ON ALIENS. ATLANTIS. TIME RIFTS. GHOST SHIPS. MAGNETIC ANOMALIES. METHANE ERUPTIONS.
UNDERWATER PYRAMIDS
KINGDOM OF THE LOST MERCORGIS
ATLANTIC OCEAN
SEA MONSTER
GIANT WHIRLPOOL
AMELIA EARHART
DIAMOND PORPOISE
THE BERMUDA TRIANGLE
SECRET FREEMASON SHADOW GOVERNMENT HEADQUARTERS
UNDERWATER CITY
THE BAHAMAS
Tropic of Cancer
CRASHED DOUGLAS DC-3 AIRCRAFT NUMBER NC16001
CUBA
TURKS AND CAICOS ISLANDS (U.K.)
DAVEY JONES' LOCKER
PEOPLE GO MAD.
HAITI
DOMINICAN REPUBLIC
JAMAICA
PEOPLE LOSE THEIR MINDS.
(U.S.)
Caribbean Sea

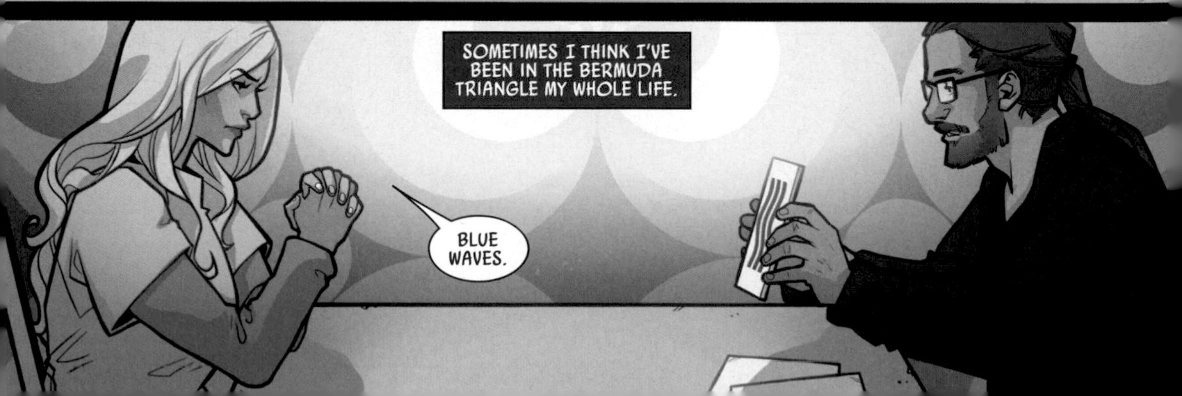
SOMETIMES I THINK I'VE BEEN IN THE BERMUDA TRIANGLE MY WHOLE LIFE.
BLUE WAVES.

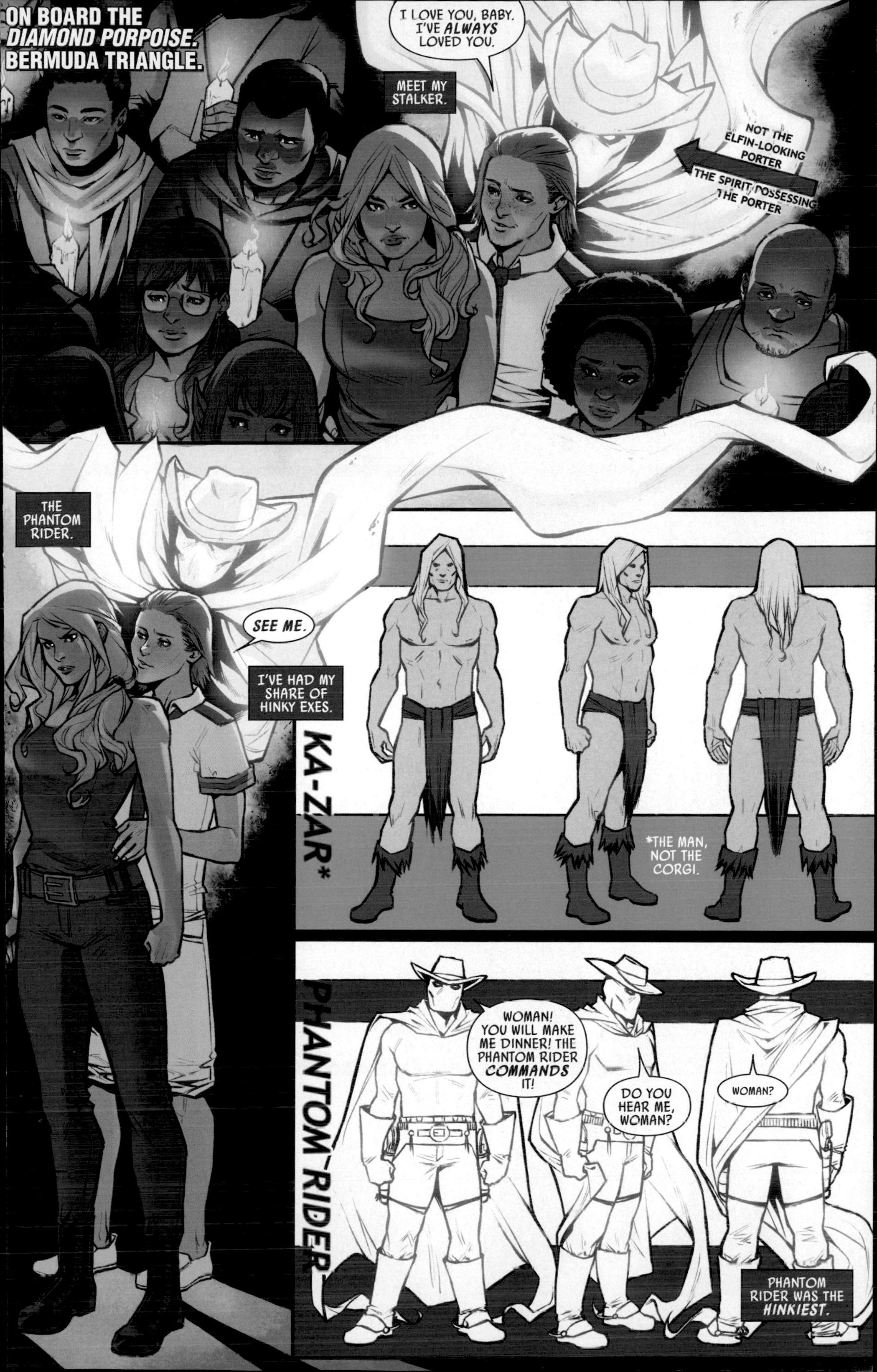
ON BOARD THE DIAMOND PORPOISE. BERMUDA TRIANGLE.
I LOVE YOU, BABY. I'VE ALWAYS LOVED YOU.
MEET MY STALKER.
NOT THE ELFIN-LOOKING PORTER
THE SPIRIT POSSESSING THE PORTER
THE PHANTOM RIDER.
SEE ME.
I'VE HAD MY SHARE OF HINKY EXES.
KA-ZAR*
*THE MAN, NOT THE CORGI.
PHANTOM RIDER
WOMAN! YOU WILL MAKE ME DINNER! THE PHANTOM RIDER COMMANDS IT!
DO YOU HEAR ME, WOMAN?
WOMAN?
PHANTOM RIDER WAS THE HINKIEST.

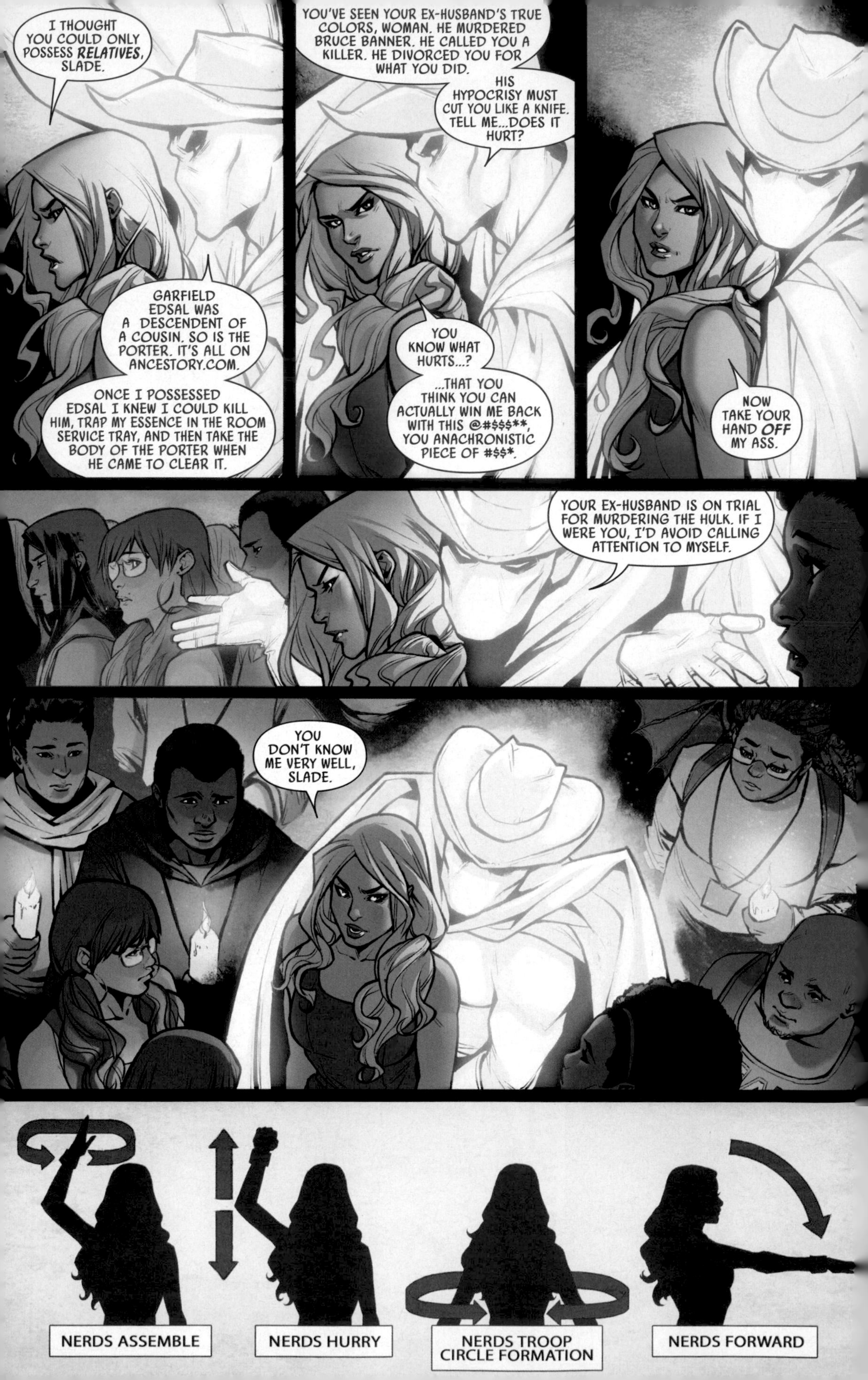
I THOUGHT YOU COULD ONLY POSSESS *RELATIVES*, SLADE.
GARFIELD EDSAL WAS A DESCENDENT OF A COUSIN. SO IS THE PORTER. IT'S ALL ON ANCESTORY.COM.
ONCE I POSSESSED EDSAL I KNEW I COULD KILL HIM, TRAP MY ESSENCE IN THE ROOM SERVICE TRAY, AND THEN TAKE THE BODY OF THE PORTER WHEN HE CAME TO CLEAR IT.
YOU'VE SEEN YOUR EX-HUSBAND'S TRUE COLORS, WOMAN. HE MURDERED BRUCE BANNER. HE CALLED YOU A KILLER. HE DIVORCED YOU FOR WHAT YOU DID.
HIS HYPOCRISY MUST CUT YOU LIKE A KNIFE. TELL ME...DOES IT HURT?
YOU KNOW WHAT HURTS...?
...THAT YOU THINK YOU CAN ACTUALLY WIN ME BACK WITH THIS @#$$$**, YOU ANACHRONISTIC PIECE OF #$$*.
NOW TAKE YOUR HAND *OFF* MY ASS.
YOUR EX-HUSBAND IS ON TRIAL FOR MURDERING THE HULK. IF I WERE YOU, I'D AVOID CALLING ATTENTION TO MYSELF.
YOU DON'T KNOW ME VERY WELL, SLADE.
NERDS ASSEMBLE
NERDS HURRY
NERDS TROOP CIRCLE FORMATION
NERDS FORWARD

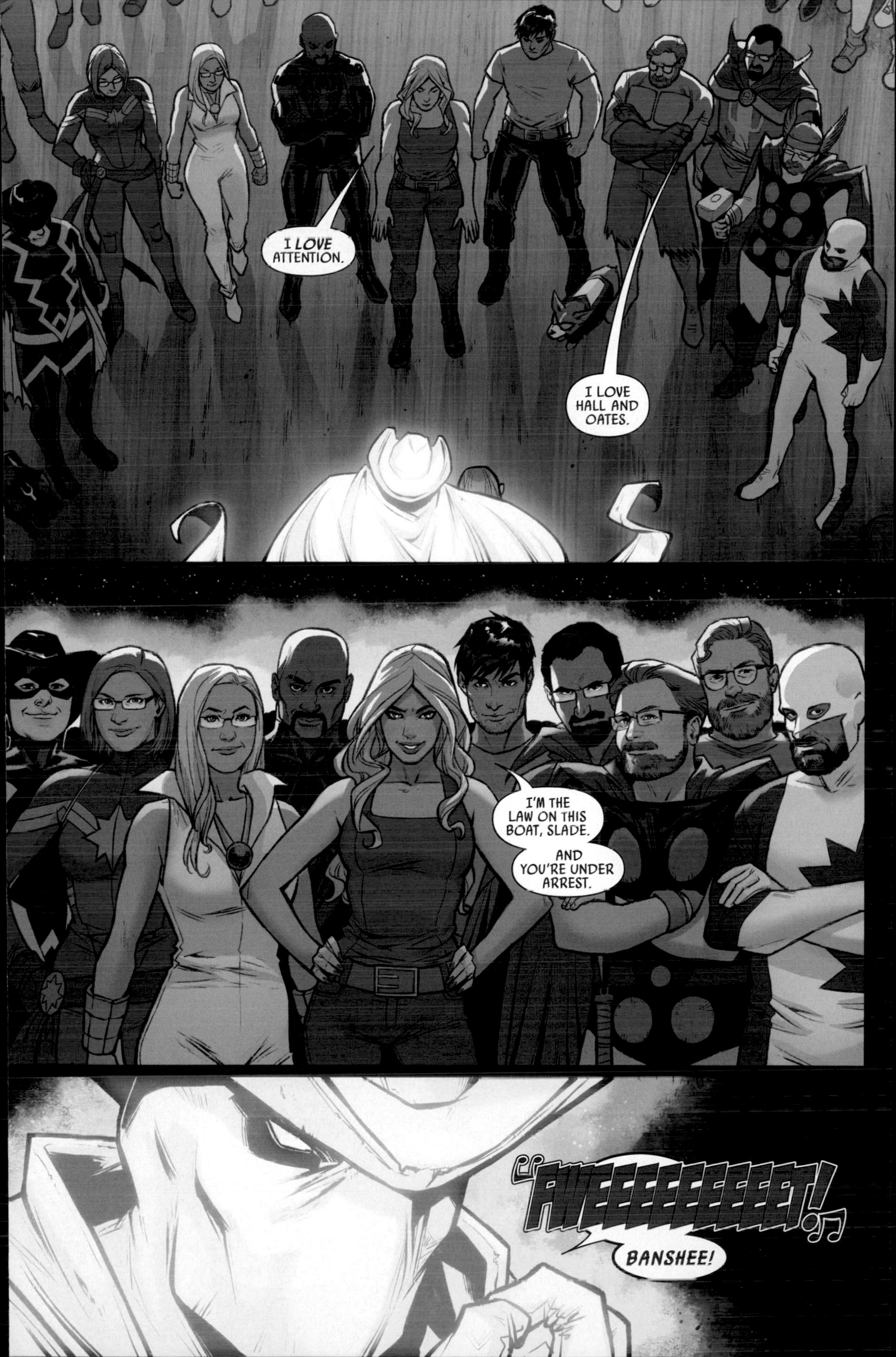
I LOVE ATTENTION.
I LOVE HALL AND OATES.
I'M THE LAW ON THIS BOAT, SLADE.
AND YOU'RE UNDER ARREST.
FWEEEEEEEEEET!
BANSHEE!

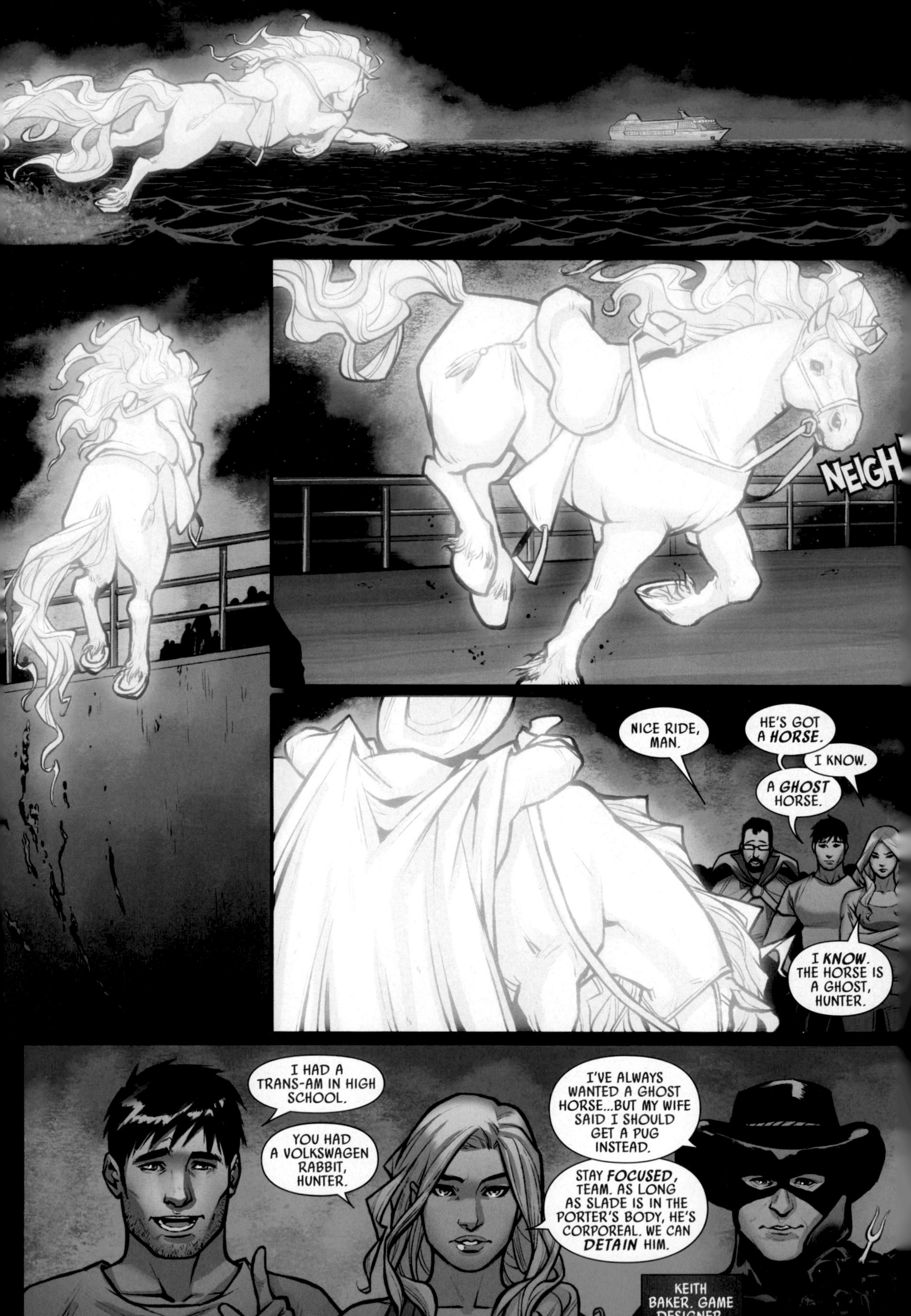
NEIGH
NICE RIDE, MAN.
HE'S GOT A HORSE.
I KNOW.
A GHOST HORSE.
I KNOW. THE HORSE IS A GHOST, HUNTER.
I HAD A TRANS-AM IN HIGH SCHOOL.
YOU HAD A VOLKSWAGEN RABBIT, HUNTER.
I'VE ALWAYS WANTED A GHOST HORSE...BUT MY WIFE SAID I SHOULD GET A PUG INSTEAD.
STAY FOCUSED, TEAM. AS LONG AS SLADE IS IN THE PORTER'S BODY, HE'S CORPOREAL. WE CAN DETAIN HIM.
KEITH BAKER. GAME DESIGNER.

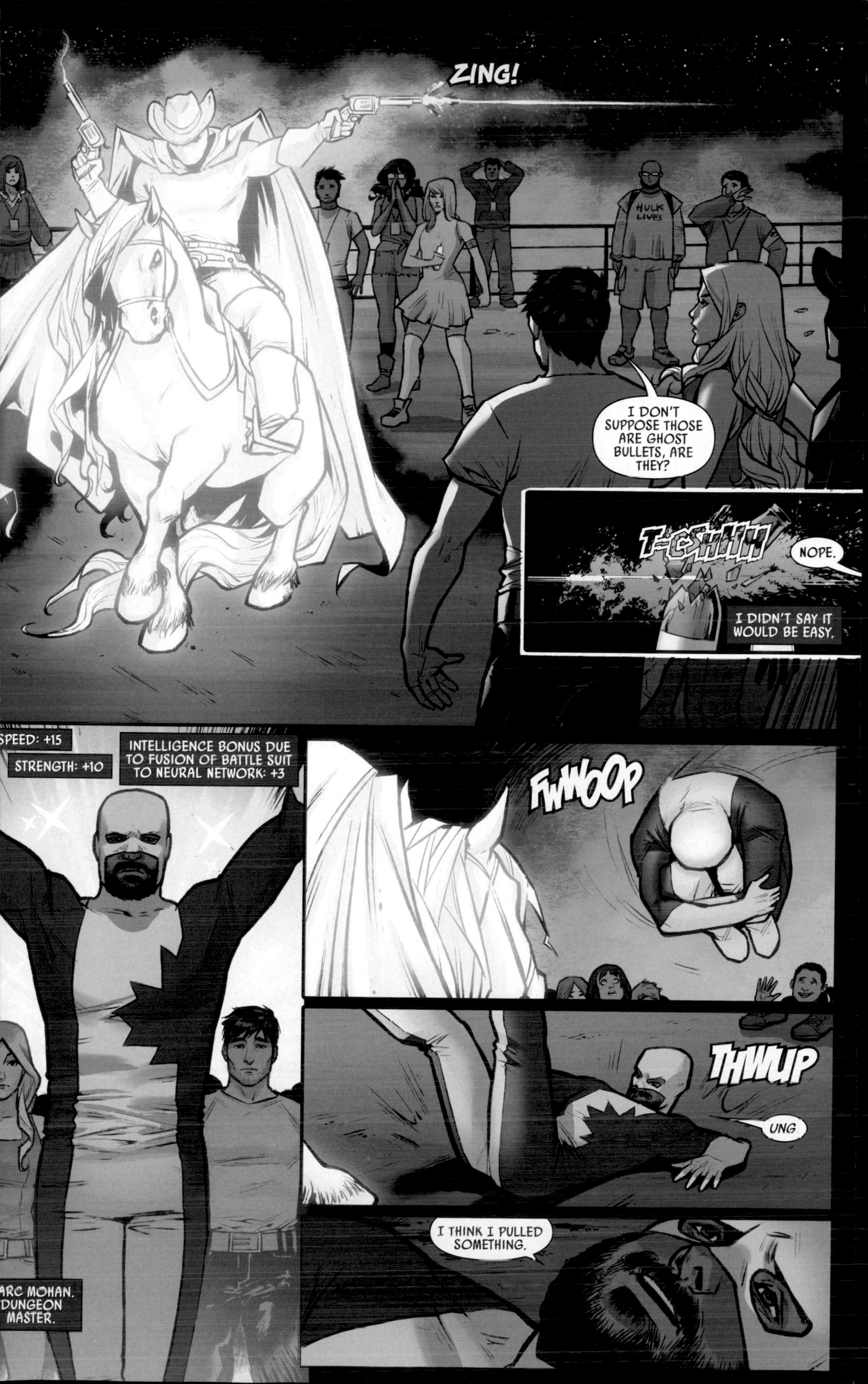
ZING!
I DON'T SUPPOSE THOSE ARE GHOST BULLETS, ARE THEY?
T-CSHHH
NOPE.
I DIDN'T SAY IT WOULD BE EASY.
SPEED: +15
STRENGTH: +10
INTELLIGENCE BONUS DUE TO FUSION OF BATTLE SUIT TO NEURAL NETWORK: +3
ARC MOHAN. DUNGEON MASTER.
FWWOOP
THWUP
UNG
I THINK I PULLED SOMETHING.

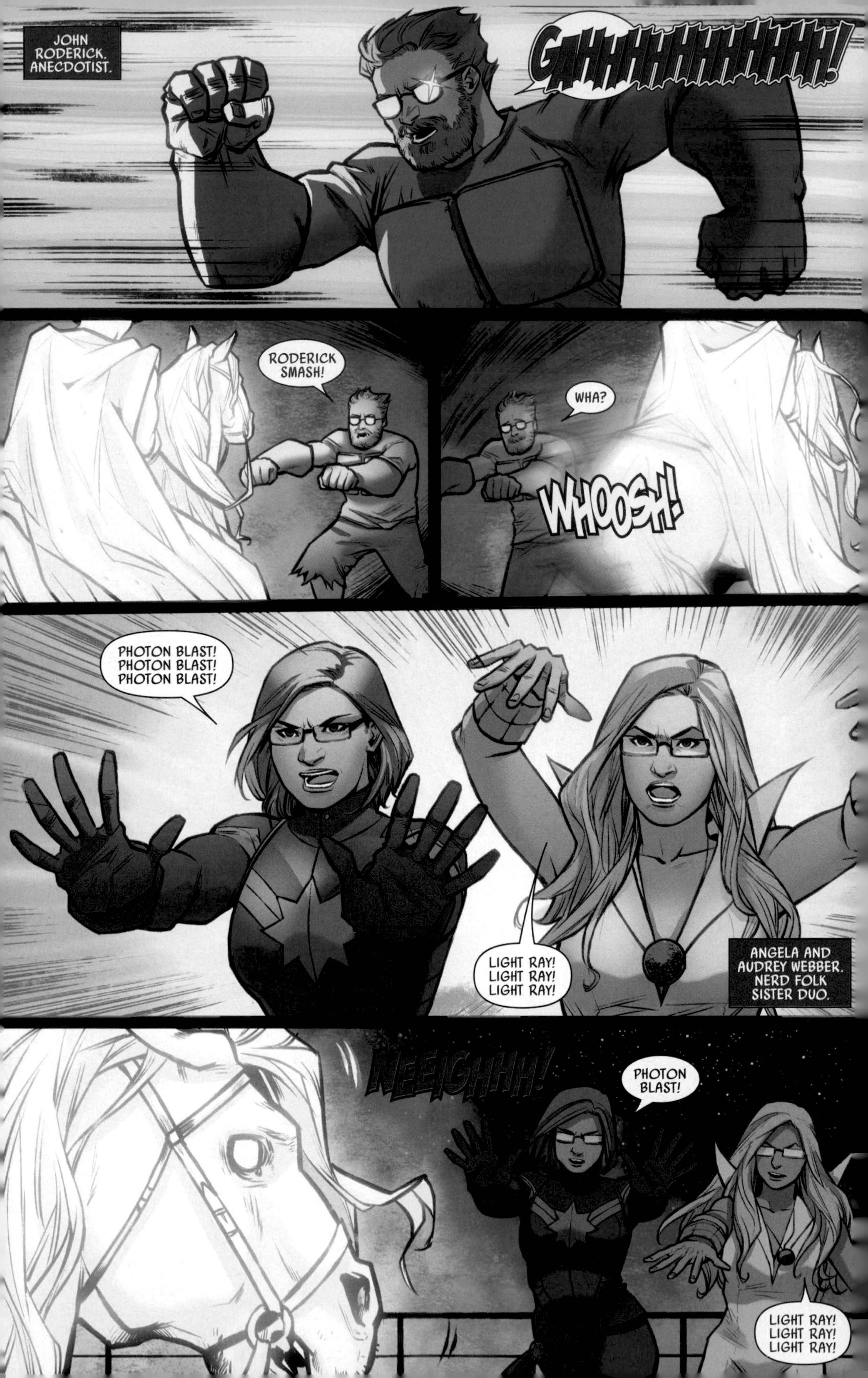

JOHN RODERICK, ANECDOTIST.
GAHHHHHHHHHH!
RODERICK SMASH!
WHA?
WHOOSH!
PHOTON BLAST! PHOTON BLAST! PHOTON BLAST!
LIGHT RAY! LIGHT RAY! LIGHT RAY!
ANGELA AND AUDREY WEBBER. NERD FOLK SISTER DUO.
NEEIGHHH!
PHOTON BLAST!
LIGHT RAY! LIGHT RAY! LIGHT RAY!

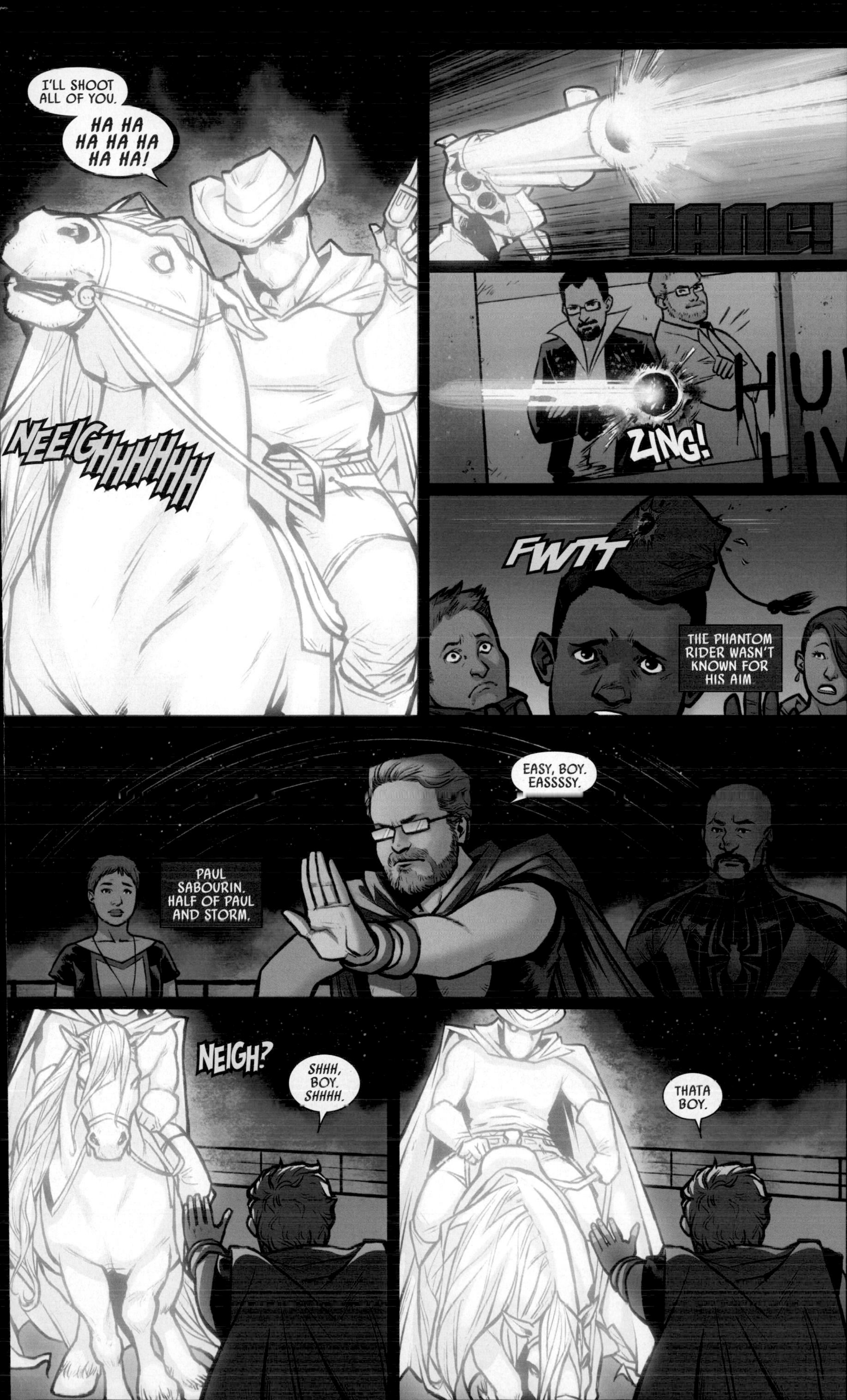
I'LL SHOOT ALL OF YOU.
HA HA HA HA HA HA HA!
NEEIGHHHHHH
BANG!
ZING!
FWTT
THE PHANTOM RIDER WASN'T KNOWN FOR HIS AIM.
EASY, BOY. EASSSSY.
PAUL SABOURIN. HALF OF PAUL AND STORM.
NEIGH?
SHHH, BOY. SHHHH.
THATA BOY.

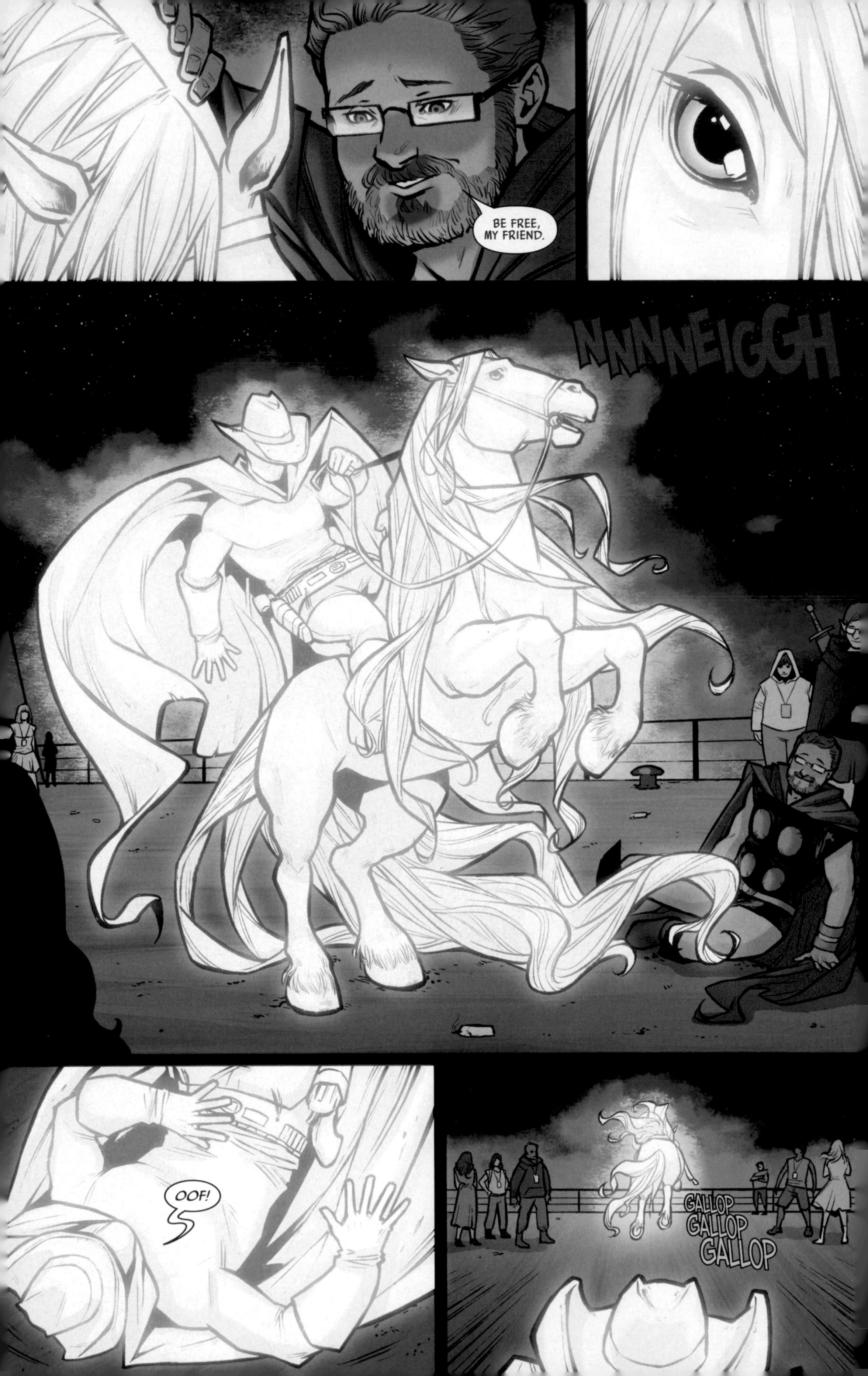
BE FREE, MY FRIEND.
NNNNEIGGH
OOF!
GALLOP
GALLOP
GALLOP

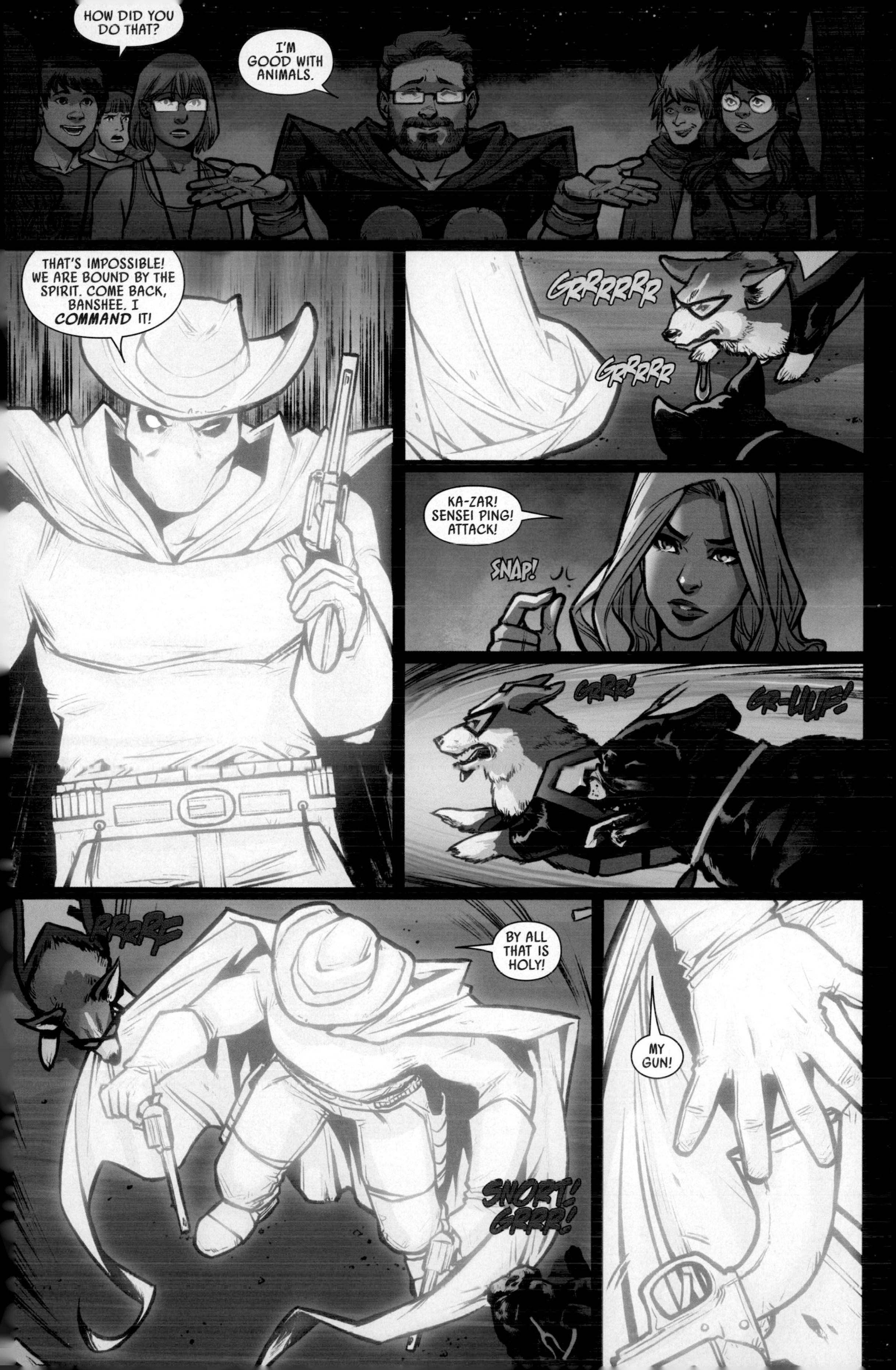
HOW DID YOU DO THAT?
I'M GOOD WITH ANIMALS.
THAT'S IMPOSSIBLE! WE ARE BOUND BY THE SPIRIT. COME BACK, BANSHEE. I COMMAND IT!
GRRRRRR
GRRRRR
KA-ZAR! SENSEI PING! ATTACK!
SNAP!
GRRR!
GR-UUF!
RRRRF
BY ALL THAT IS HOLY!
SNORT! GRRR!
MY GUN!

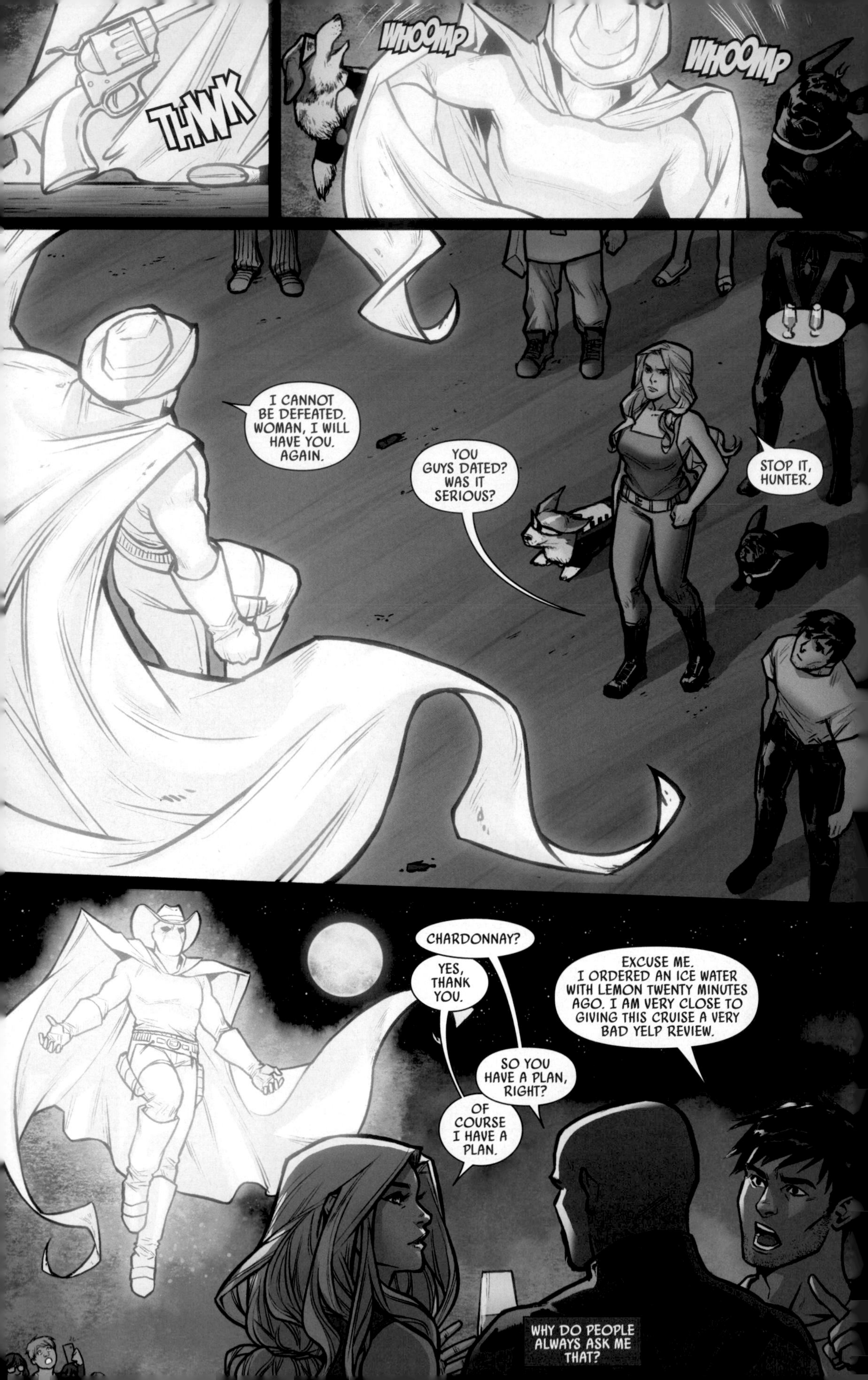
THWK
WHOOMP
WHOOMP
I CANNOT BE DEFEATED. WOMAN, I WILL HAVE YOU. AGAIN.
YOU GUYS DATED? WAS IT SERIOUS?
STOP IT, HUNTER.
CHARDONNAY?
YES, THANK YOU.
EXCUSE ME. I ORDERED AN ICE WATER WITH LEMON TWENTY MINUTES AGO. I AM VERY CLOSE TO GIVING THIS CRUISE A VERY BAD YELP REVIEW.
SO YOU HAVE A PLAN, RIGHT?
OF COURSE I HAVE A PLAN.
WHY DO PEOPLE ALWAYS ASK ME THAT?

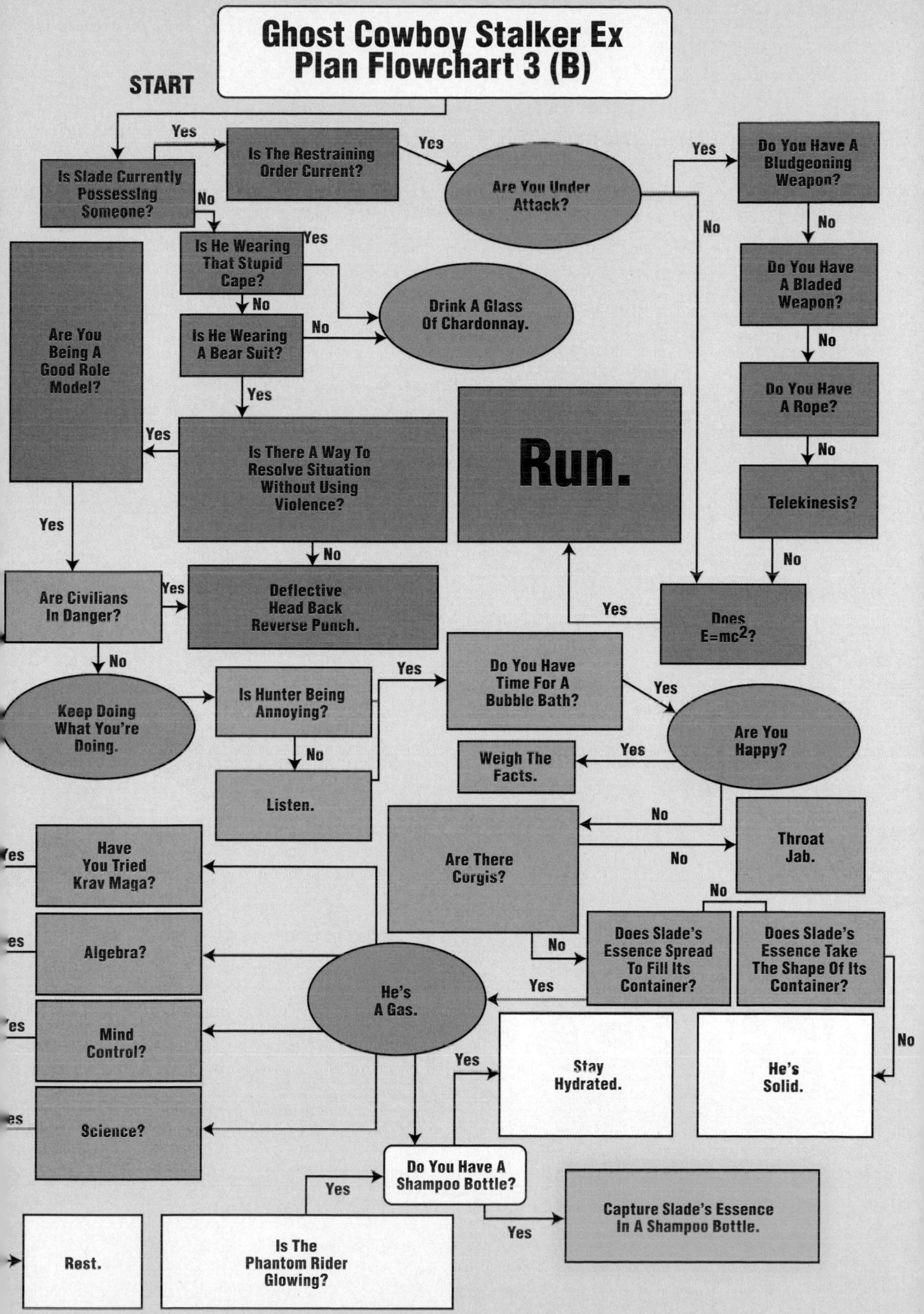

Ghost Cowboy Stalker Ex Plan Flowchart 3 (B)
START
Is Slade Currently Possessing Someone?
Yes
No
Is The Restraining Order Current?
Are You Under Attack?
Yes
No
Do You Have A Bludgeoning Weapon?
No
Do You Have A Bladed Weapon?
No
Do You Have A Rope?
No
Telekinesis?
No
Is He Wearing That Stupid Cape?
Yes
No
Is He Wearing A Bear Suit?
No
Yes
Drink A Glass Of Chardonnay.
Are You Being A Good Role Model?
Yes
Is There A Way To Resolve Situation Without Using Violence?
Yes
No
Run.
Does E=mc2?
Yes
Are Civilians In Danger?
Yes
No
Deflective Head Back Reverse Punch.
Keep Doing What You're Doing.
Is Hunter Being Annoying?
Yes
No
Listen.
Do You Have Time For A Bubble Bath?
Yes
Are You Happy?
Yes
Weigh The Facts.
No
Are There Corgis?
No
Throat Jab.
No
No
Does Slade's Essence Spread To Fill Its Container?
Does Slade's Essence Take The Shape Of Its Container?
Yes
No
He's A Gas.
Yes
Stay Hydrated.
He's Solid.
'es
Have You Tried Krav Maga?
es
Algebra?
'es
Mind Control?
es
Science?
Do You Have A Shampoo Bottle?
Yes
Yes
Capture Slade's Essence In A Shampoo Bottle.
Rest.
Is The Phantom Rider Glowing?

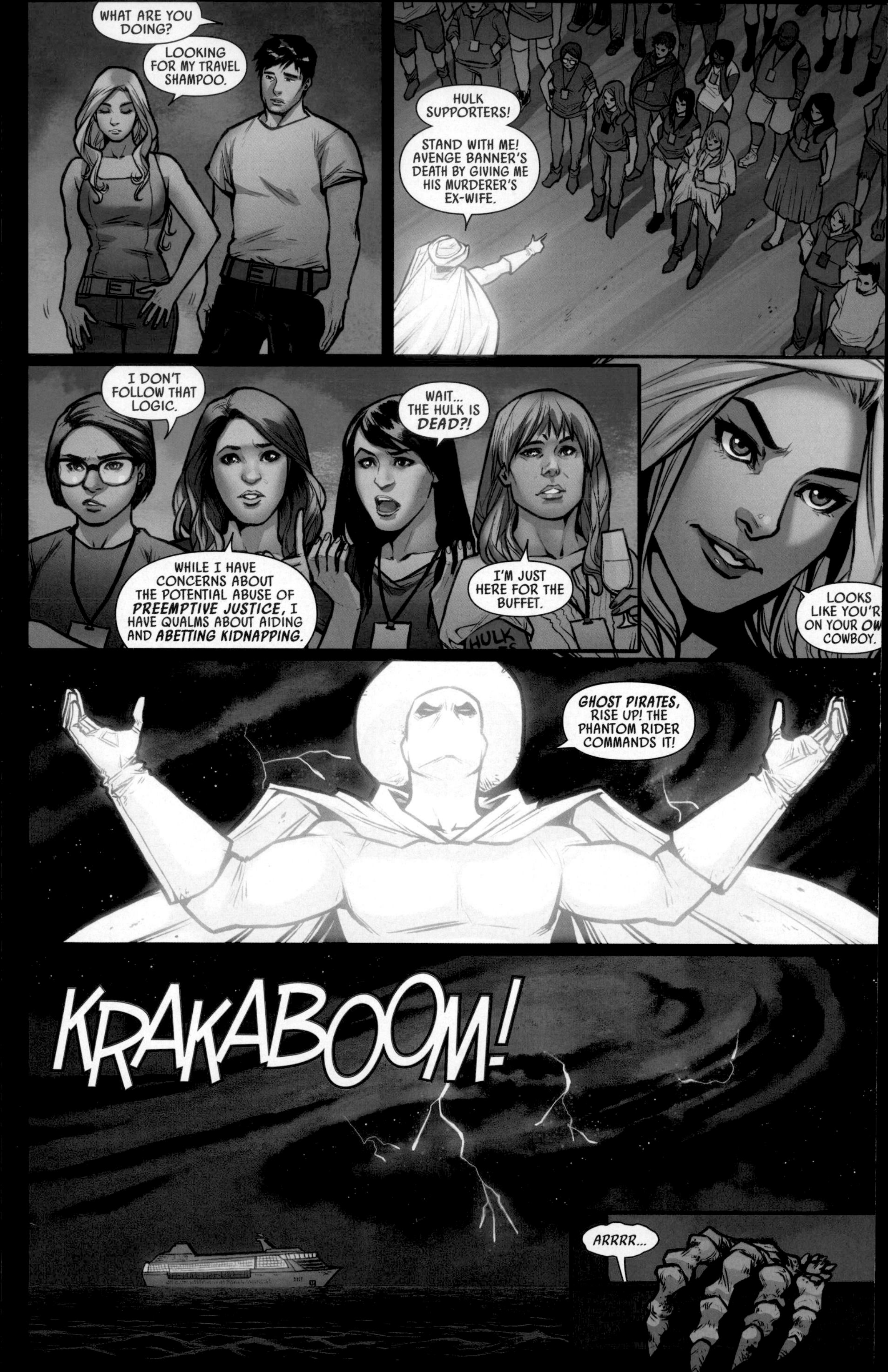
WHAT ARE YOU DOING?
LOOKING FOR MY TRAVEL SHAMPOO.
HULK SUPPORTERS!
STAND WITH ME! AVENGE BANNER'S DEATH BY GIVING ME HIS MURDERER'S EX-WIFE.
I DON'T FOLLOW THAT LOGIC.
WAIT... THE HULK IS DEAD?!
WHILE I HAVE CONCERNS ABOUT THE POTENTIAL ABUSE OF PREEMPTIVE JUSTICE, I HAVE QUALMS ABOUT AIDING AND ABETTING KIDNAPPING.
I'M JUST HERE FOR THE BUFFET.
LOOKS LIKE YOU'R ON YOUR OW COWBOY.
GHOST PIRATES, RISE UP! THE PHANTOM RIDER COMMANDS IT!
KRAKABOOM!
ARRRR...

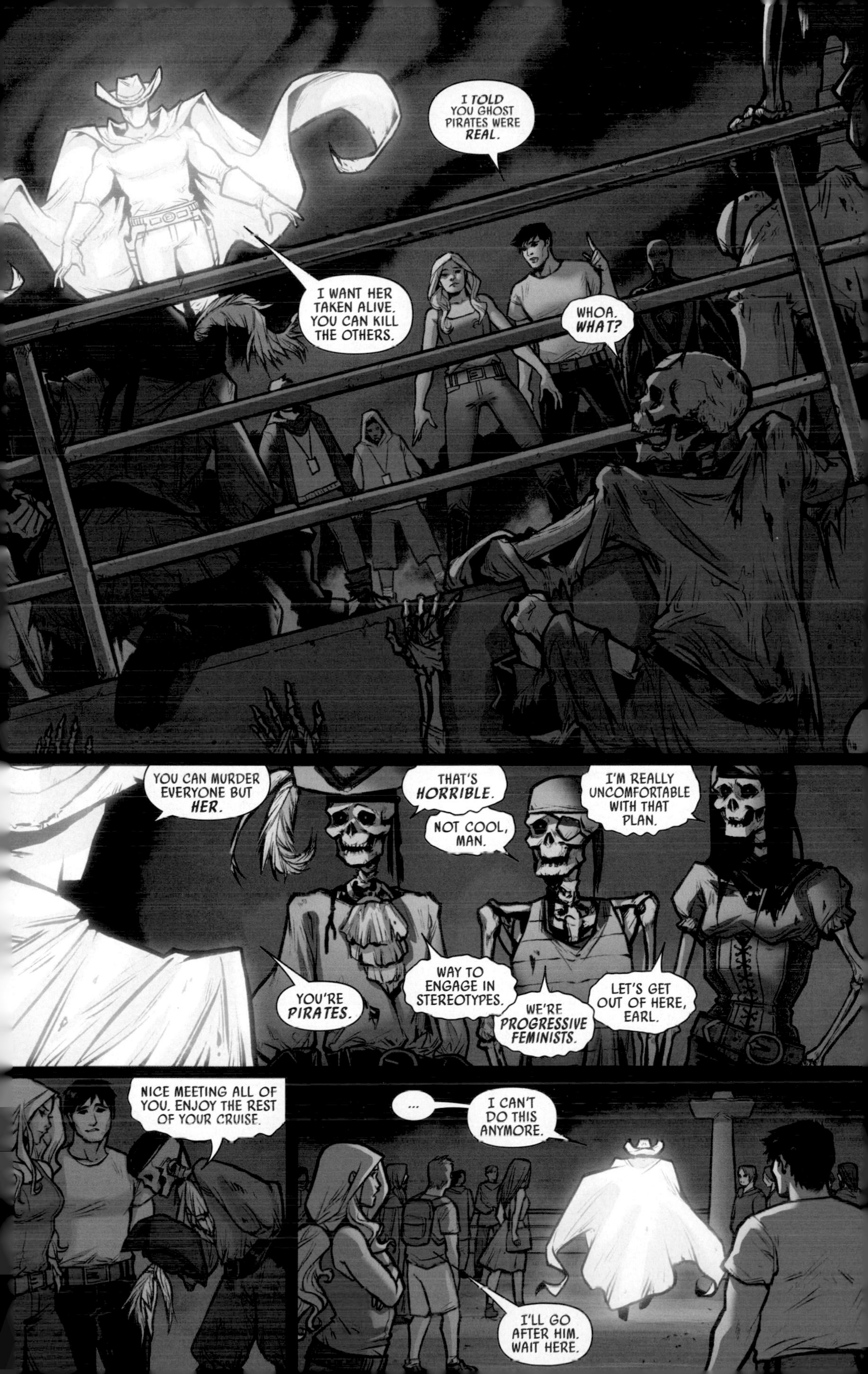
I TOLD YOU GHOST PIRATES WERE REAL.
I WANT HER TAKEN ALIVE. YOU CAN KILL THE OTHERS.
WHOA. WHAT?
YOU CAN MURDER EVERYONE BUT HER.
THAT'S HORRIBLE.
NOT COOL, MAN.
I'M REALLY UNCOMFORTABLE WITH THAT PLAN.
YOU'RE PIRATES.
WAY TO ENGAGE IN STEREOTYPES.
WE'RE PROGRESSIVE FEMINISTS.
LET'S GET OUT OF HERE, EARL.
NICE MEETING ALL OF YOU. ENJOY THE REST OF YOUR CRUISE.
...
I CAN'T DO THIS ANYMORE.
I'LL GO AFTER HIM. WAIT HERE.

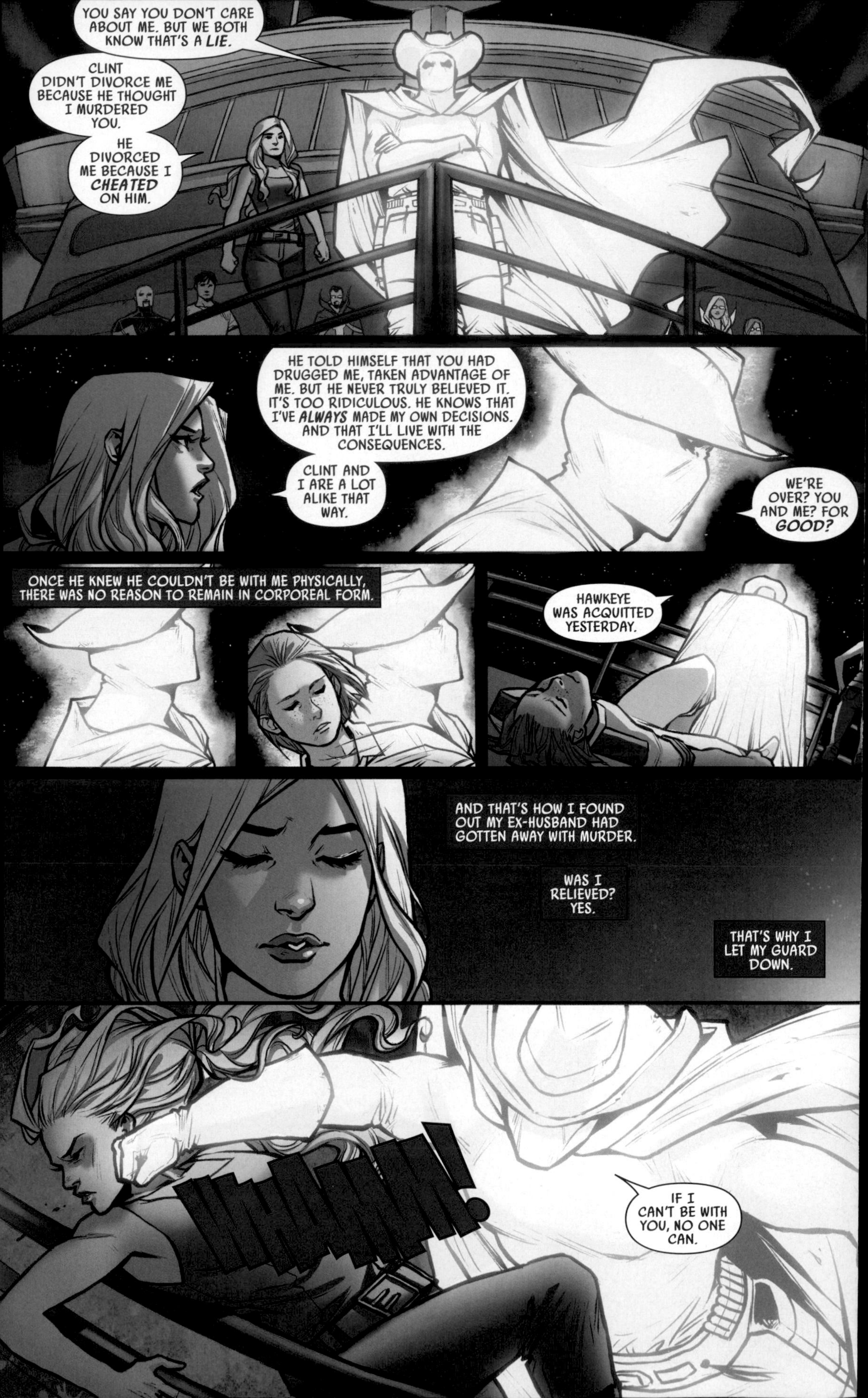
YOU SAY YOU DON'T CARE ABOUT ME. BUT WE BOTH KNOW THAT'S A LIE.
CLINT DIDN'T DIVORCE ME BECAUSE HE THOUGHT I MURDERED YOU.
HE DIVORCED ME BECAUSE I CHEATED ON HIM.
HE TOLD HIMSELF THAT YOU HAD DRUGGED ME, TAKEN ADVANTAGE OF ME. BUT HE NEVER TRULY BELIEVED IT. IT'S TOO RIDICULOUS. HE KNOWS THAT I'VE ALWAYS MADE MY OWN DECISIONS. AND THAT I'LL LIVE WITH THE CONSEQUENCES.
CLINT AND I ARE A LOT ALIKE THAT WAY.
WE'RE OVER? YOU AND ME? FOR GOOD?
ONCE HE KNEW HE COULDN'T BE WITH ME PHYSICALLY, THERE WAS NO REASON TO REMAIN IN CORPOREAL FORM.
HAWKEYE WAS ACQUITTED YESTERDAY.
AND THAT'S HOW I FOUND OUT MY EX-HUSBAND HAD GOTTEN AWAY WITH MURDER.
WAS I RELIEVED? YES.
THAT'S WHY I LET MY GUARD DOWN.
IF I CAN'T BE WITH YOU, NO ONE CAN.

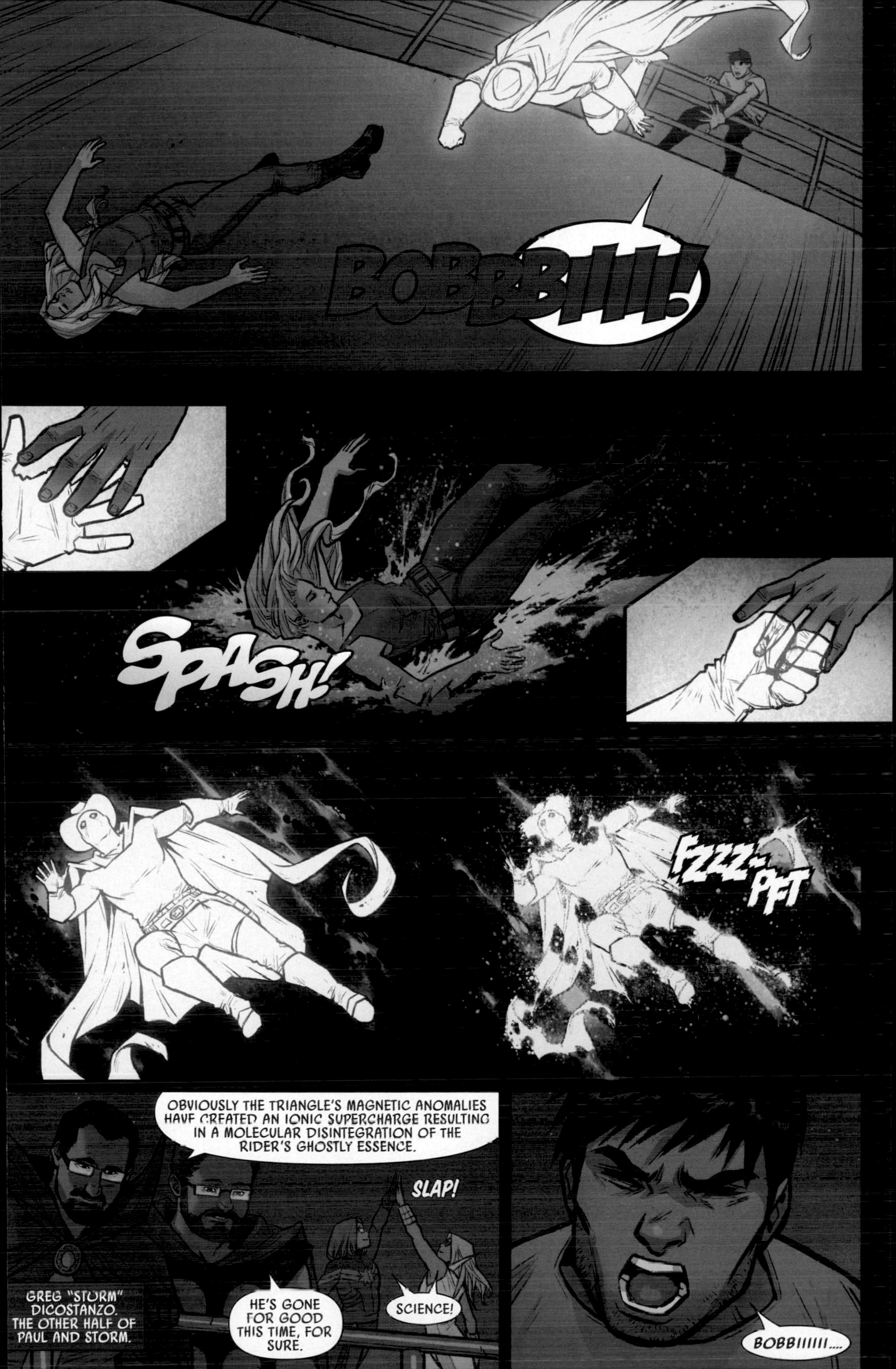
BOBBBIIII!
SPASH!
FZZZ-PFT
OBVIOUSLY THE TRIANGLE'S MAGNETIC ANOMALIES HAVE CREATED AN IONIC SUPERCHARGE RESULTING IN A MOLECULAR DISINTEGRATION OF THE RIDER'S GHOSTLY ESSENCE.
SLAP!
GREG "STORM" DICOSTANZO. THE OTHER HALF OF PAUL AND STORM.
HE'S GONE FOR GOOD THIS TIME, FOR SURE.
SCIENCE!
BOBBIIIIII....

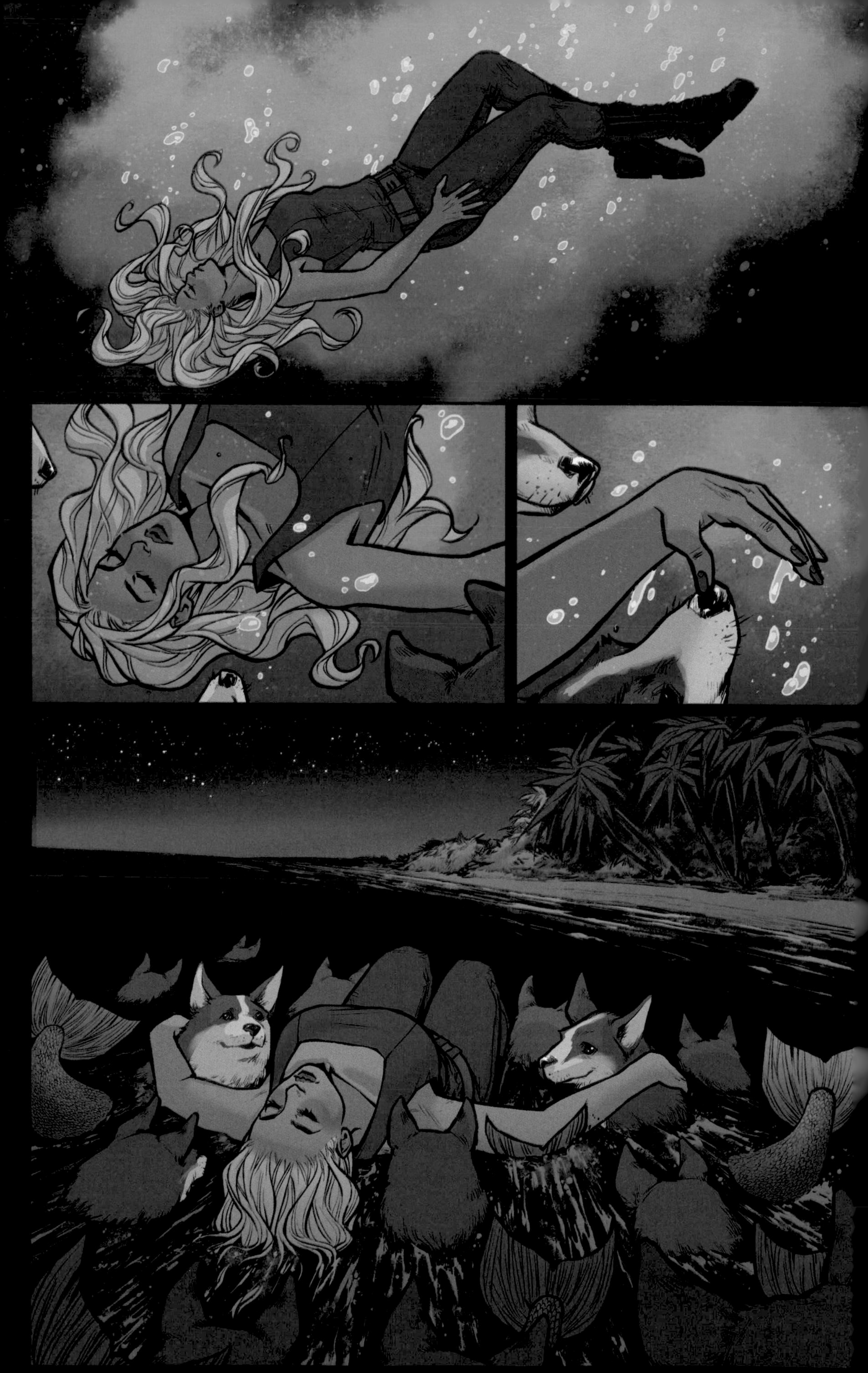

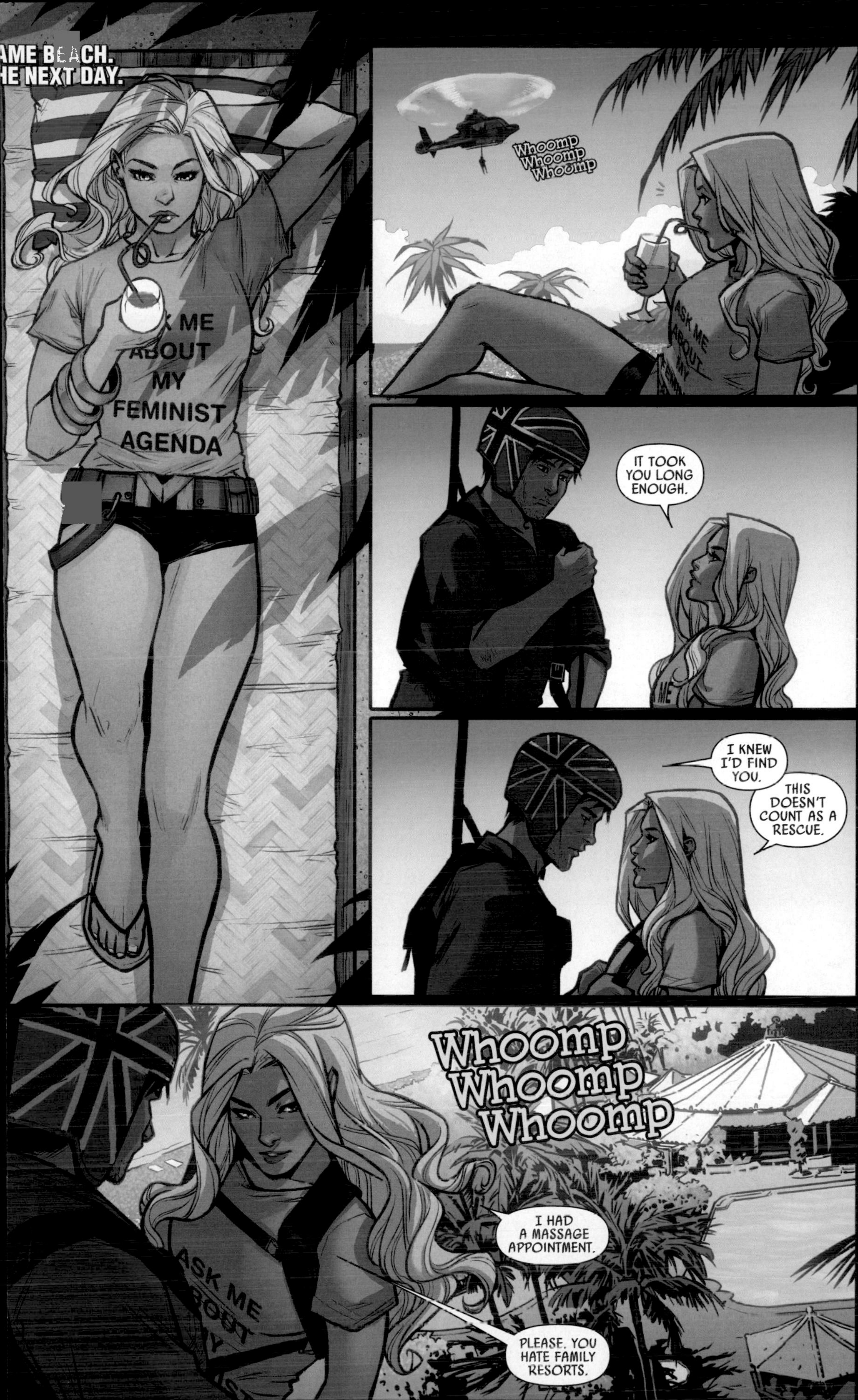
AME BEACH.
HE NEXT DAY.
K ME ABOUT MY FEMINIST AGENDA
Whoomp Whoomp Whoomp
IT TOOK YOU LONG ENOUGH.
I KNEW I'D FIND YOU.
THIS DOESN'T COUNT AS A RESCUE.
Whoomp Whoomp Whoomp
I HAD A MASSAGE APPOINTMENT.
PLEASE. YOU HATE FAMILY RESORTS.

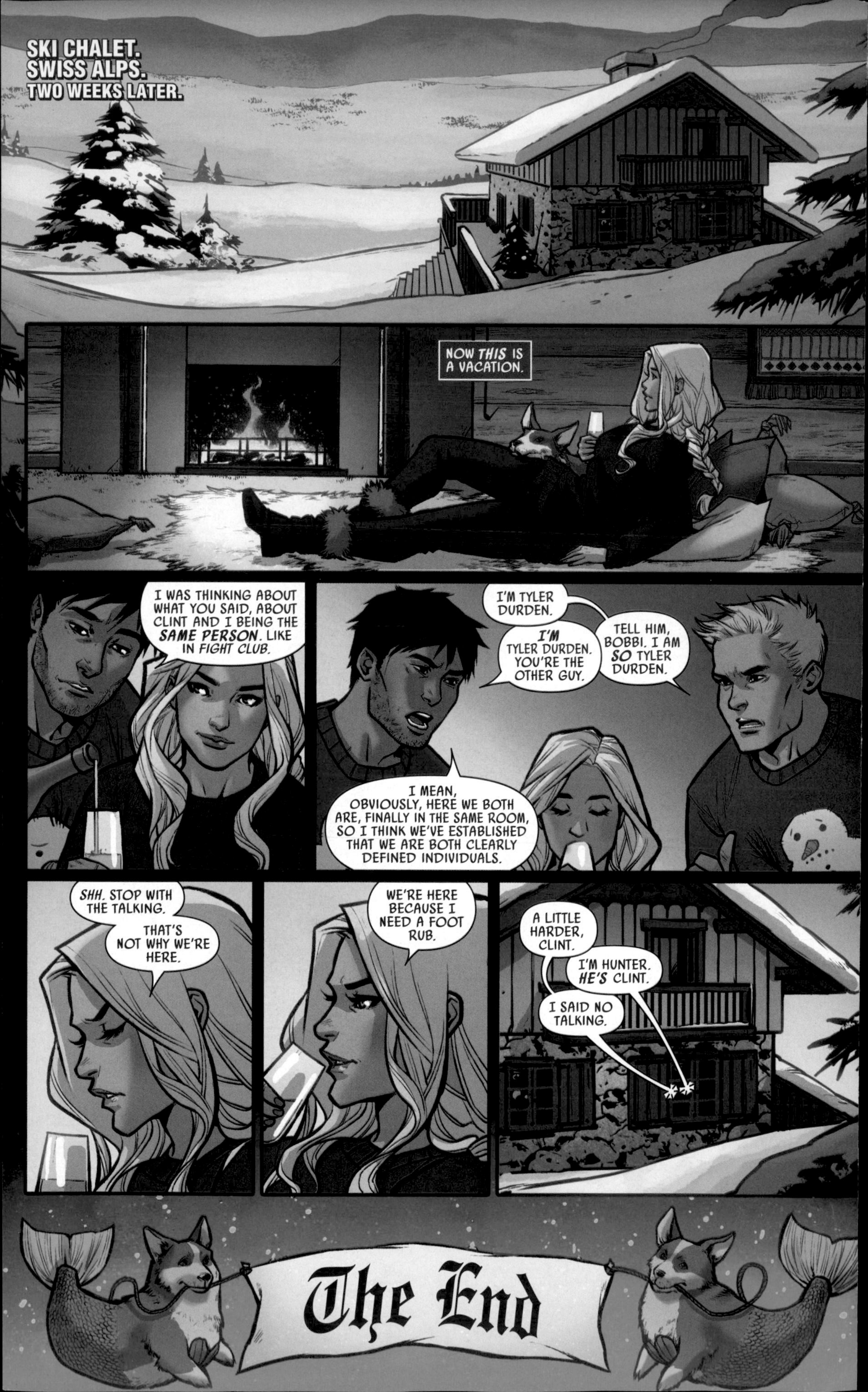
SKI CHALET.
SWISS ALPS.
TWO WEEKS LATER.
NOW THIS IS A VACATION.
I WAS THINKING ABOUT WHAT YOU SAID, ABOUT CLINT AND I BEING THE SAME PERSON. LIKE IN FIGHT CLUB.
I'M TYLER DURDEN.
I'M TYLER DURDEN. YOU'RE THE OTHER GUY.
TELL HIM, BOBBI. I AM SO TYLER DURDEN.
I MEAN, OBVIOUSLY, HERE WE BOTH ARE, FINALLY IN THE SAME ROOM, SO I THINK WE'VE ESTABLISHED THAT WE ARE BOTH CLEARLY DEFINED INDIVIDUALS.
SHH. STOP WITH THE TALKING.
THAT'S NOT WHY WE'RE HERE.
WE'RE HERE BECAUSE I NEED A FOOT RUB.
A LITTLE HARDER, CLINT.
I'M HUNTER. HE'S CLINT.
I SAID NO TALKING.
The End

The first issue of MOCKINGBIRD ended with an apology. "None of that made any sense at all." I was sure the jig was up. That you'd see through me and send me packing. But look at us! Eight issues later!

This is the last issue in this little run. And I'm going to end it with a thank you note. Thank you. All of you. For showing up.

I'm not a comic book writer. I have no idea how I got here. I was having dinner with friends and then...it all gets a bit hazy. When I came to, I was writing MOCKINGBIRD for Marvel. Eight issues later, I'm still dizzy.

I love Bobbi. She has swagger and confidence. She likes herself. She doesn't second-guess her instincts. She knows she's awesome. Obviously, we're a lot alike. At least we share the same sense of humor.

This is my favorite issue. I'm so proud of it. We knew it was going to be our last, and everyone brought their A-game. So it's a great one to go out on. I have to give Marvel credit, because when I sent the script in to my editor, Katie Kubert, I was pretty sure she was going to tell me all the reasons why I couldn't do it. It's a crazy script. I figured, what the heck, right? I just put it all in. Mercorgis. Ghost pirates. Alpine threesomes. I kept checking my email to see if Katie had responded. Then, there it was. An email from her. I have Gmail, so I could see the first line of her email before I even clicked on it. "THIS SCRIPT IS RIDICULOUS..."

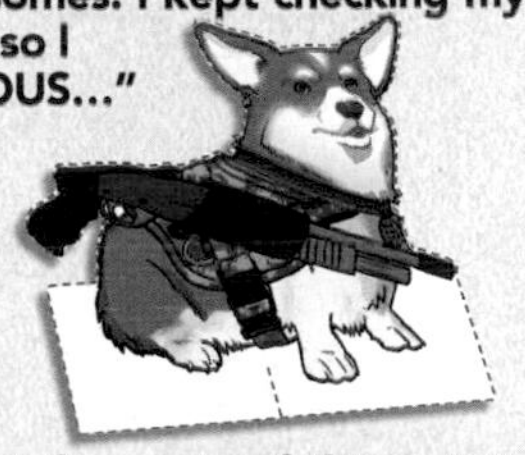

Crap.

Well, I'd tried.

Then I clicked on the email. "THIS SCRIPT IS RIDICULOUSLY AMAZING."

Always click on the email. That's the lesson there.

Katie is no longer at Marvel, but she is a huge part of MOCKINGBIRD. And she fought for parts of this script–including having Clint show up at the end. Thank you, Katie Kubert. I am so pleased to have gotten to work with you.

Christina Harrington was the assistant editor on this series, but that title doesn't even begin to cover all she brought to this book. I could always, always count on her. She has been a real champion of Bobbi's and of mine. Thank you, Christina.

The brilliant Manny Mederos did terrific back pages, in all kinds of styles, from paper dolls (his Clint Barton paper dolls are priceless) to yoga poses, to restraining orders. He was always able to take whatever concept I threw at him and do something clever and funny and smart.

Carlos Lao did the recap pages at the front of each issue. The Daily Blowhole is still my favorite thing ever, second only to the Kazakhstan matchbook he came up with for #3. Thanks, Carlos.

Sean Parsons was our inker on issues #4, #6, and #7. He is so smart and gifted, and really made Kate's drawings sing. Plus, he brought real vision and collaboration to the project. He was completely invested. Thank you, Sean.

Joëlle Jones has done every one of our covers. Joëlle and I once spent an evening together drinking hard liquor at a Portland bar up the street from my house. Who knew it was to be the beginning of such a fruitful creative friendship? Your covers are magnificent, Joëlle. They radiate style, sass, and glamor. Thank you.

Our colorist! Rachelle Rosenberg. Take a look at the hallway wallpaper on the nerd cruise. I gave her a few key words as direction for that wallpaper. Palm Beach. LOVE BOAT. Big print. Palm fronds. Now flip back in this issue and take a look at what she came up with. Believe me, you'll know it when you see it. That's a brilliant colorist. She found what I was seeing in my head, only even better. I just love it so much. One of the early directions I gave Rachelle was this: anything you've ever wanted to try as colorist, do it here. She has brought such dazzle and style and humor to this work. Colorists are underpaid and undervalued. But trust me, they make or break a book. And Rachelle made this one special from the start. Thank you, Rachelle.

Ibrahim Moustafa was our guest artist on issue #5. I am such a huge fan of his work on HIGH CRIMES (with Chris Sebela). Thank you, Ibrahim; you are amazing. That layout you did of S.H.I.E.L.D.'s underground medical complex still knocks my socks off.

Our letterer is Joe Caramagna. MOCKINGBIRD issues are really hard to letter. I have so many background jokes and signs and t-shirts and book jackets and maps and style shifts. And a lot of it is really small. It takes Joe twice as long to do one of my issues, and he gets paid the same page rate. Sometimes, I would send Joe hand-scribbled sketches of what I was imagining. Sometimes I sent font references. He's a genius, if you ask me. Thanks, Joe.

Tom Brevoort, I blame you for this whole thing. Tom is the one who offered me the gig, and he edited the first two issues along with Alanna Smith. I still had so much to learn, and they walked me through the process with such patience and grace. Thank you, Tom and Alanna.

Kate Niemczyk. Where do I begin? Kate, you have brought Bobbi to life. "Our Bobbi," you called her in your first email to me. You have been game for all my shenanigans. You have put up with my early micromanaging. You created a character who is unapologetically beautiful, beautiful on her own terms, separate from the male gaze, but still not afraid to bask in it. Also, you draw the best corgi since Tasha Tudor. I have loved working with you. I have loved opening every layout you've sent, because it has always been thrilling. This issue, in particular, is your very best work. Did you know you could draw such excellent mercorgis? Thank you, Kate. A thousand times, thank you.

And thank you, reader person. You have given us a great gift. You have allowed us the privilege of spending time in your company and in the company of some pretty spectacular characters. Thank you, from all of us, for that.

Maybe we'll see you around.

Until then,
Yours,
Chelsea.

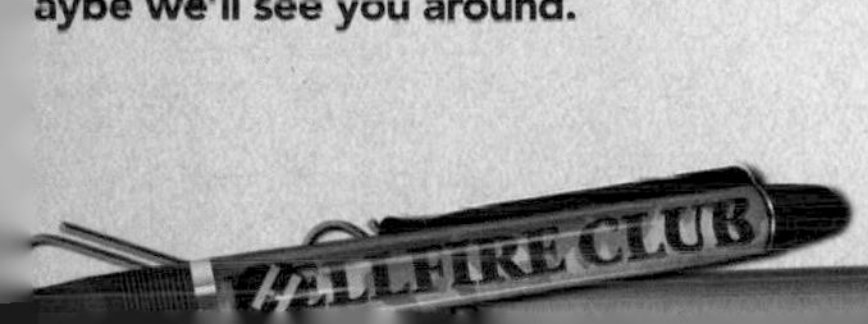
HELLFIRE CLUB

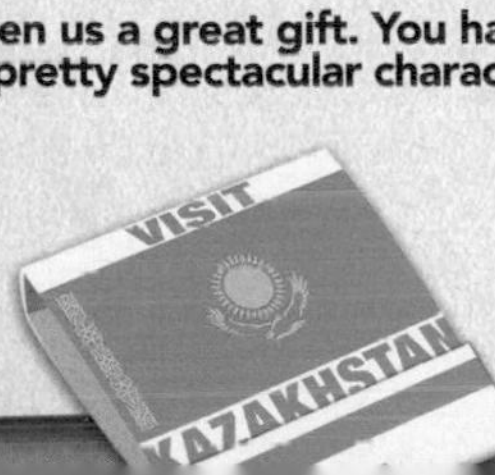
VISIT
KAZAKHSTAN

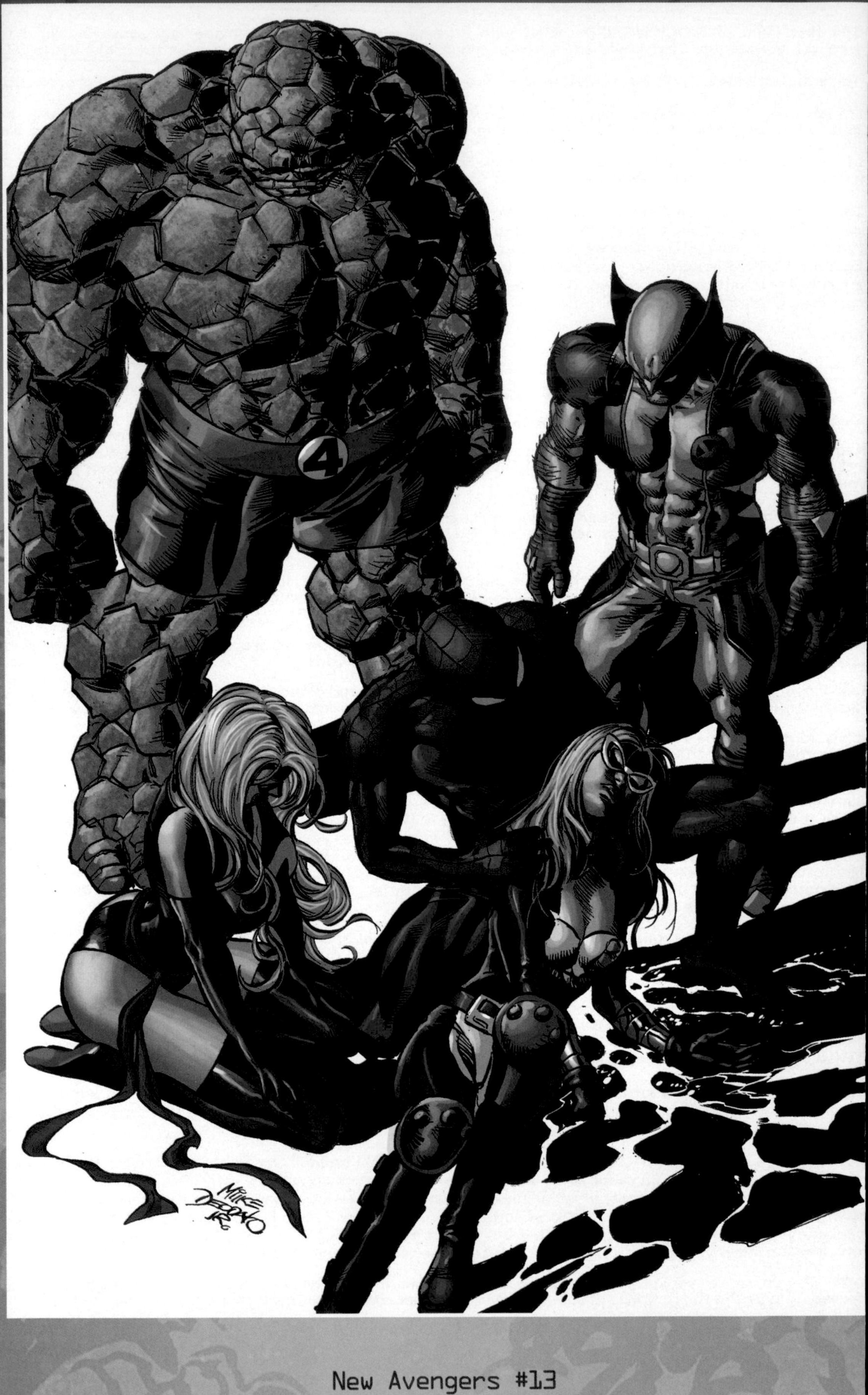
MIKE DEODATO JR.

New Avengers #13

EARTH'S MIGHTIEST HEROES, UNITED AGAINST A COMMON THREAT! ON THAT DAY THE AVENGERS WERE BORN, TO FIGHT FOES THAT NO SINGLE HERO COULD WITHSTAND!

NEW AVENGERS

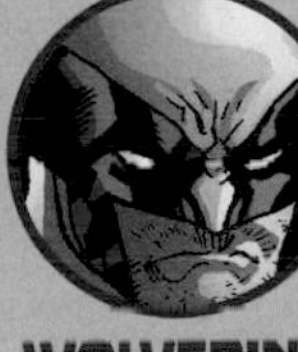
WOLVERINE

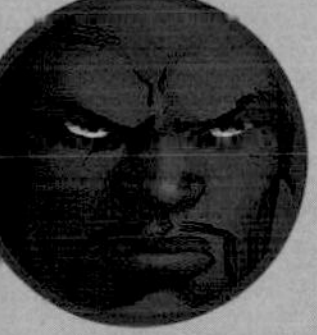
LUKE CAGE

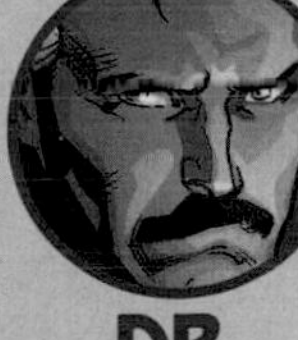
DR. STRANGE

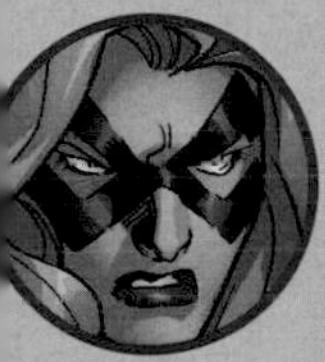
MS. MARVEL

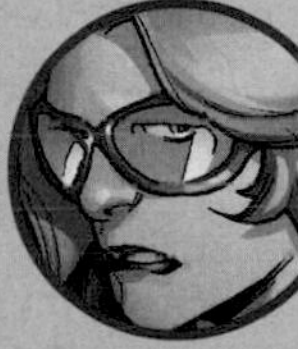
MOCKINGBIRD

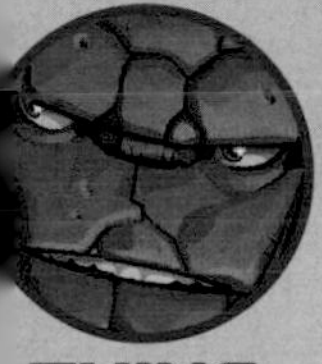
THING

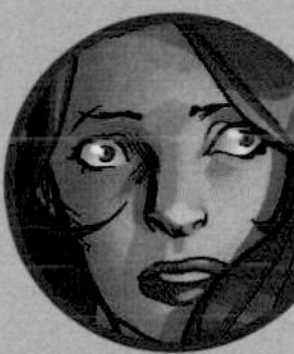
JESSICA JONES

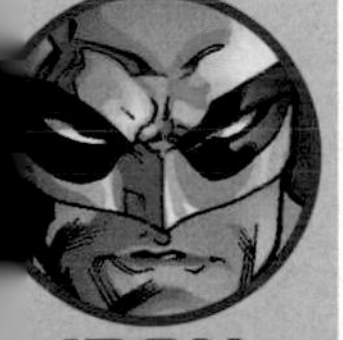
IRON FIST

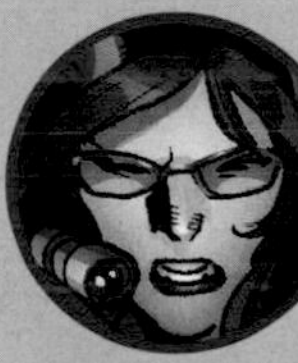
VICTORIA HAND

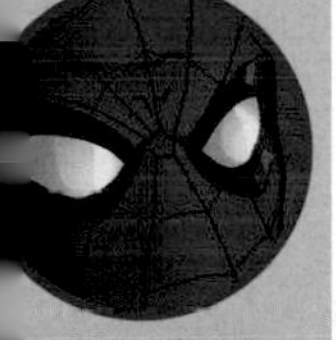
SPIDER-MAN

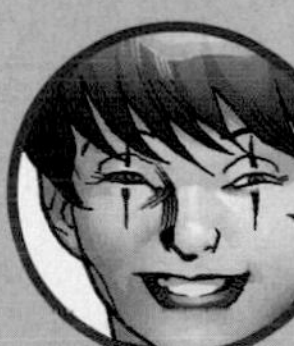
SQUIRREL GIRL

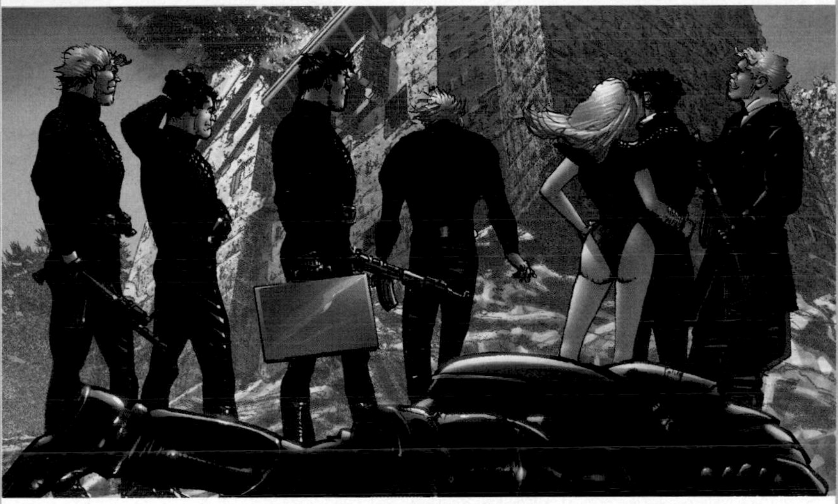

AVENGERS COMMANDER STEVE ROGERS HAS GIVEN LUKE CAGE, JESSICA JONES, MS. MARVEL, MOCKINGBIRD, SPIDER-MAN, WOLVERINE, IRON FIST, DOCTOR STRANGE, AND THE THING THE KEYS TO AVENGERS MANSION, A CONTROVERSIAL LIAISON IN THE FORM OF VICTORIA HAND, AND FREE REIN TO PROTECT THE WORLD ANY WAY THEY SEE FIT.

IN THE LATE NINETEEN-FIFTIES: NICK FURY IS SPENDING HIS TIME HUNTING DOWN NAZI WAR CRIMINALS WHEN THE PRESIDENT ASKS HIM TO PUT TOGETHER AN AVENGERS INITIATIVE FOR A SPECIAL SECRET MISSION. THE TEAM CONSISTS OF HIS PARTNER DUM DUM DUGAN; VICTOR CREED, A.K.A. SABRETOOTH; NAMORA, AN ATLANTEAN PRINCESS; SERGEI KRAVINOFF, A.K.A. KRAVEN THE HUNTER; ULYSSES BLOODSTONE, MYSTICALLY ENHANCED MONSTER HUNTER; DOMINIC FORTUNE, SUPER-SOLDIER-FOR-HIRE; AND ERNST SABLINOVA, A.K.A. THE SILVER SABLE.

HAVING TRACKED THE RED SKULL TO SWEDEN, THE AVENGERS DISCOVER THE SKULL HAS CREATED HIS OWN TWISTED VERSION OF CAPTAIN AMERICA. DESTROYING THE EVIL CAP, THE TEAM TAKES OUT THE SKULL AS WELL, WHO TURNS OUT NOT TO BE THE ORIGINAL HIMSELF, BUT A SUCCESSOR. RECOVERING THE SKULL'S BRIEFCASE, FURY FINDS SOME VERY CURIOUS CONTENTS…

IN THE PRESENT: NORMAN OSBORN'S DEFUNCT ORGANIZATION H.A.M.M.E.R. IS SETTING UP SHOP AGAIN, BUT THE NEW AVENGERS STOP THEM AND THEIR NEW LEADER SUPERIA BEFORE THEY EVEN GET STARTED. THE ENSUING BATTLE HAS ALREADY CLAIMED A VICTIM…MOCKINGBIRD IS DOWN.

THE NEW AVENGERS TEAM UP WITH MOCKINGBIRD'S EX-HUSBAND HAWKEYE AND SPIDER-WOMAN AND SCRAMBLE TO FIND SUPERIA. MEANWHILE, SUPERIA CONFRONTS THE AVENGERS' LIAISON, AND FORMER H.A.M.M.E.R. AGENT VICTORIA HAND, WHO REVEALS SHE IS STILL A H.A.M.M.E.R. LOYALIST. OR IS SHE?

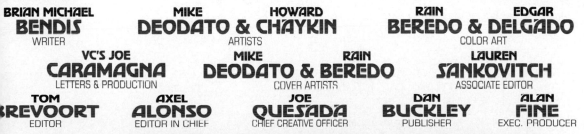

BRIAN MICHAEL BENDIS
WRITER

MIKE DEODATO & HOWARD CHAYKIN
ARTISTS

RAIN BEREDO & EDGAR DELGADO
COLOR ART

VC'S JOE CARAMAGNA
LETTERS & PRODUCTION

MIKE DEODATO & RAIN BEREDO
COVER ARTISTS

LAUREN SANKOVITCH
ASSOCIATE EDITOR

TOM BREVOORT
EDITOR

AXEL ALONSO
EDITOR IN CHIEF

JOE QUESADA
CHIEF CREATIVE OFFICER

DAN BUCKLEY
PUBLISHER

ALAN FINE
EXEC. PRODUCER

SPECIAL THANKS TO STUART VANDAL, MICHAEL HOSKIN, RONALD BYRD AND KEVIN GARCIA

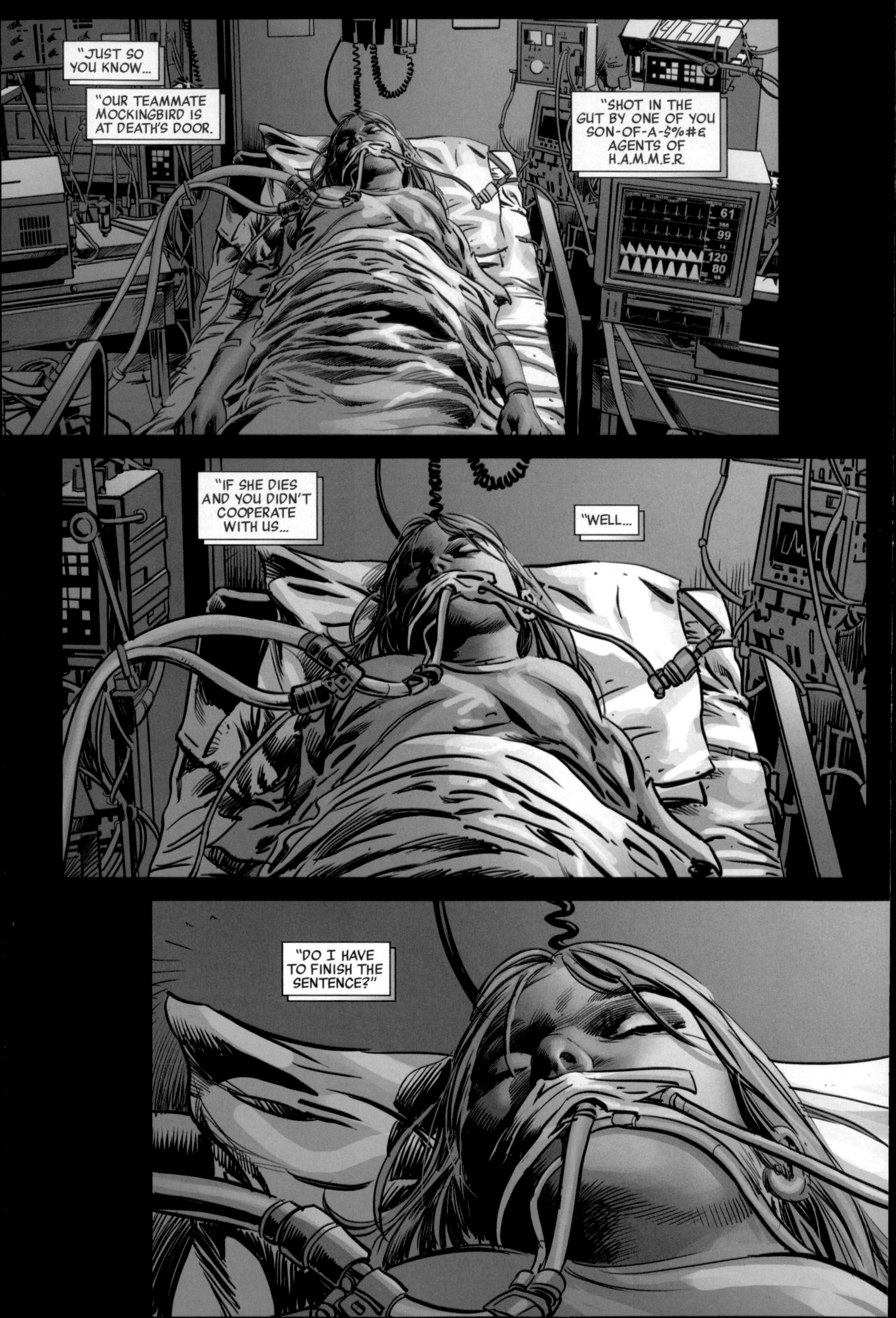
"JUST SO YOU KNOW...
"OUR TEAMMATE MOCKINGBIRD IS AT DEATH'S DOOR.
"SHOT IN THE GUT BY ONE OF YOU SON-OF-A-$%#& AGENTS OF H.A.M.M.E.R.
"IF SHE DIES AND YOU DIDN'T COOPERATE WITH US...
"WELL...
"DO I HAVE TO FINISH THE SENTENCE?"

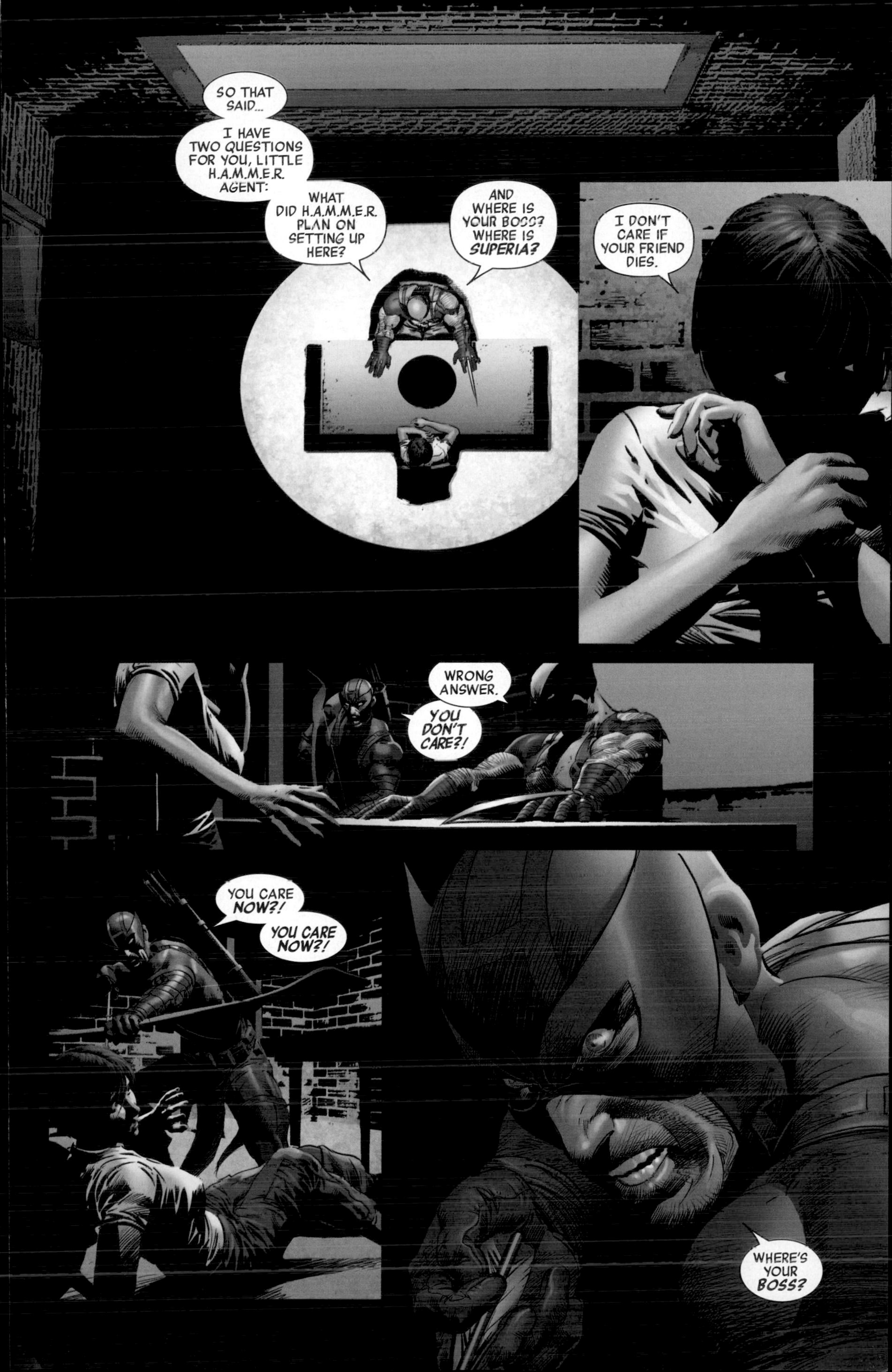

SO THAT SAID...
I HAVE TWO QUESTIONS FOR YOU, LITTLE H.A.M.M.E.R. AGENT:
WHAT DID H.A.M.M.E.R. PLAN ON SETTING UP HERE?
AND WHERE IS YOUR BOSS? WHERE IS SUPERIA?
I DON'T CARE IF YOUR FRIEND DIES.
WRONG ANSWER.
YOU DON'T CARE?!
YOU CARE NOW?!
YOU CARE NOW?!
WHERE'S YOUR BOSS?

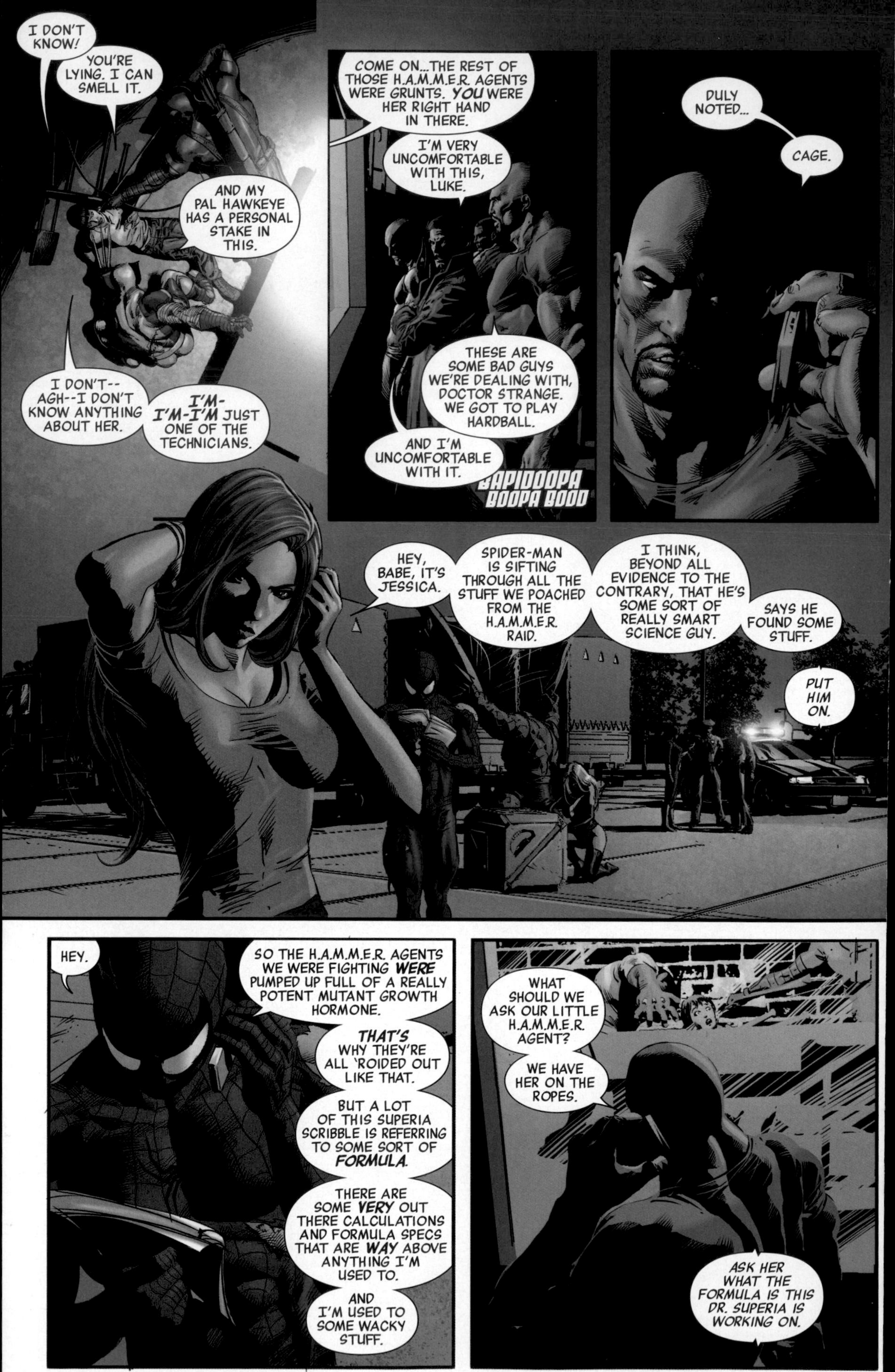
I DON'T KNOW!
YOU'RE LYING. I CAN SMELL IT.
AND MY PAL HAWKEYE HAS A PERSONAL STAKE IN THIS.
I DON'T-- AGH--I DON'T KNOW ANYTHING ABOUT HER.
I'M- I'M-I'M JUST ONE OF THE TECHNICIANS.
COME ON...THE REST OF THOSE H.A.M.M.E.R. AGENTS WERE GRUNTS. YOU WERE HER RIGHT HAND IN THERE.
I'M VERY UNCOMFORTABLE WITH THIS, LUKE.
THESE ARE SOME BAD GUYS WE'RE DEALING WITH, DOCTOR STRANGE. WE GOT TO PLAY HARDBALL.
AND I'M UNCOMFORTABLE WITH IT.
BAPIDOOPA BOOPA BOOD
DULY NOTED...
CAGE.
HEY, BABE, IT'S JESSICA.
SPIDER-MAN IS SIFTING THROUGH ALL THE STUFF WE POACHED FROM THE H.A.M.M.E.R. RAID.
I THINK, BEYOND ALL EVIDENCE TO THE CONTRARY, THAT HE'S SOME SORT OF REALLY SMART SCIENCE GUY.
SAYS HE FOUND SOME STUFF.
PUT HIM ON.
HEY.
SO THE H.A.M.M.E.R AGENTS WE WERE FIGHTING WERE PUMPED UP FULL OF A REALLY POTENT MUTANT GROWTH HORMONE.
THAT'S WHY THEY'RE ALL 'ROIDED OUT LIKE THAT.
BUT A LOT OF THIS SUPERIA SCRIBBLE IS REFERRING TO SOME SORT OF FORMULA.
THERE ARE SOME VERY OUT THERE CALCULATIONS AND FORMULA SPECS THAT ARE WAY ABOVE ANYTHING I'M USED TO.
AND I'M USED TO SOME WACKY STUFF.
WHAT SHOULD WE ASK OUR LITTLE H.A.M.M.E.R. AGENT?
WE HAVE HER ON THE ROPES.
ASK HER WHAT THE FORMULA IS THIS DR. SUPERIA IS WORKING ON.

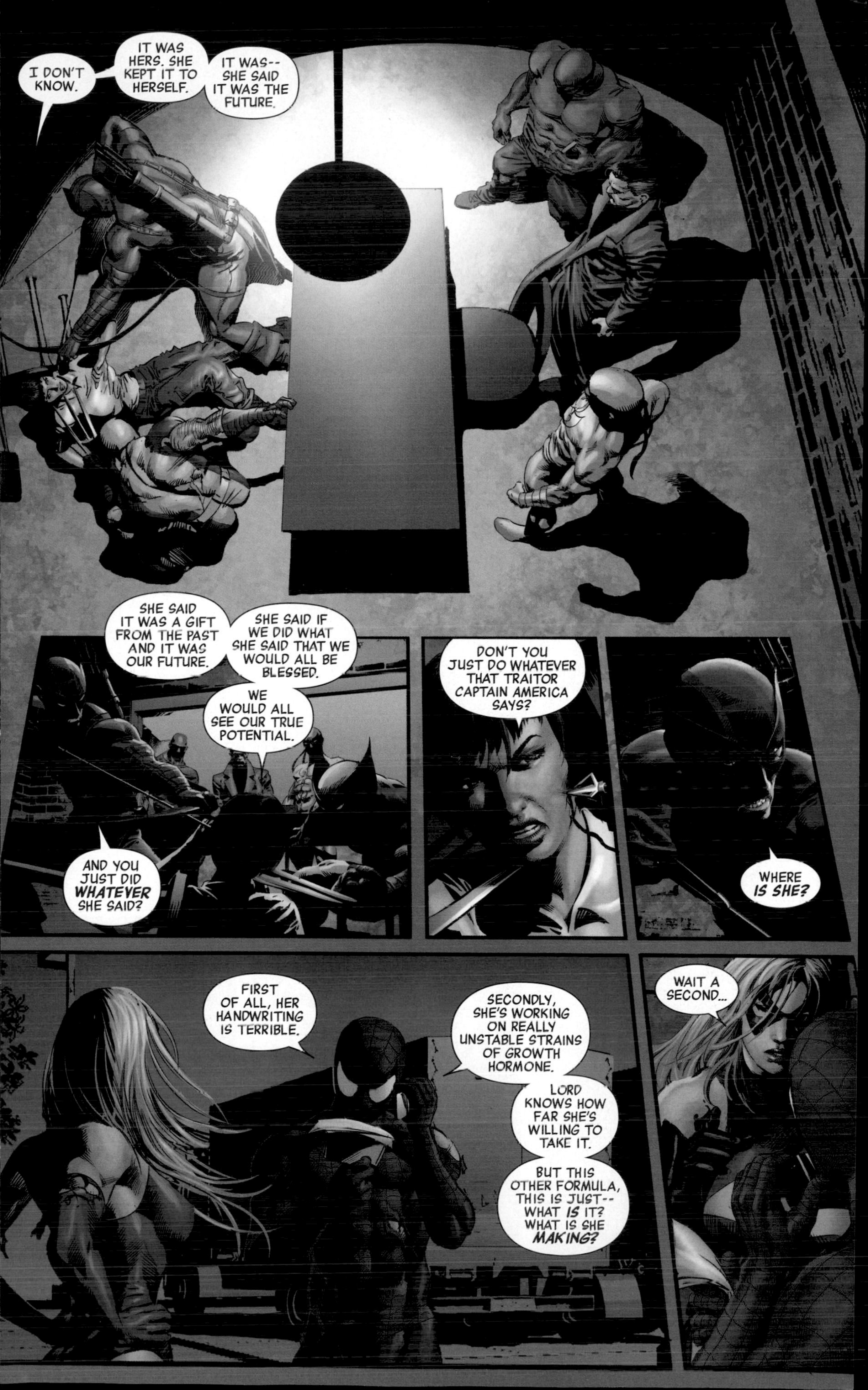
I DON'T KNOW.
IT WAS HERS. SHE KEPT IT TO HERSELF.
IT WAS-- SHE SAID IT WAS THE FUTURE.
SHE SAID IT WAS A GIFT FROM THE PAST AND IT WAS OUR FUTURE.
SHE SAID IF WE DID WHAT SHE SAID THAT WE WOULD ALL BE BLESSED.
WE WOULD ALL SEE OUR TRUE POTENTIAL.
AND YOU JUST DID WHATEVER SHE SAID?
DON'T YOU JUST DO WHATEVER THAT TRAITOR CAPTAIN AMERICA SAYS?
WHERE IS SHE?
FIRST OF ALL, HER HANDWRITING IS TERRIBLE.
SECONDLY, SHE'S WORKING ON REALLY UNSTABLE STRAINS OF GROWTH HORMONE.
LORD KNOWS HOW FAR SHE'S WILLING TO TAKE IT.
BUT THIS OTHER FORMULA, THIS IS JUST-- WHAT IS IT? WHAT IS SHE MAKING?
WAIT A SECOND...

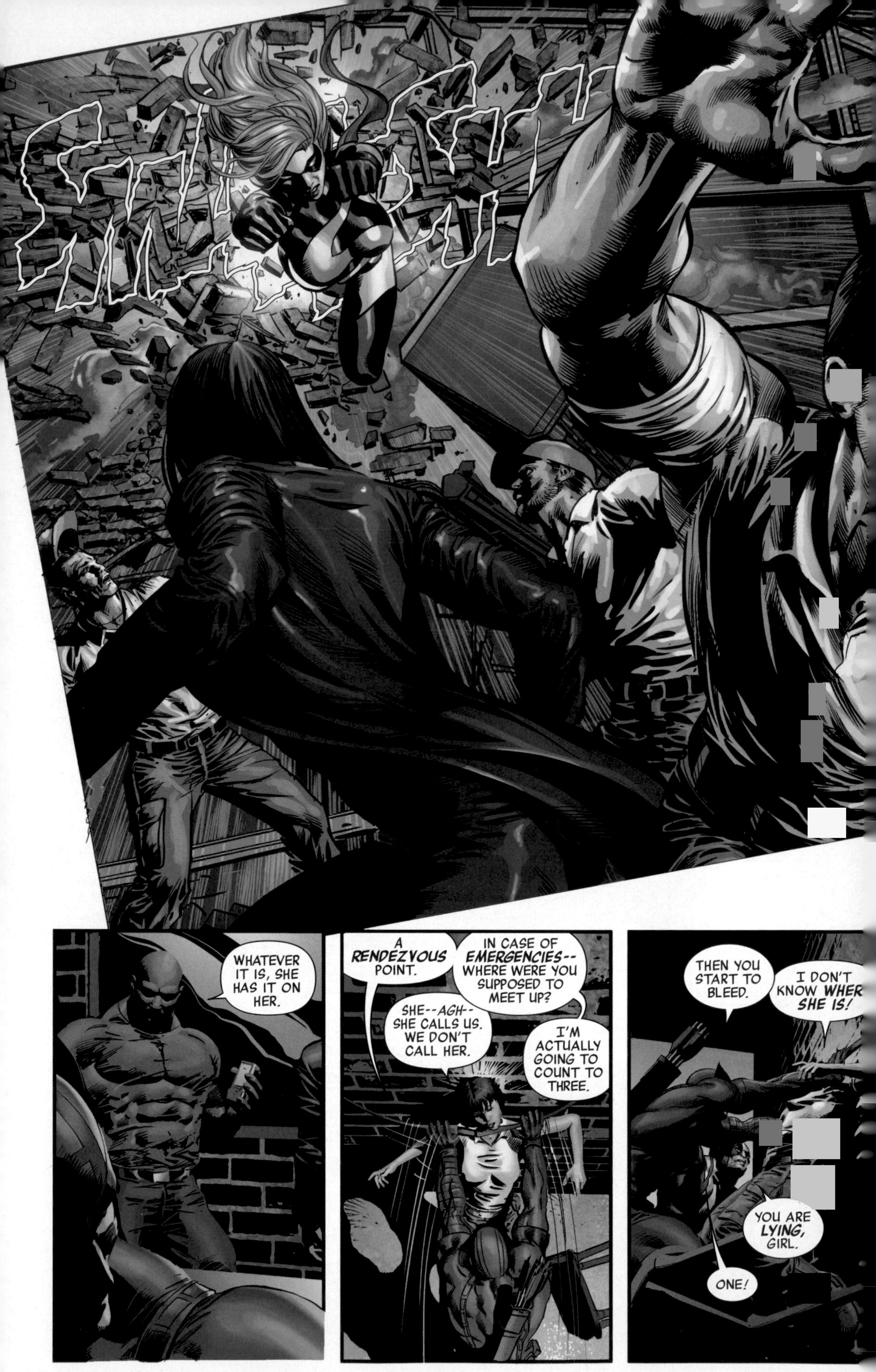
WHATEVER IT IS, SHE HAS IT ON HER.
A *RENDEZVOUS* POINT.
IN CASE OF *EMERGENCIES*-- WHERE WERE YOU SUPPOSED TO MEET UP?
SHE--*AGH*-- SHE CALLS US. WE DON'T CALL HER.
I'M ACTUALLY GOING TO COUNT TO THREE.
THEN YOU START TO BLEED.
I DON'T KNOW **WHER**
SHE IS!
YOU ARE ***LYING,*** GIRL.
ONE!

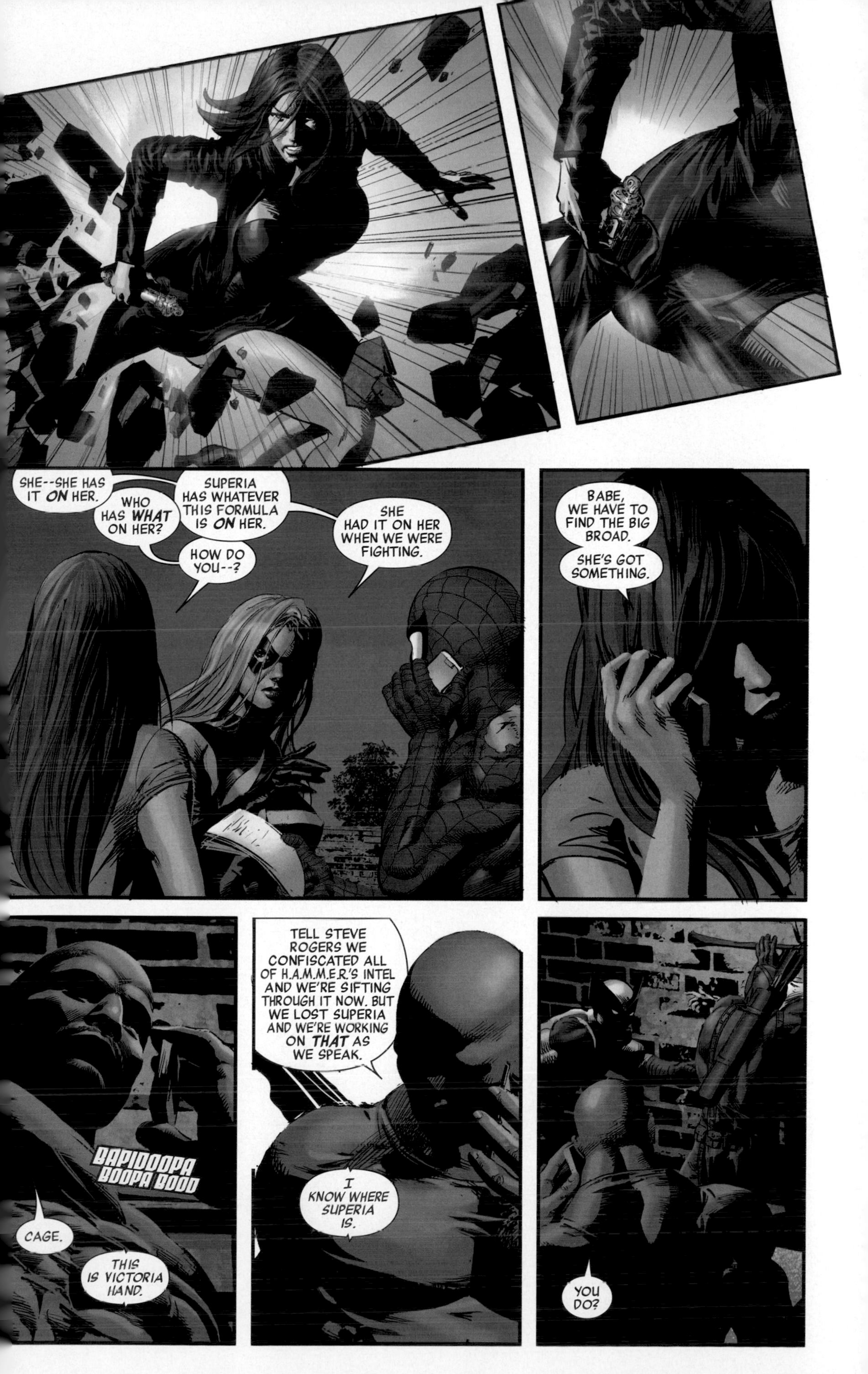
SHE--SHE HAS IT ON HER.
WHO HAS WHAT ON HER?
SUPERIA HAS WHATEVER THIS FORMULA IS ON HER.
HOW DO YOU--?
SHE HAD IT ON HER WHEN WE WERE FIGHTING.
BABE, WE HAVE TO FIND THE BIG BROAD.
SHE'S GOT SOMETHING.
BAPIDOOPA BOOPA BOOD
CAGE.
THIS IS VICTORIA HAND.
TELL STEVE ROGERS WE CONFISCATED ALL OF H.A.M.M.E.R.'S INTEL AND WE'RE SIFTING THROUGH IT NOW. BUT WE LOST SUPERIA AND WE'RE WORKING ON THAT AS WE SPEAK.
I KNOW WHERE SUPERIA IS.
YOU DO?

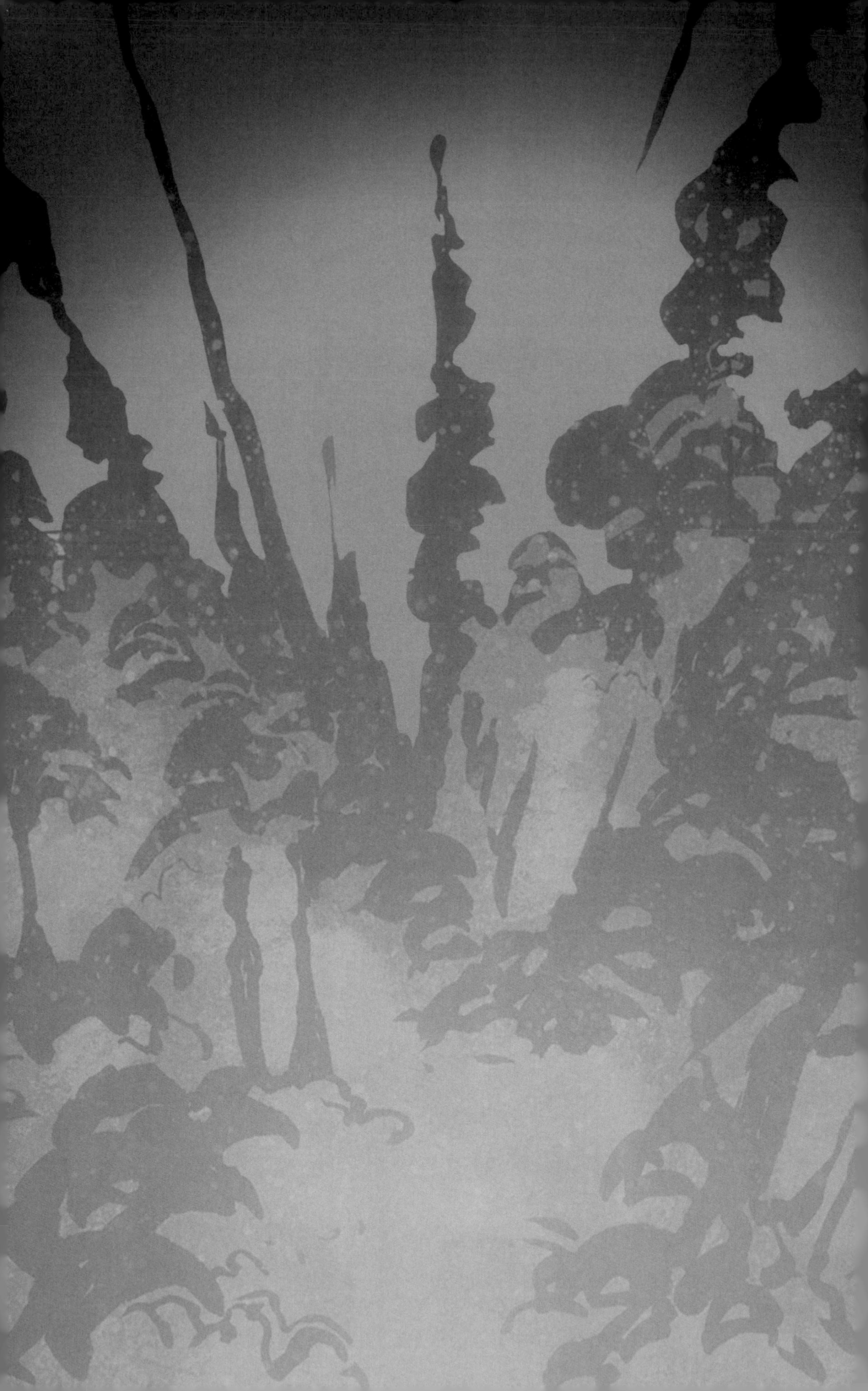

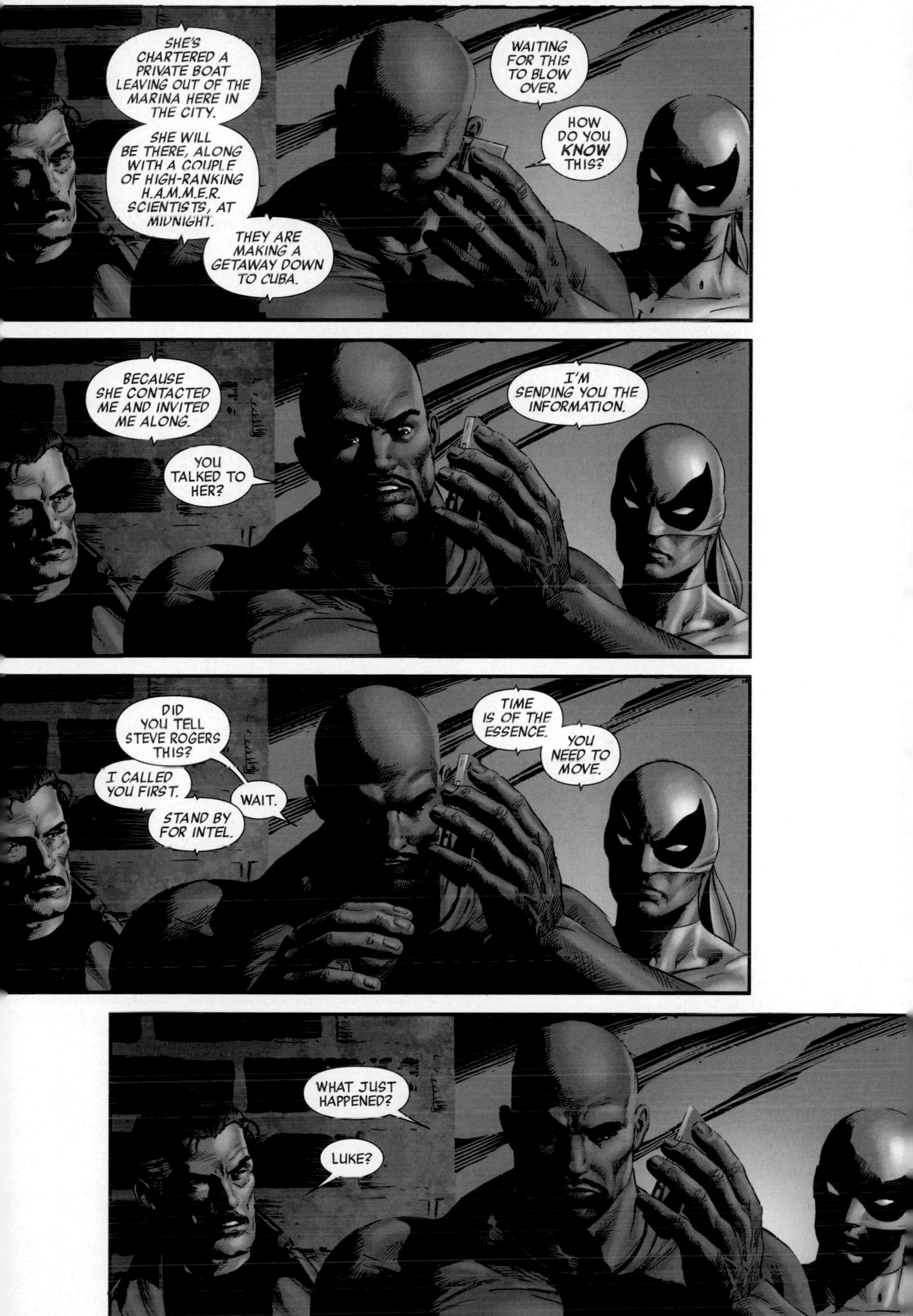
SHE'S CHARTERED A PRIVATE BOAT LEAVING OUT OF THE MARINA HERE IN THE CITY.
SHE WILL BE THERE, ALONG WITH A COUPLE OF HIGH-RANKING H.A.M.M.E.R. SCIENTISTS, AT MIDNIGHT.
THEY ARE MAKING A GETAWAY DOWN TO CUBA.
WAITING FOR THIS TO BLOW OVER.
HOW DO YOU KNOW THIS?
BECAUSE SHE CONTACTED ME AND INVITED ME ALONG.
YOU TALKED TO HER?
I'M SENDING YOU THE INFORMATION.
DID YOU TELL STEVE ROGERS THIS?
I CALLED YOU FIRST.
STAND BY FOR INTEL.
WAIT.
TIME IS OF THE ESSENCE.
YOU NEED TO MOVE.
WHAT JUST HAPPENED?
LUKE?

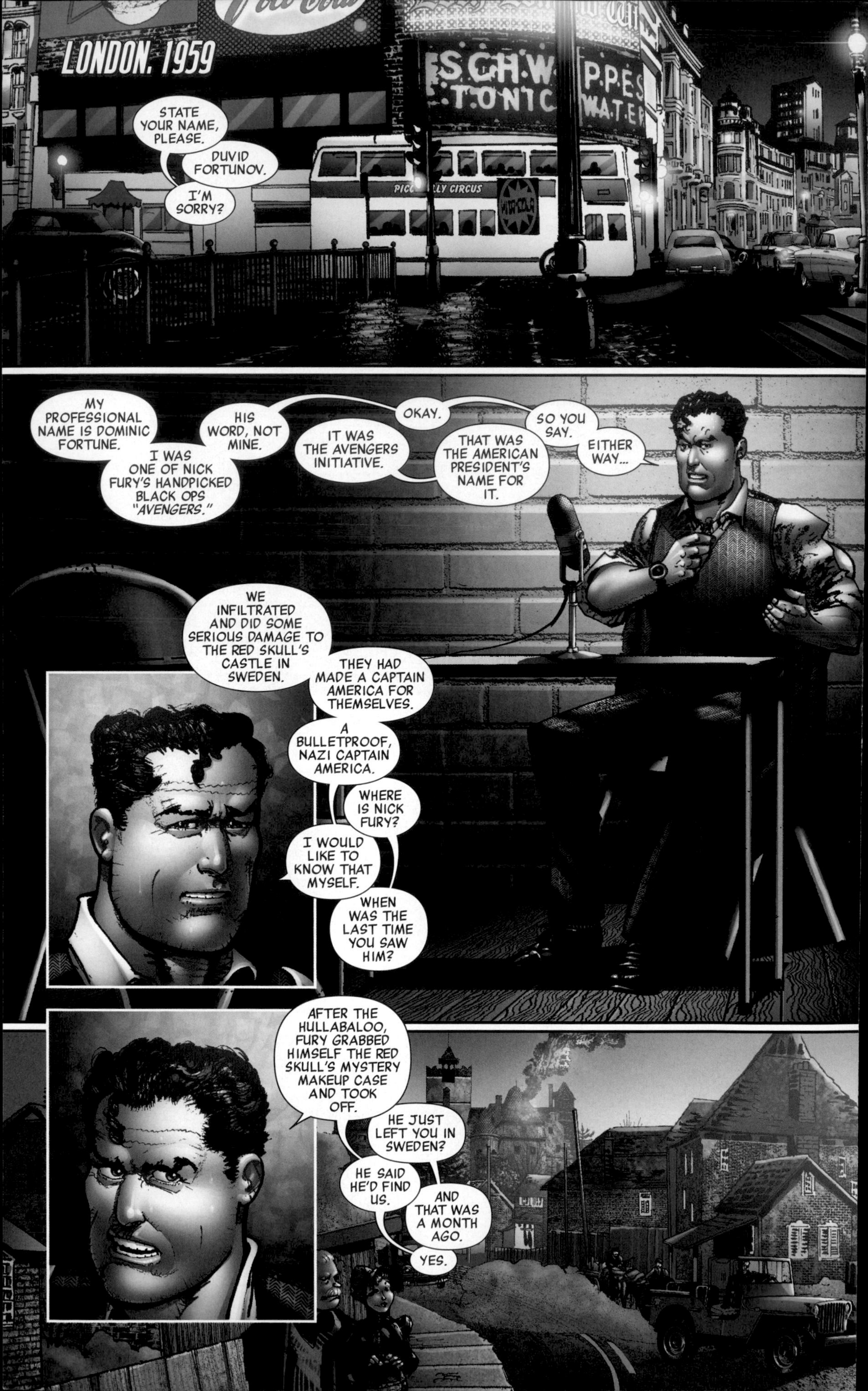
LONDON. 1959
SCHWEPPES TONIC WATER
PICCADILLY CIRCUS
STATE YOUR NAME, PLEASE.
DUVID FORTUNOV.
I'M SORRY?
MY PROFESSIONAL NAME IS DOMINIC FORTUNE.
I WAS ONE OF NICK FURY'S HANDPICKED BLACK OPS "AVENGERS."
HIS WORD, NOT MINE.
OKAY.
IT WAS THE AVENGERS INITIATIVE.
SO YOU SAY.
THAT WAS THE AMERICAN PRESIDENT'S NAME FOR IT.
EITHER WAY...
WE INFILTRATED AND DID SOME SERIOUS DAMAGE TO THE RED SKULL'S CASTLE IN SWEDEN.
THEY HAD MADE A CAPTAIN AMERICA FOR THEMSELVES.
A BULLETPROOF, NAZI CAPTAIN AMERICA.
WHERE IS NICK FURY?
I WOULD LIKE TO KNOW THAT MYSELF.
WHEN WAS THE LAST TIME YOU SAW HIM?
AFTER THE HULLABALOO, FURY GRABBED HIMSELF THE RED SKULL'S MYSTERY MAKEUP CASE AND TOOK OFF.
HE JUST LEFT YOU IN SWEDEN?
HE SAID HE'D FIND US.
AND THAT WAS A MONTH AGO.
YES.

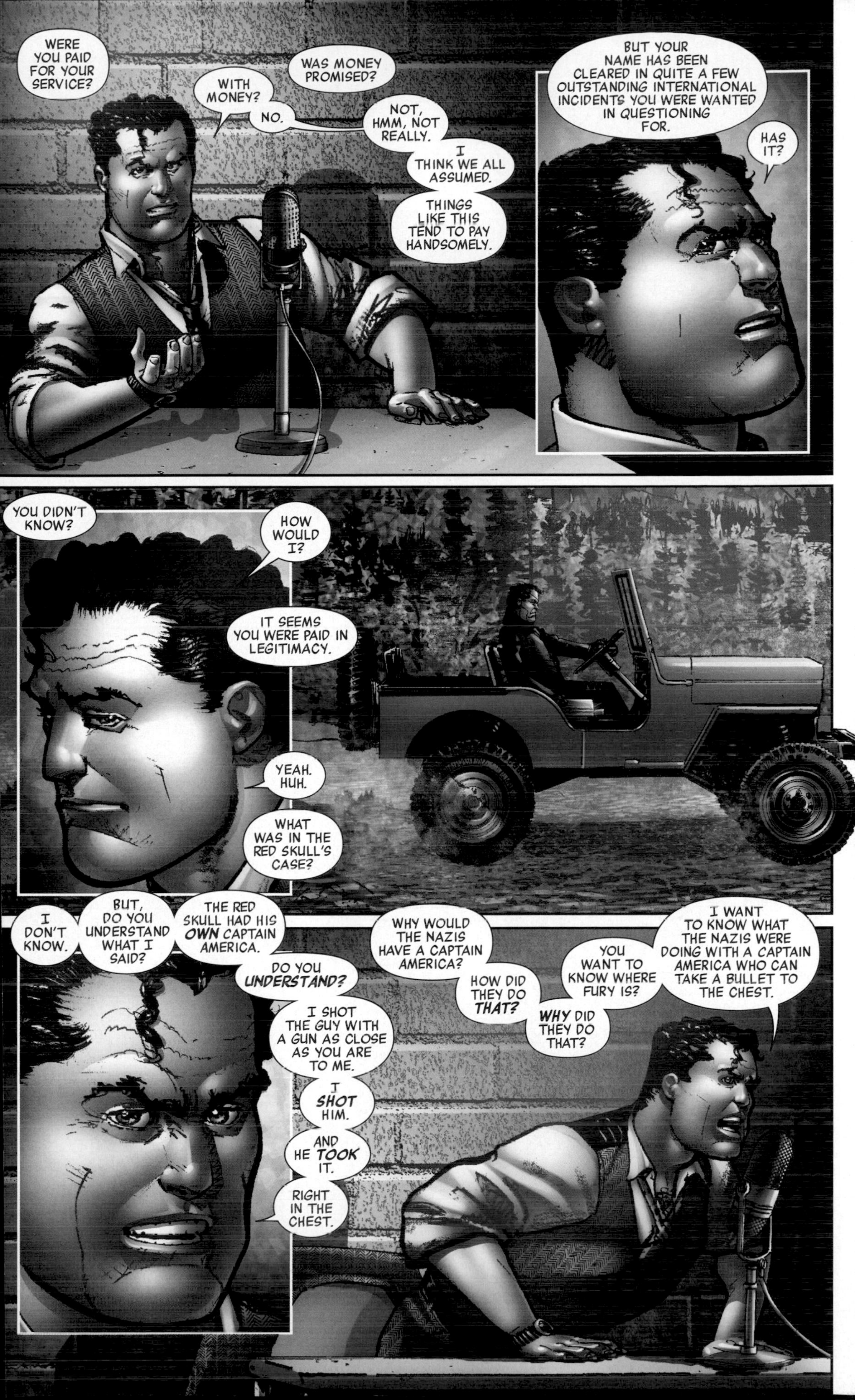
WERE YOU PAID FOR YOUR SERVICE?
WITH MONEY?
NO.
WAS MONEY PROMISED?
NOT, HMM, NOT REALLY.
I THINK WE ALL ASSUMED.
THINGS LIKE THIS TEND TO PAY HANDSOMELY.
BUT YOUR NAME HAS BEEN CLEARED IN QUITE A FEW OUTSTANDING INTERNATIONAL INCIDENTS YOU WERE WANTED IN QUESTIONING FOR.
HAS IT?
YOU DIDN'T KNOW?
HOW WOULD I?
IT SEEMS YOU WERE PAID IN LEGITIMACY.
YEAH. HUH.
WHAT WAS IN THE RED SKULL'S CASE?
I DON'T KNOW.
BUT, DO YOU UNDERSTAND WHAT I SAID?
THE RED SKULL HAD HIS **OWN** CAPTAIN AMERICA.
DO YOU **UNDERSTAND?**
I SHOT THE GUY WITH A GUN AS CLOSE AS YOU ARE TO ME.
I **SHOT** HIM.
AND HE **TOOK** IT.
RIGHT IN THE CHEST.
WHY WOULD THE NAZIS HAVE A CAPTAIN AMERICA?
HOW DID THEY DO **THAT?**
WHY DID THEY DO THAT?
YOU WANT TO KNOW WHERE FURY IS?
I WANT TO KNOW WHAT THE NAZIS WERE DOING WITH A CAPTAIN AMERICA WHO CAN TAKE A BULLET TO THE CHEST.

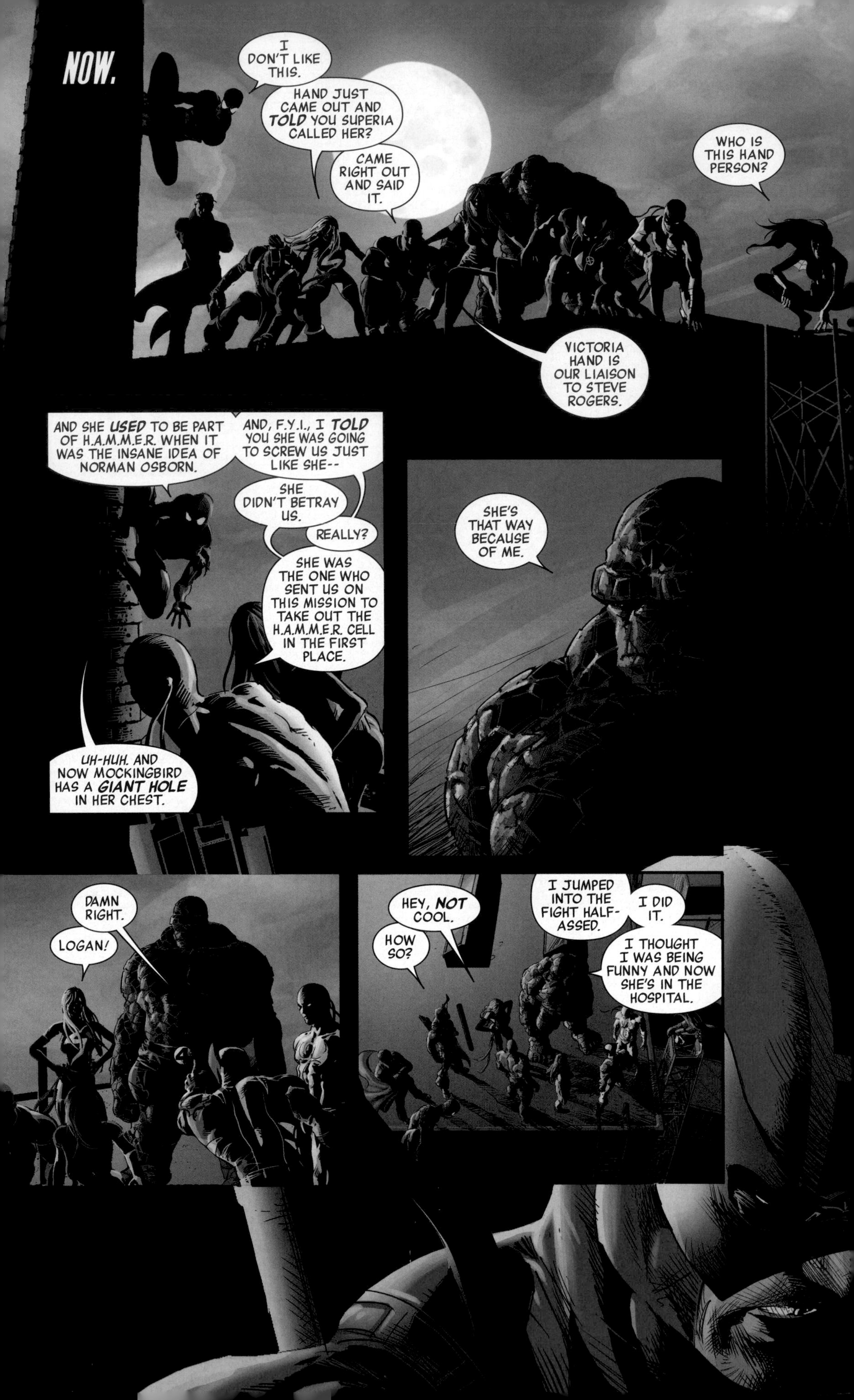
NOW.
I DON'T LIKE THIS.
HAND JUST CAME OUT AND TOLD YOU SUPERIA CALLED HER?
CAME RIGHT OUT AND SAID IT.
WHO IS THIS HAND PERSON?
VICTORIA HAND IS OUR LIAISON TO STEVE ROGERS.
AND SHE USED TO BE PART OF H.A.M.M.E.R. WHEN IT WAS THE INSANE IDEA OF NORMAN OSBORN.
AND, F.Y.I., I TOLD YOU SHE WAS GOING TO SCREW US JUST LIKE SHE--
SHE DIDN'T BETRAY US.
REALLY?
SHE WAS THE ONE WHO SENT US ON THIS MISSION TO TAKE OUT THE H.A.M.M.E.R. CELL IN THE FIRST PLACE.
UH-HUH. AND NOW MOCKINGBIRD HAS A GIANT HOLE IN HER CHEST.
SHE'S THAT WAY BECAUSE OF ME.
DAMN RIGHT.
LOGAN!
HEY, NOT COOL.
HOW SO?
I JUMPED INTO THE FIGHT HALF-ASSED.
I DID IT.
I THOUGHT I WAS BEING FUNNY AND NOW SHE'S IN THE HOSPITAL.

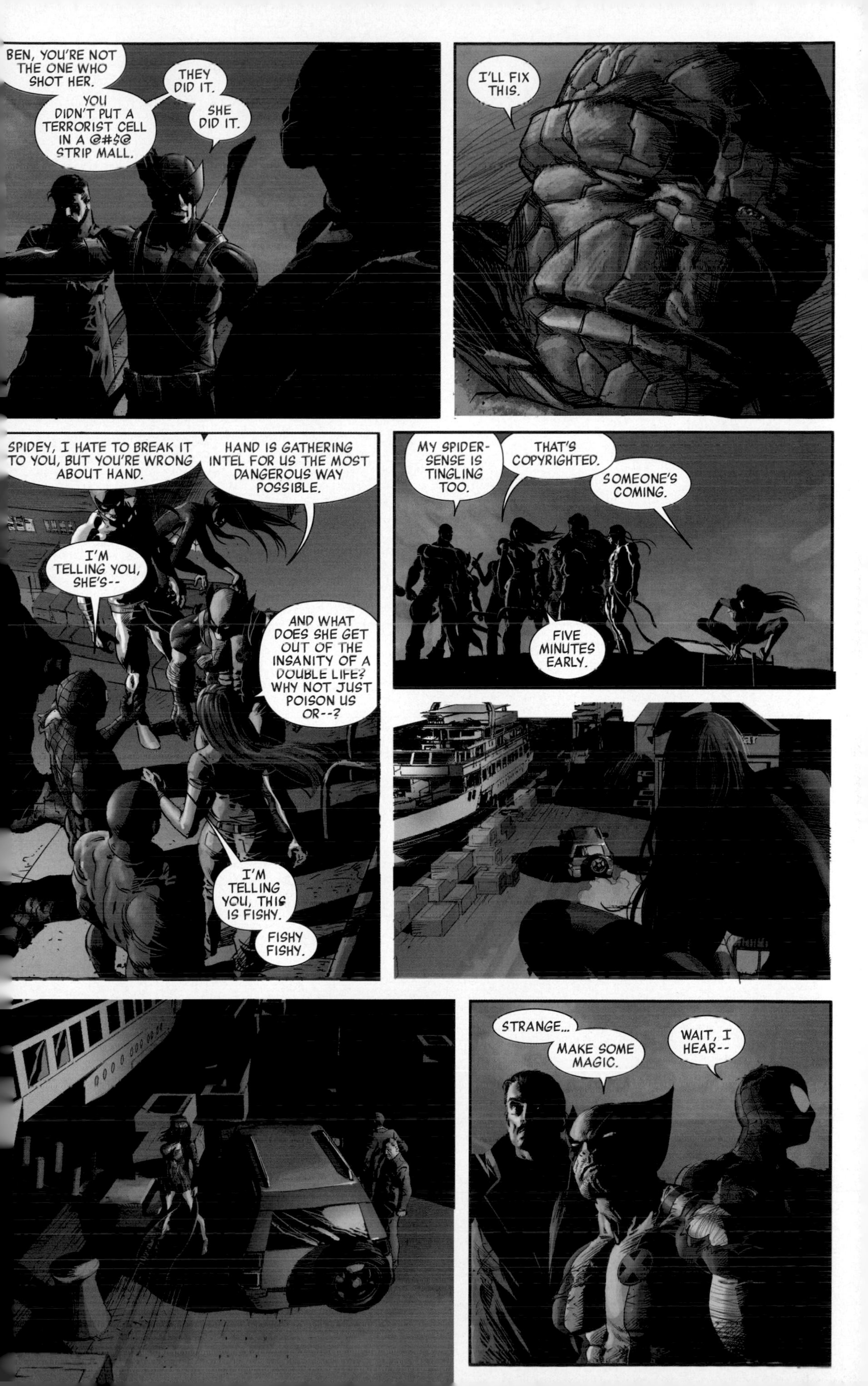
BEN, YOU'RE NOT THE ONE WHO SHOT HER.
THEY DID IT.
YOU DIDN'T PUT A TERRORIST CELL IN A @#$@ STRIP MALL.
SHE DID IT.
I'LL FIX THIS.
SPIDEY, I HATE TO BREAK IT TO YOU, BUT YOU'RE WRONG ABOUT HAND.
HAND IS GATHERING INTEL FOR US THE MOST DANGEROUS WAY POSSIBLE.
I'M TELLING YOU, SHE'S--
AND WHAT DOES SHE GET OUT OF THE INSANITY OF A DOUBLE LIFE? WHY NOT JUST POISON US OR--?
I'M TELLING YOU, THIS IS FISHY.
FISHY FISHY.
MY SPIDER-SENSE IS TINGLING TOO.
THAT'S COPYRIGHTED.
SOMEONE'S COMING.
FIVE MINUTES EARLY.
STRANGE...
MAKE SOME MAGIC.
WAIT, I HEAR--

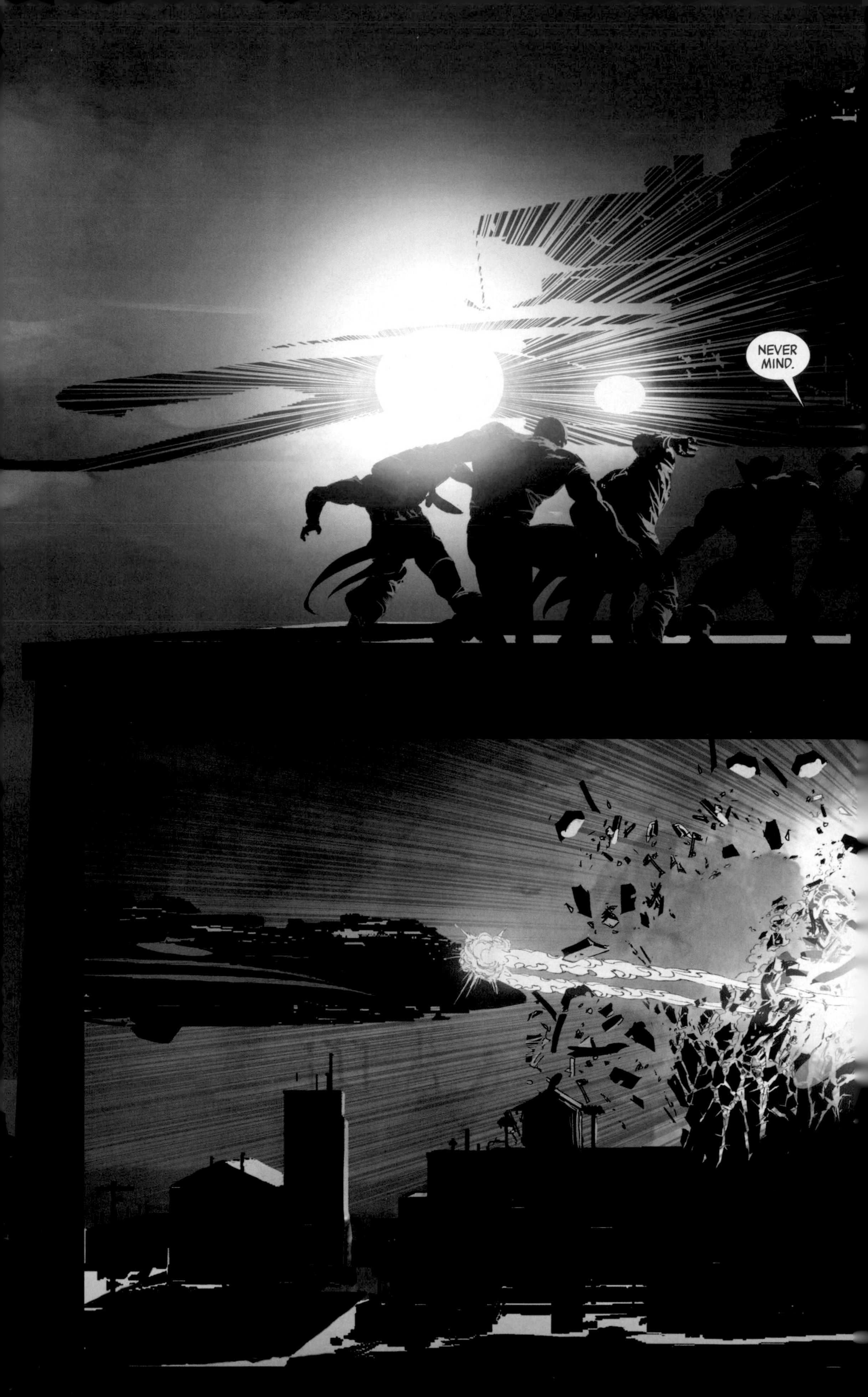
NEVER MIND.

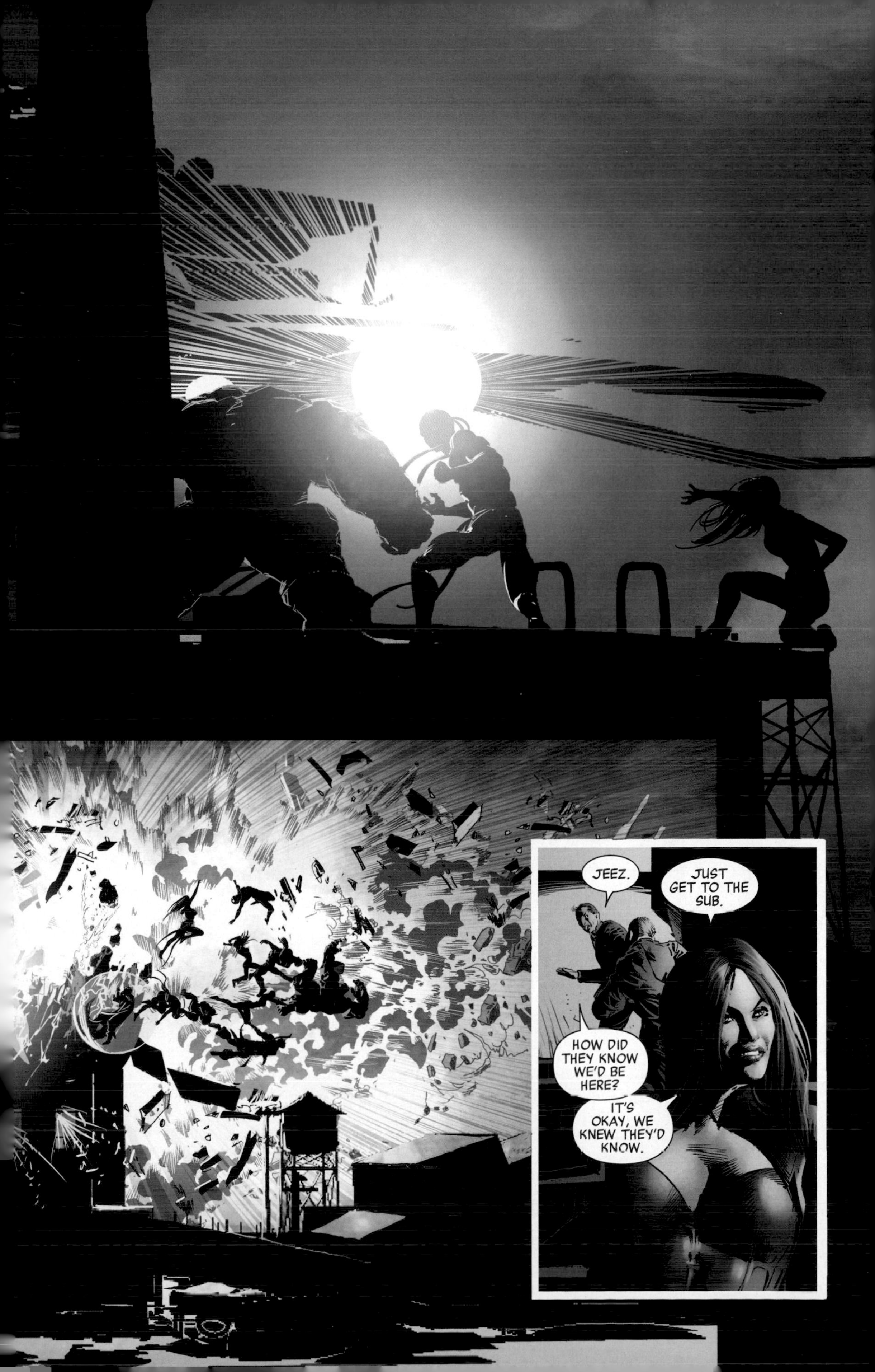
JEEZ.
JUST GET TO THE SUB.
HOW DID THEY KNOW WE'D BE HERE?
IT'S OKAY, WE KNEW THEY'D KNOW.

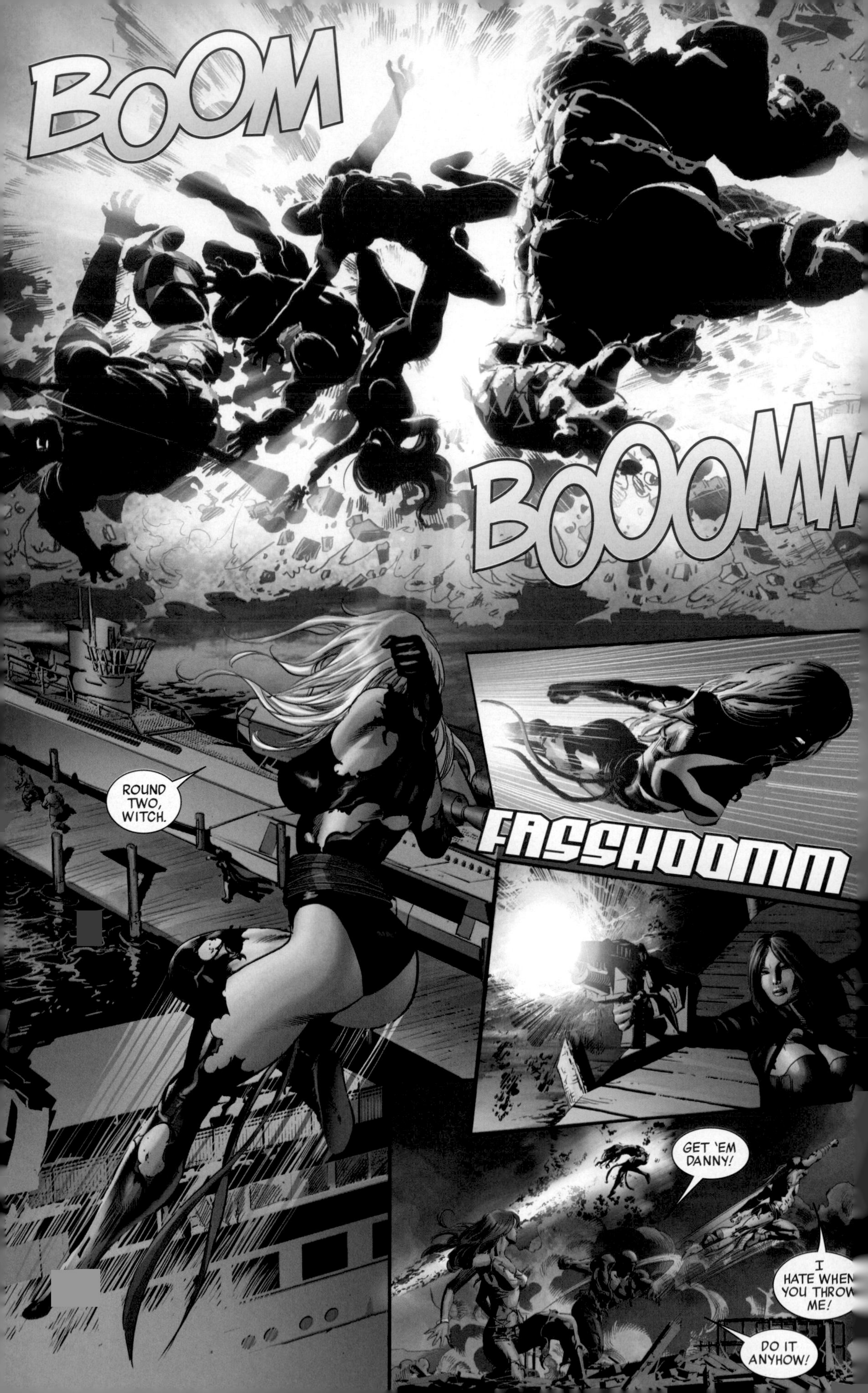
BOOM
BOOOMM
ROUND TWO, WITCH.
FASSHOOMM
GET 'EM DANNY!
I HATE WHEN YOU THROW ME!
DO IT ANYHOW!

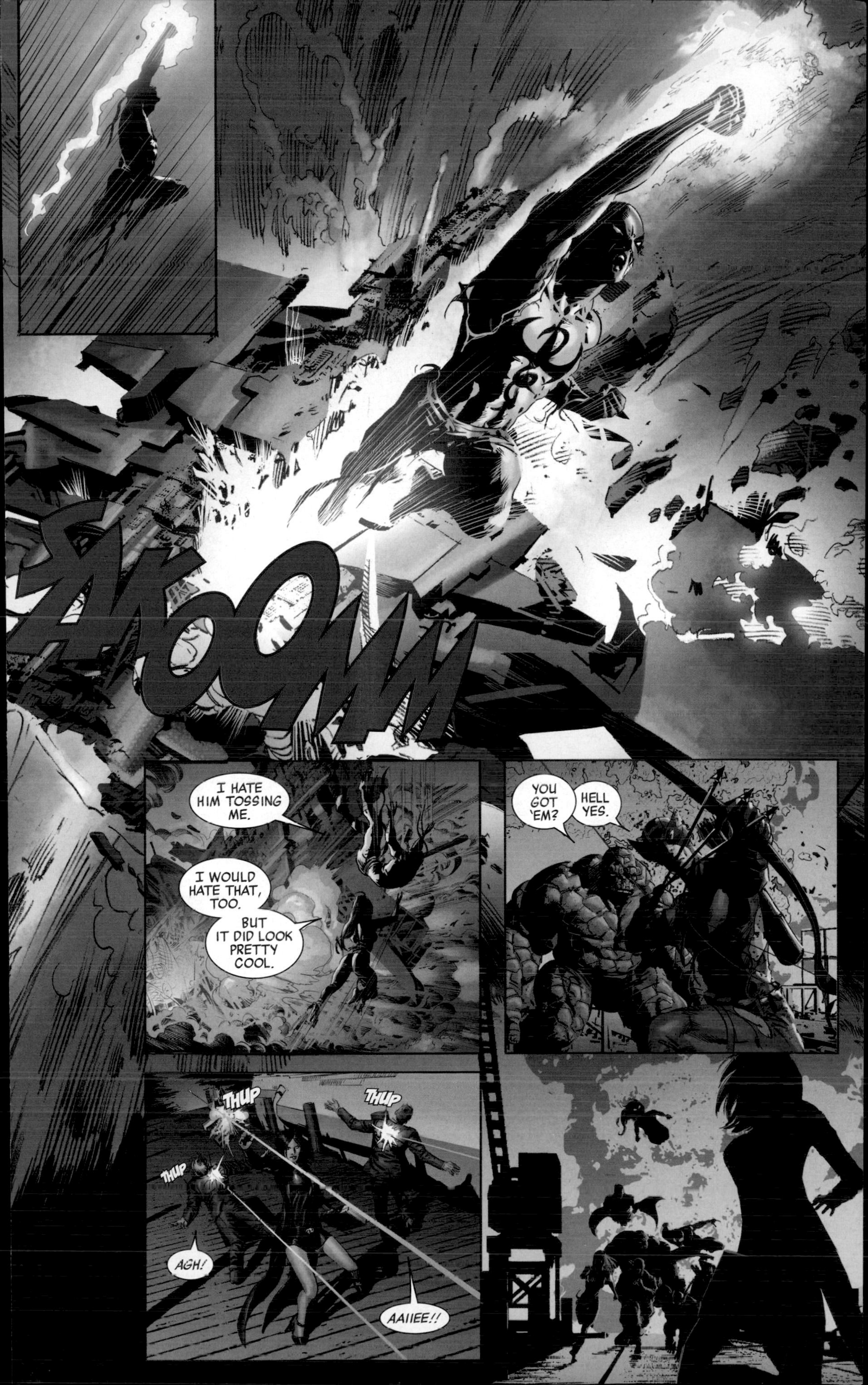
WHOOM
I HATE HIM TOSSING ME.
I WOULD HATE THAT, TOO.
BUT IT DID LOOK PRETTY COOL.
YOU GOT 'EM?
HELL YES.
THUP
THUP
THUP
AGH!
AAIIEE!!

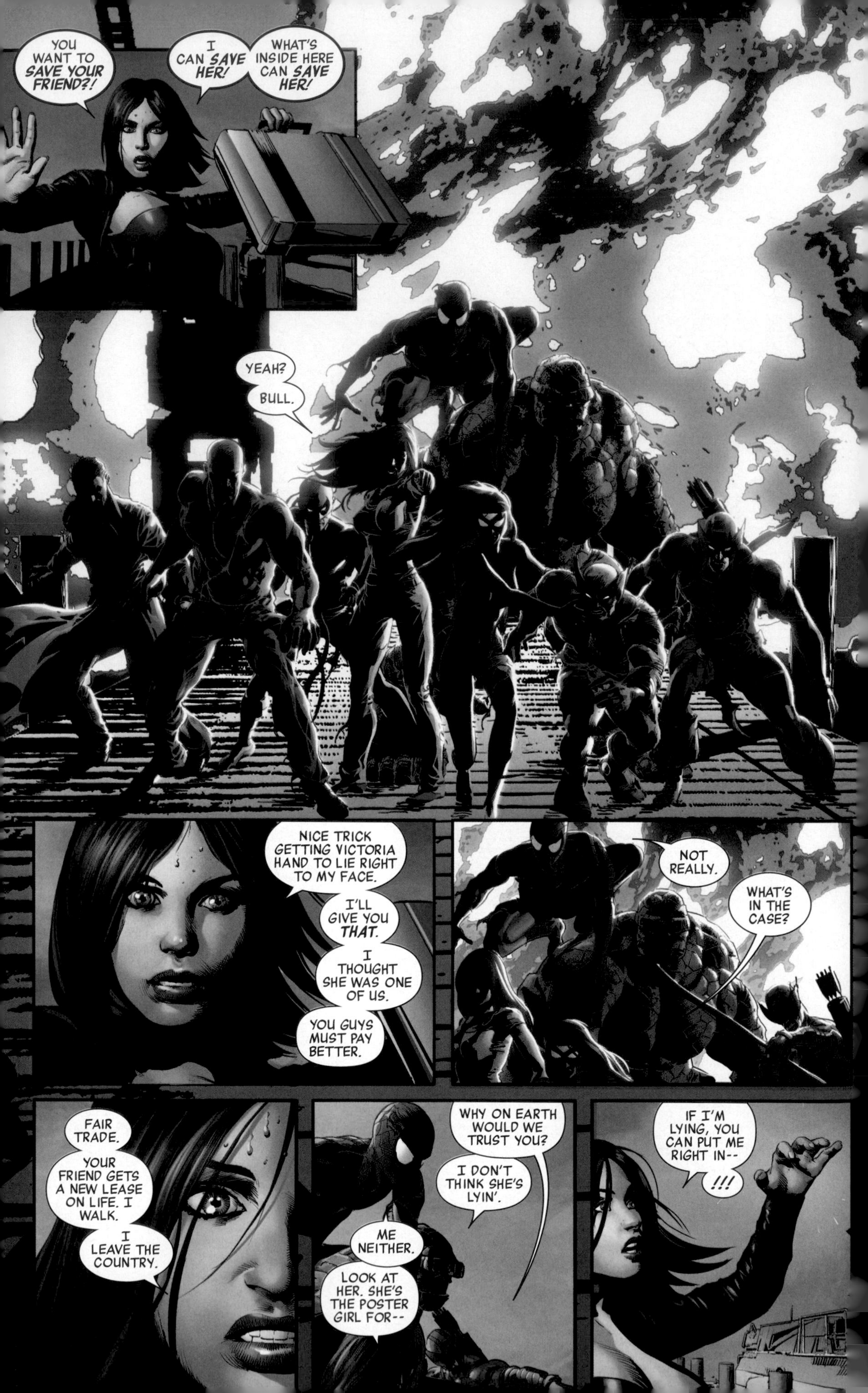
YOU WANT TO SAVE YOUR FRIEND?!
I CAN SAVE HER!
WHAT'S INSIDE HERE CAN SAVE HER!
YEAH?
BULL.
NICE TRICK GETTING VICTORIA HAND TO LIE RIGHT TO MY FACE.
I'LL GIVE YOU THAT.
I THOUGHT SHE WAS ONE OF US.
YOU GUYS MUST PAY BETTER.
NOT REALLY.
WHAT'S IN THE CASE?
FAIR TRADE.
YOUR FRIEND GETS A NEW LEASE ON LIFE. I WALK.
I LEAVE THE COUNTRY.
WHY ON EARTH WOULD WE TRUST YOU?
I DON'T THINK SHE'S LYIN'.
ME NEITHER.
LOOK AT HER. SHE'S THE POSTER GIRL FOR--
IF I'M LYING, YOU CAN PUT ME RIGHT IN--
!!!

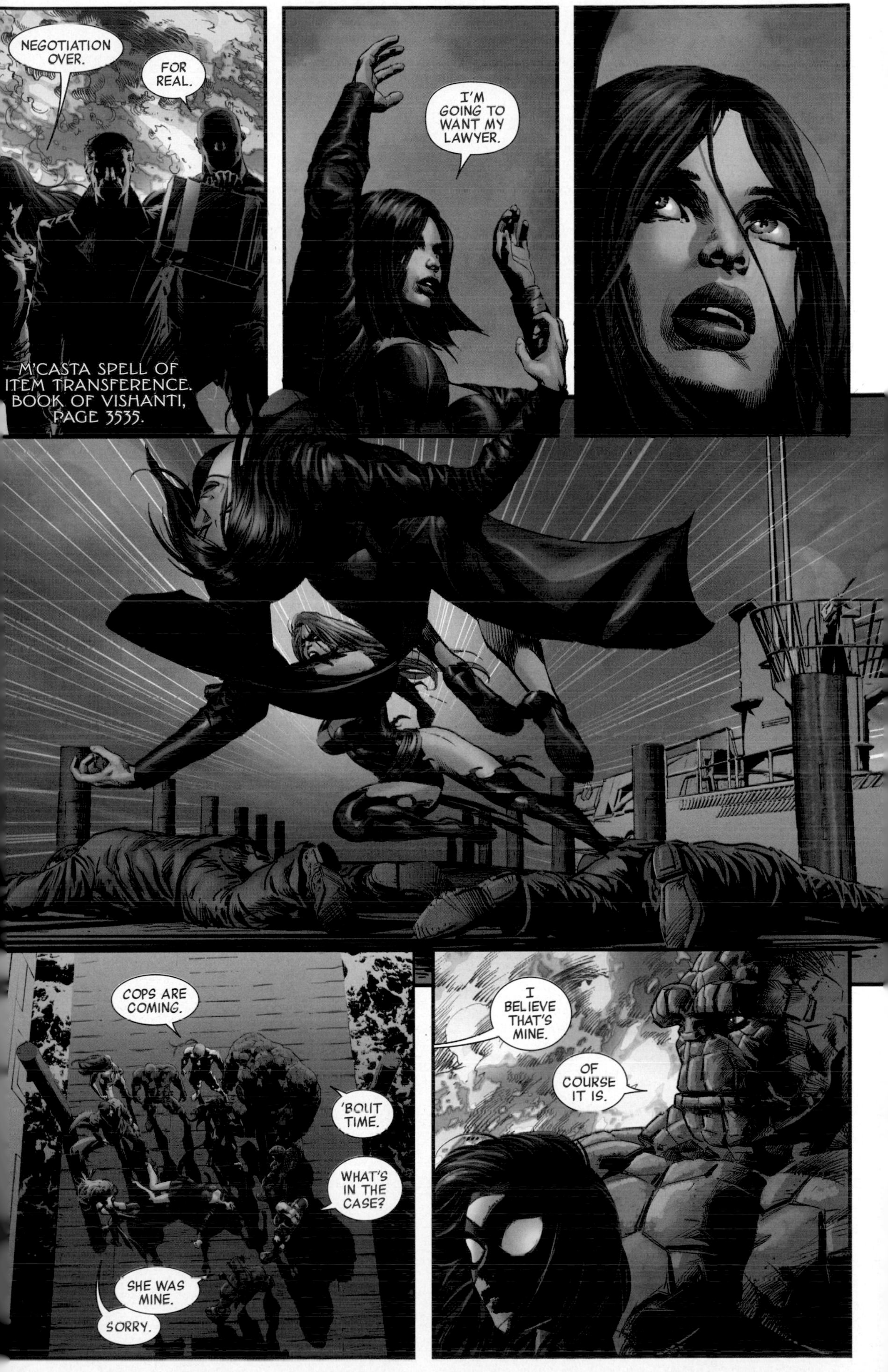
NEGOTIATION OVER.
FOR REAL.
M'CASTA SPELL OF ITEM TRANSFERENCE. BOOK OF VISHANTI, PAGE 3535.
I'M GOING TO WANT MY LAWYER.
COPS ARE COMING.
'BOUT TIME.
WHAT'S IN THE CASE?
SHE WAS MINE.
SORRY.
I BELIEVE THAT'S MINE.
OF COURSE IT IS.

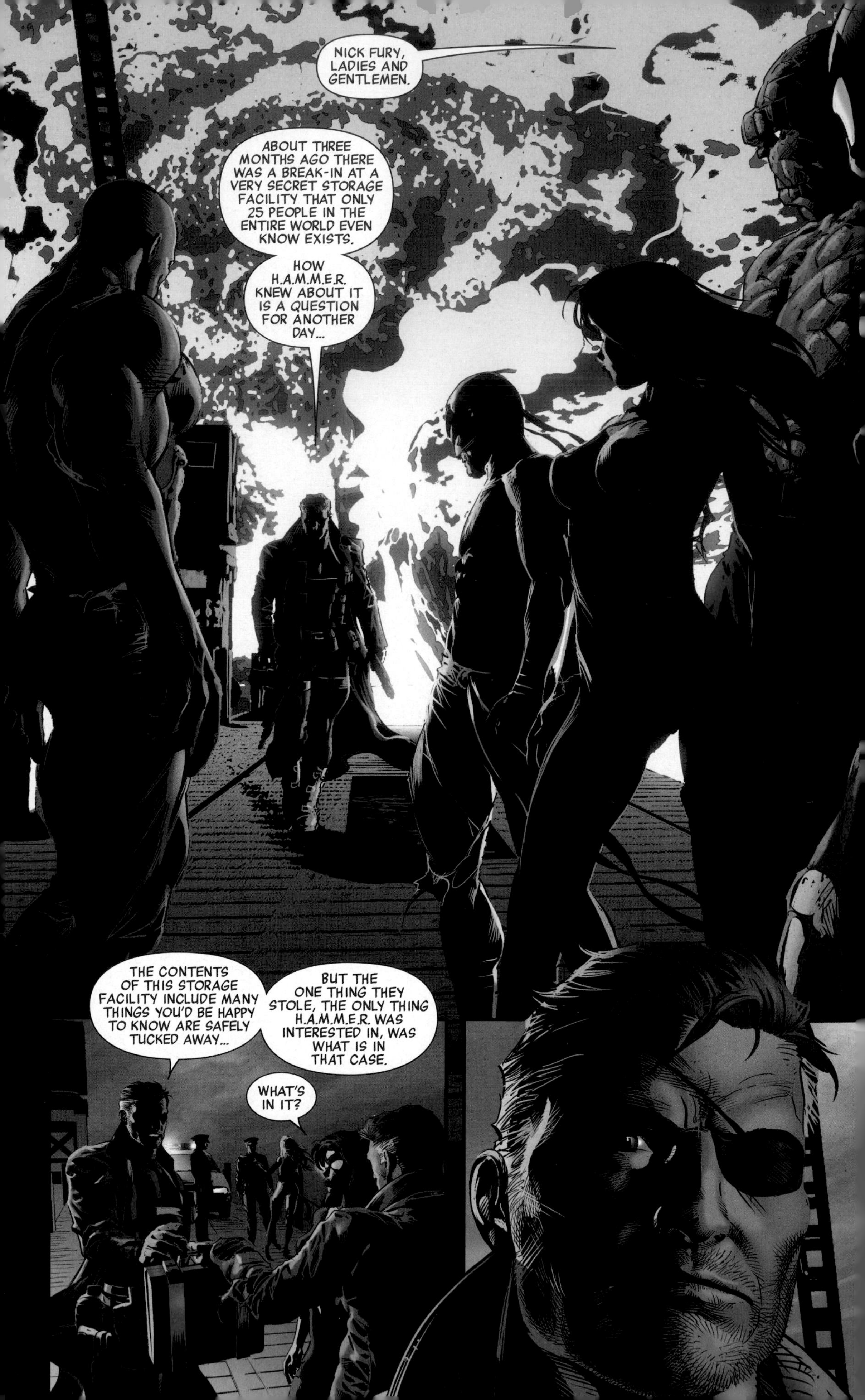
NICK FURY, LADIES AND GENTLEMEN.
ABOUT THREE MONTHS AGO THERE WAS A BREAK-IN AT A VERY SECRET STORAGE FACILITY THAT ONLY 25 PEOPLE IN THE ENTIRE WORLD EVEN KNOW EXISTS.
HOW H.A.M.M.E.R. KNEW ABOUT IT IS A QUESTION FOR ANOTHER DAY...
THE CONTENTS OF THIS STORAGE FACILITY INCLUDE MANY THINGS YOU'D BE HAPPY TO KNOW ARE SAFELY TUCKED AWAY...
BUT THE ONE THING THEY STOLE, THE ONLY THING H.A.M.M.E.R. WAS INTERESTED IN, WAS WHAT IS IN THAT CASE.
WHAT'S IN IT?

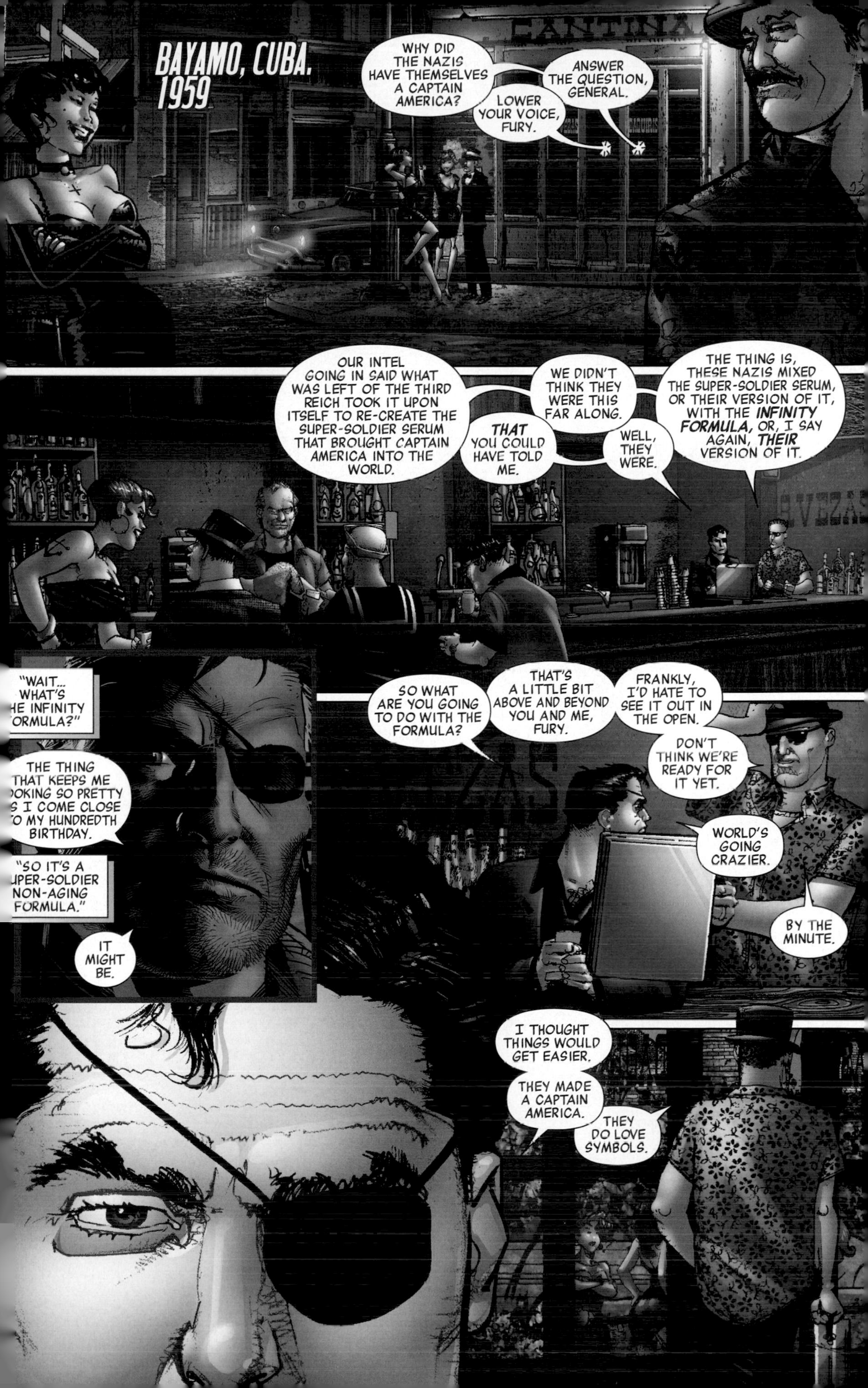
BAYAMO, CUBA. 1959
CANTINA
WHY DID THE NAZIS HAVE THEMSELVES A CAPTAIN AMERICA?
ANSWER THE QUESTION, GENERAL.
LOWER YOUR VOICE, FURY.
OUR INTEL GOING IN SAID WHAT WAS LEFT OF THE THIRD REICH TOOK IT UPON ITSELF TO RE-CREATE THE SUPER-SOLDIER SERUM THAT BROUGHT CAPTAIN AMERICA INTO THE WORLD.
WE DIDN'T THINK THEY WERE THIS FAR ALONG.
THAT YOU COULD HAVE TOLD ME.
WELL, THEY WERE.
THE THING IS, THESE NAZIS MIXED THE SUPER-SOLDIER SERUM, OR THEIR VERSION OF IT, WITH THE INFINITY FORMULA, OR, I SAY AGAIN, THEIR VERSION OF IT.
"WAIT... WHAT'S THE INFINITY FORMULA?"
THE THING THAT KEEPS ME LOOKING SO PRETTY AS I COME CLOSE TO MY HUNDREDTH BIRTHDAY.
"SO IT'S A SUPER-SOLDIER NON-AGING FORMULA."
IT MIGHT BE.
SO WHAT ARE YOU GOING TO DO WITH THE FORMULA?
THAT'S A LITTLE BIT ABOVE AND BEYOND YOU AND ME, FURY.
FRANKLY, I'D HATE TO SEE IT OUT IN THE OPEN.
DON'T THINK WE'RE READY FOR IT YET.
WORLD'S GOING CRAZIER.
BY THE MINUTE.
I THOUGHT THINGS WOULD GET EASIER.
THEY MADE A CAPTAIN AMERICA.
THEY DO LOVE SYMBOLS.

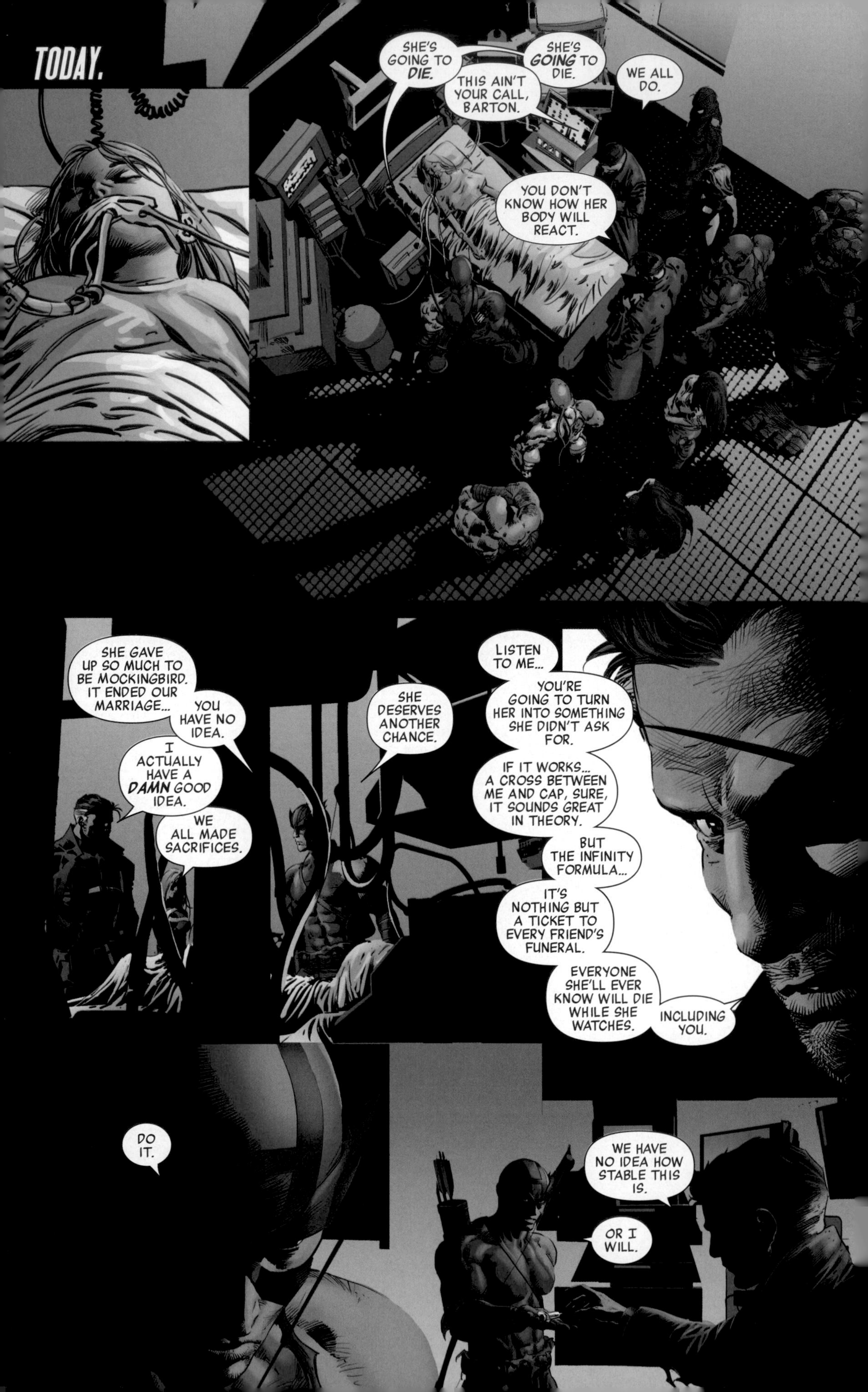
TODAY.
SHE'S GOING TO DIE.
SHE'S GOING TO DIE.
THIS AIN'T YOUR CALL, BARTON.
WE ALL DO.
YOU DON'T KNOW HOW HER BODY WILL REACT.
SHE GAVE UP SO MUCH TO BE MOCKINGBIRD. IT ENDED OUR MARRIAGE...
YOU HAVE NO IDEA.
I ACTUALLY HAVE A DAMN GOOD IDEA.
WE ALL MADE SACRIFICES.
SHE DESERVES ANOTHER CHANCE.
LISTEN TO ME...
YOU'RE GOING TO TURN HER INTO SOMETHING SHE DIDN'T ASK FOR.
IF IT WORKS... A CROSS BETWEEN ME AND CAP, SURE, IT SOUNDS GREAT IN THEORY.
BUT THE INFINITY FORMULA...
IT'S NOTHING BUT A TICKET TO EVERY FRIEND'S FUNERAL.
EVERYONE SHE'LL EVER KNOW WILL DIE WHILE SHE WATCHES.
INCLUDING YOU.
DO IT.
WE HAVE NO IDEA HOW STABLE THIS IS.
OR I WILL.

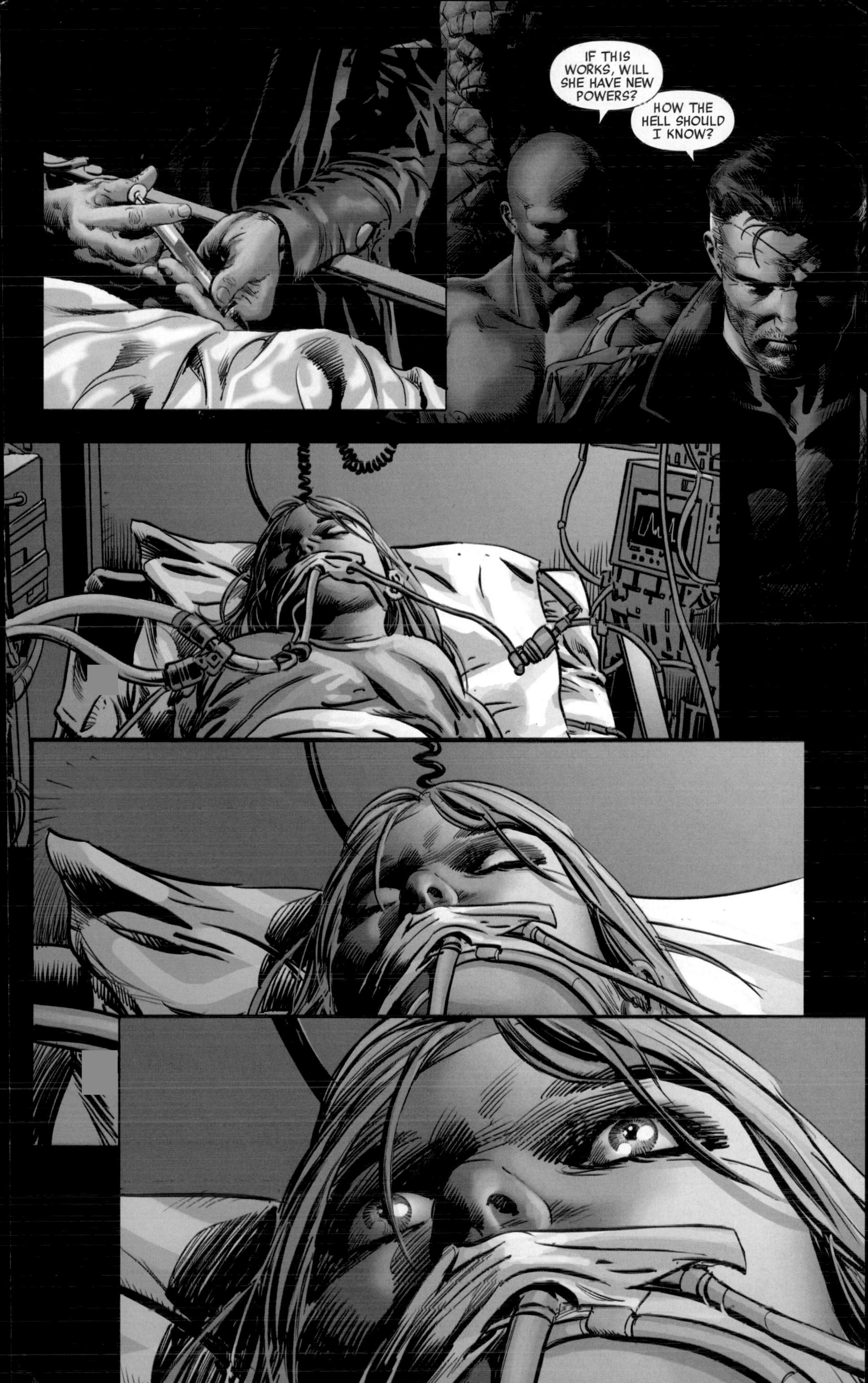
IF THIS WORKS, WILL SHE HAVE NEW POWERS?
HOW THE HELL SHOULD I KNOW?

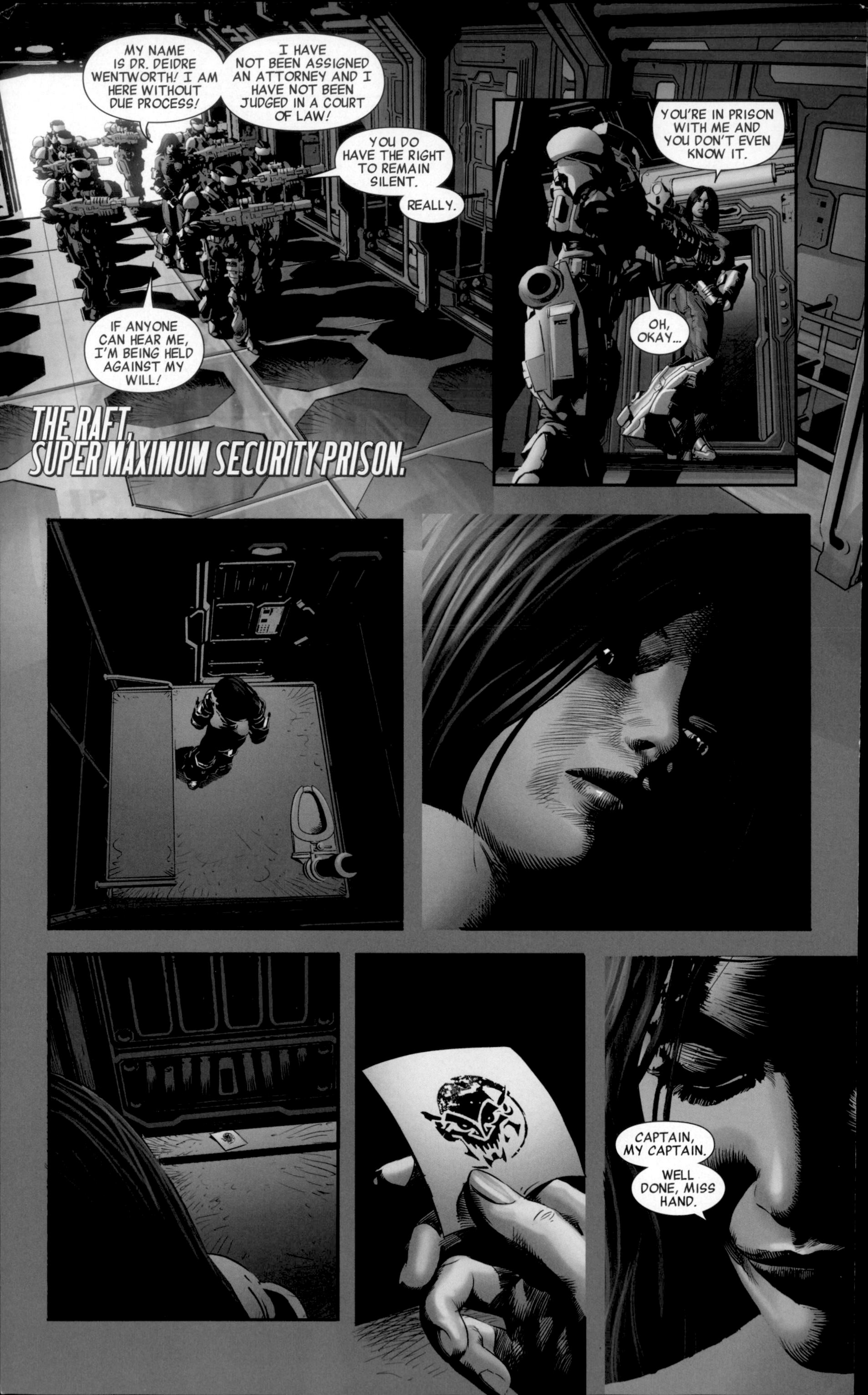
MY NAME IS DR. DEIDRE WENTWORTH! I AM HERE WITHOUT DUE PROCESS!
I HAVE NOT BEEN ASSIGNED AN ATTORNEY AND I HAVE NOT BEEN JUDGED IN A COURT OF LAW!
YOU DO HAVE THE RIGHT TO REMAIN SILENT.
REALLY.
IF ANYONE CAN HEAR ME, I'M BEING HELD AGAINST MY WILL!
THE RAFT, SUPER MAXIMUM SECURITY PRISON.
YOU'RE IN PRISON WITH ME AND YOU DON'T EVEN KNOW IT.
OH, OKAY...
CAPTAIN, MY CAPTAIN.
WELL DONE, MISS HAND.

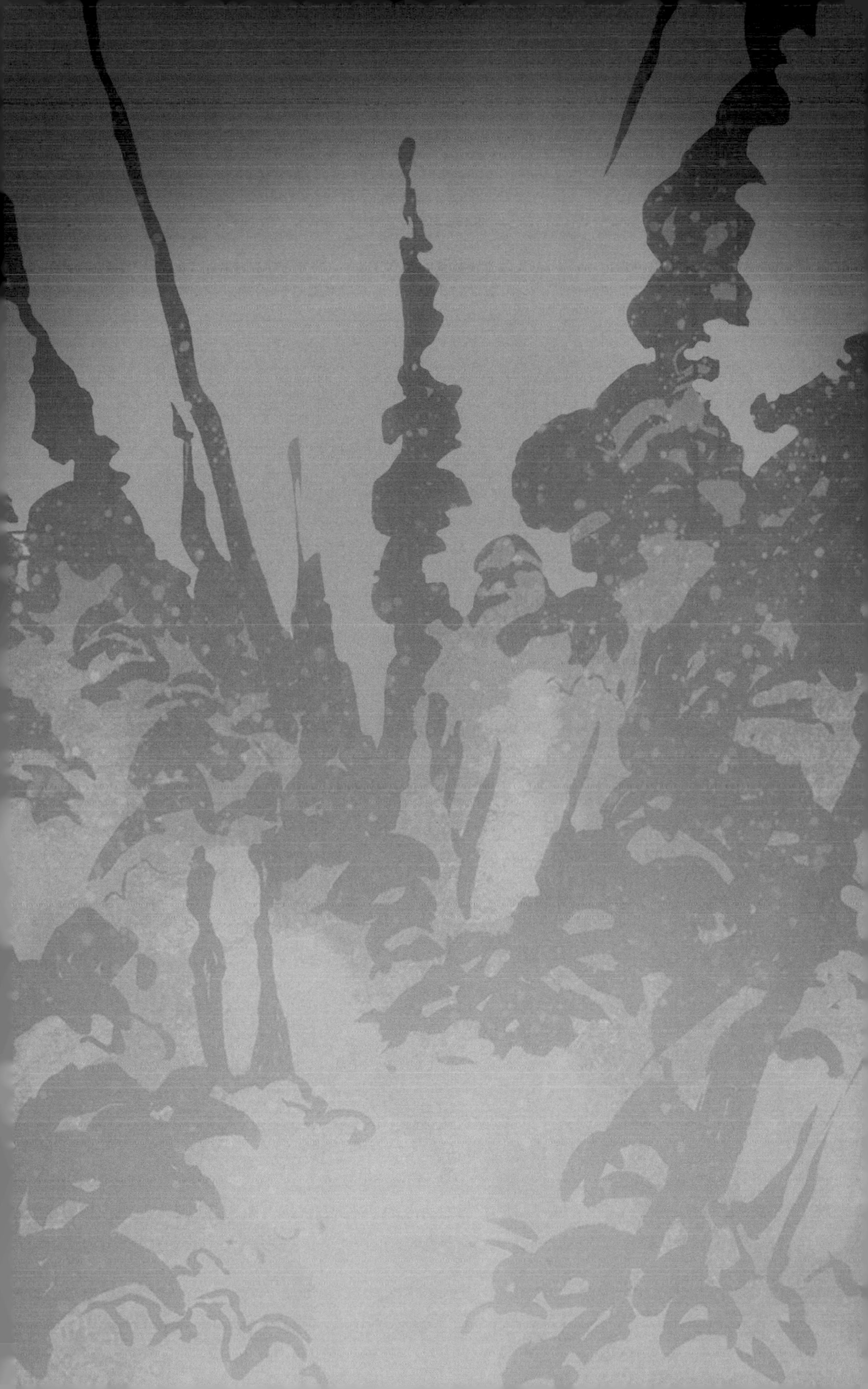

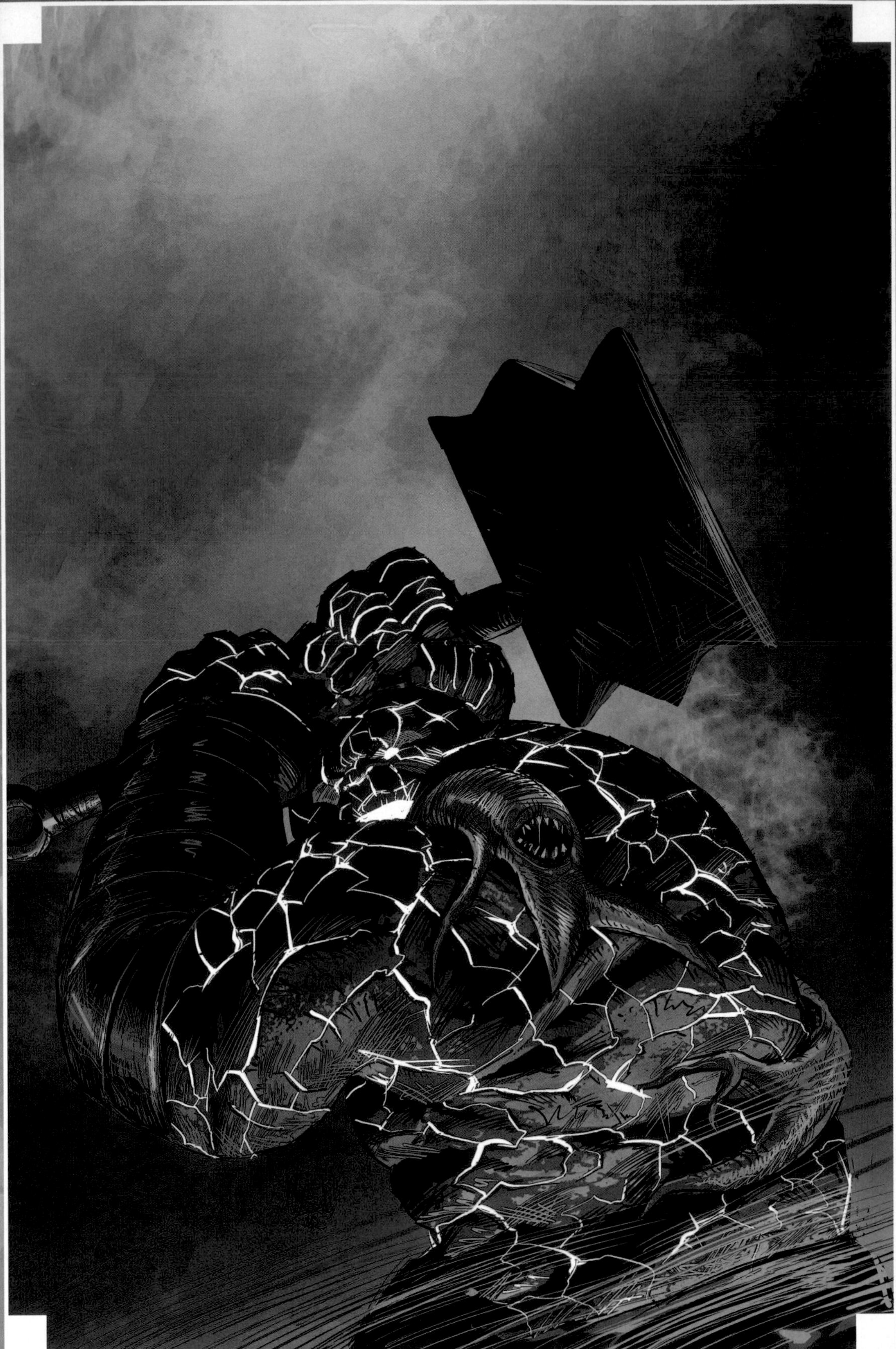

New Avengers #14

NEW AVENGERS

WOLVERINE

DR. STRANGE

EARTH'S MIGHTIEST HEROES, UNITED AGAINST A COMMON THREAT! ON THAT DAY THE AVENGERS WERE BORN, TO FIGHT FOES THAT NO SINGLE HERO COULD WITHSTAND!

LUKE CAGE

MS. MARVEL

THING

IRON FIST

SPIDER-MAN

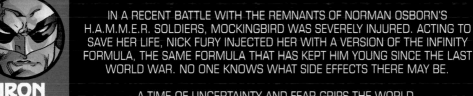

MOCKINGBIRD

JESSICA JONES

VICTORIA HAND

SQUIRREL GIRL

AVENGERS COMMANDER STEVE ROGERS HAS GIVEN LUKE CAGE, JESSICA JONES, MS. MARVEL, MOCKINGBIRD, SPIDER-MAN, WOLVERINE, IRON FIST, DOCTOR STRANGE, AND THE THING THE KEYS TO AVENGERS MANSION, A LIAISON IN THE CONTROVERSIAL FORM OF VICTORIA HAND, AND FREE REIN TO PROTECT THE WORLD ANY WAY THEY SEE FIT.

IN A RECENT BATTLE WITH THE REMNANTS OF NORMAN OSBORN'S H.A.M.M.E.R. SOLDIERS, MOCKINGBIRD WAS SEVERELY INJURED. ACTING TO SAVE HER LIFE, NICK FURY INJECTED HER WITH A VERSION OF THE INFINITY FORMULA, THE SAME FORMULA THAT HAS KEPT HIM YOUNG SINCE THE LAST WORLD WAR. NO ONE KNOWS WHAT SIDE EFFECTS THERE MAY BE.

A TIME OF UNCERTAINTY AND FEAR GRIPS THE WORLD.

SIN, THE DAUGHTER OF THE RED SKULL, HAS UNLEASHED AN ANCIENT EVIL INTO THE WORLD: THE FORGOTTEN ASGARDIAN GOD KNOWN ONLY AS THE SERPENT! WITH HIS HAMMER-WIELDING MINIONS, THE SERPENT DEVASTATES THE EARTH IN HIS MARCH TOWARDS REVENGE ON ODIN AND ASGARD.

SENSING THE SERPENT'S RETURN, ODIN ORDERS THE ASGARDIANS TO WITHDRAW FROM EARTH AND DRAGS HIS REBELLIOUS SON THOR WITH HIM.

SIN LEADS AN ATTACK ON THE U.S. CAPITAL, RAZING ALL IN THEIR PATH. HER BLOODY ARMY CONTINUES TO MARCH NORTH, TO NEW YORK, AND THE AVENGERS STAND IN THEIR WAY.

BRIAN MICHAEL BENDIS — WRITER

MIKE DEODATO — ARTIST

RAIN BEREDO — COLOR ART

VC'S JOE CARAMAGNA — LETTERS & PRODUCTION

MIKE DEODATO & RAIN BEREDO — COVER ARTISTS

LAUREN SANKOVITCH — ASSOCIATE EDITOR

TOM BREVOORT — EDITOR

AXEL ALONSO — EDITOR IN CHIEF

JOE QUESADA — CHIEF CREATIVE OFFICER

DAN BUCKLEY — PUBLISHER

ALAN FINE — EXEC. PRODUCER

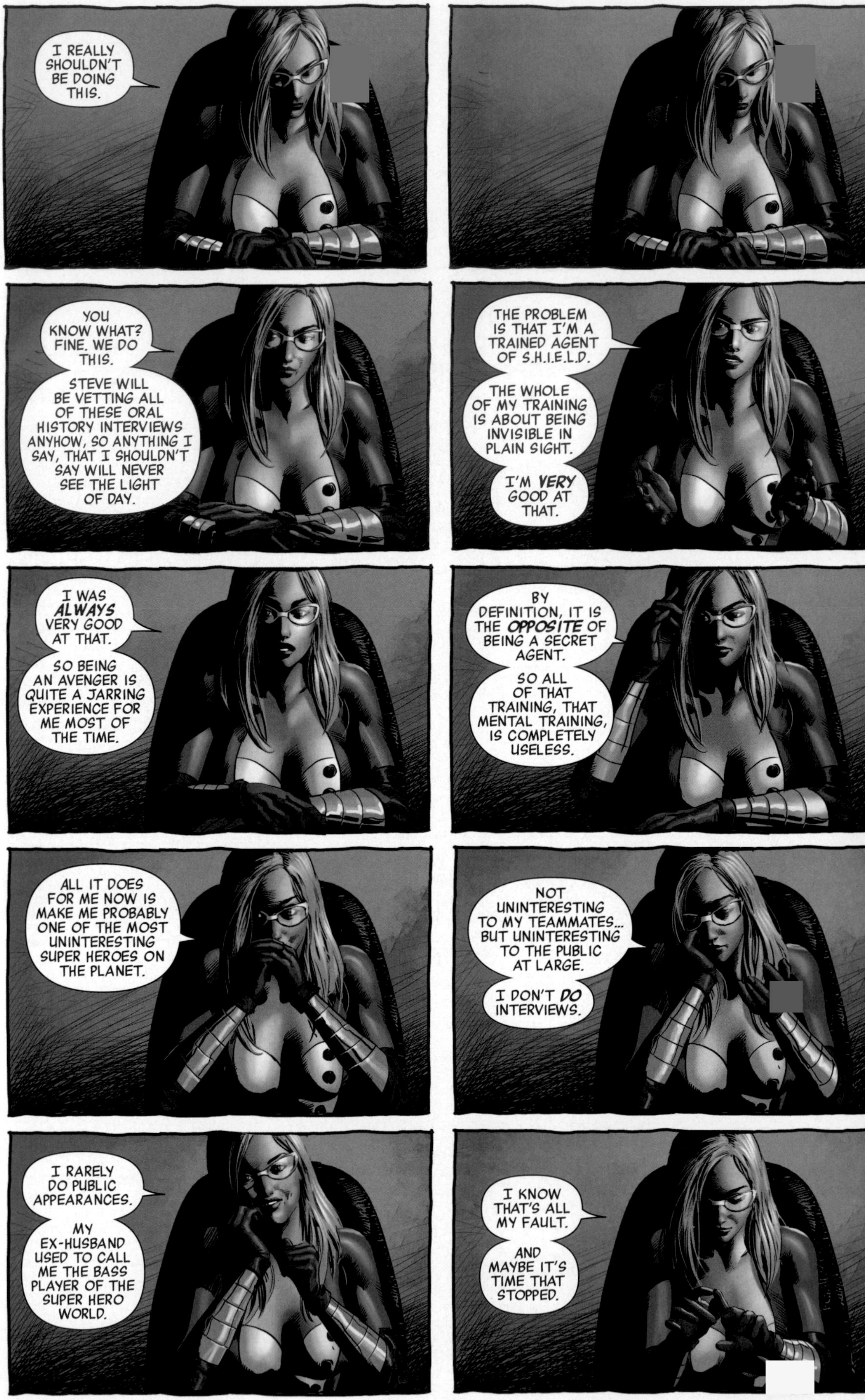

I REALLY SHOULDN'T BE DOING THIS.
YOU KNOW WHAT? FINE. WE DO THIS.
STEVE WILL BE VETTING ALL OF THESE ORAL HISTORY INTERVIEWS ANYHOW, SO ANYTHING I SAY, THAT I SHOULDN'T SAY WILL NEVER SEE THE LIGHT OF DAY.
THE PROBLEM IS THAT I'M A TRAINED AGENT OF S.H.I.E.L.D.
THE WHOLE OF MY TRAINING IS ABOUT BEING INVISIBLE IN PLAIN SIGHT.
I'M *VERY* GOOD AT THAT.
I WAS *ALWAYS* VERY GOOD AT THAT.
SO BEING AN AVENGER IS QUITE A JARRING EXPERIENCE FOR ME MOST OF THE TIME.
BY DEFINITION, IT IS THE *OPPOSITE* OF BEING A SECRET AGENT.
SO ALL OF THAT TRAINING, THAT MENTAL TRAINING, IS COMPLETELY USELESS.
ALL IT DOES FOR ME NOW IS MAKE ME PROBABLY ONE OF THE MOST UNINTERESTING SUPER HEROES ON THE PLANET.
NOT UNINTERESTING TO MY TEAMMATES... BUT UNINTERESTING TO THE PUBLIC AT LARGE.
I DON'T *DO* INTERVIEWS.
I RARELY DO PUBLIC APPEARANCES.
MY EX-HUSBAND USED TO CALL ME THE BASS PLAYER OF THE SUPER HERO WORLD.
I KNOW THAT'S ALL MY FAULT.
AND MAYBE IT'S TIME THAT STOPPED.

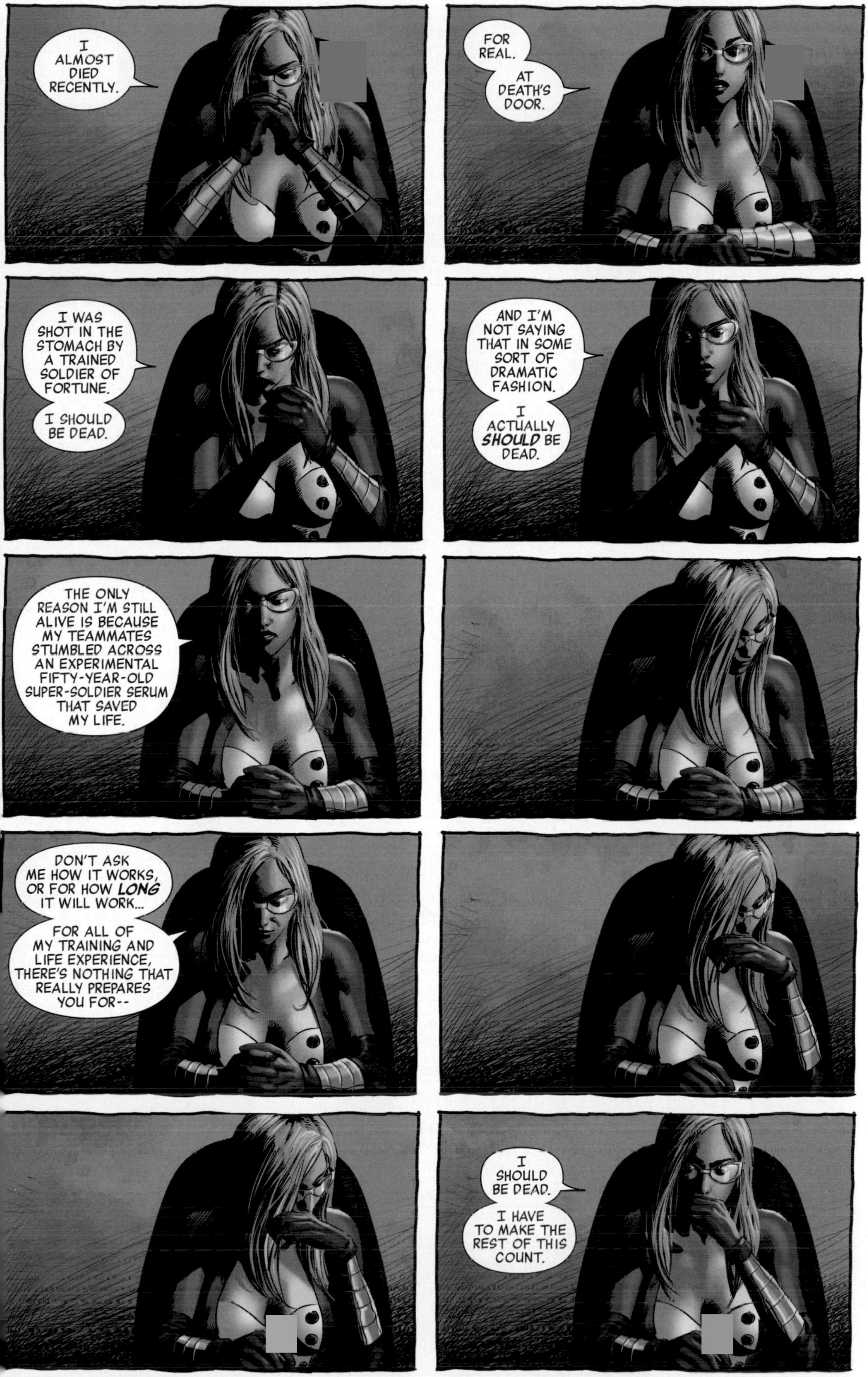
I ALMOST DIED RECENTLY.
FOR REAL.
AT DEATH'S DOOR.
I WAS SHOT IN THE STOMACH BY A TRAINED SOLDIER OF FORTUNE.
I SHOULD BE DEAD.
AND I'M NOT SAYING THAT IN SOME SORT OF DRAMATIC FASHION.
I ACTUALLY *SHOULD* BE DEAD.
THE ONLY REASON I'M STILL ALIVE IS BECAUSE MY TEAMMATES STUMBLED ACROSS AN EXPERIMENTAL FIFTY-YEAR-OLD SUPER-SOLDIER SERUM THAT SAVED MY LIFE.
DON'T ASK ME HOW IT WORKS, OR FOR HOW *LONG* IT WILL WORK...
FOR ALL OF MY TRAINING AND LIFE EXPERIENCE, THERE'S NOTHING THAT REALLY PREPARES YOU FOR--
I SHOULD BE DEAD.
I HAVE TO MAKE THE REST OF THIS COUNT.

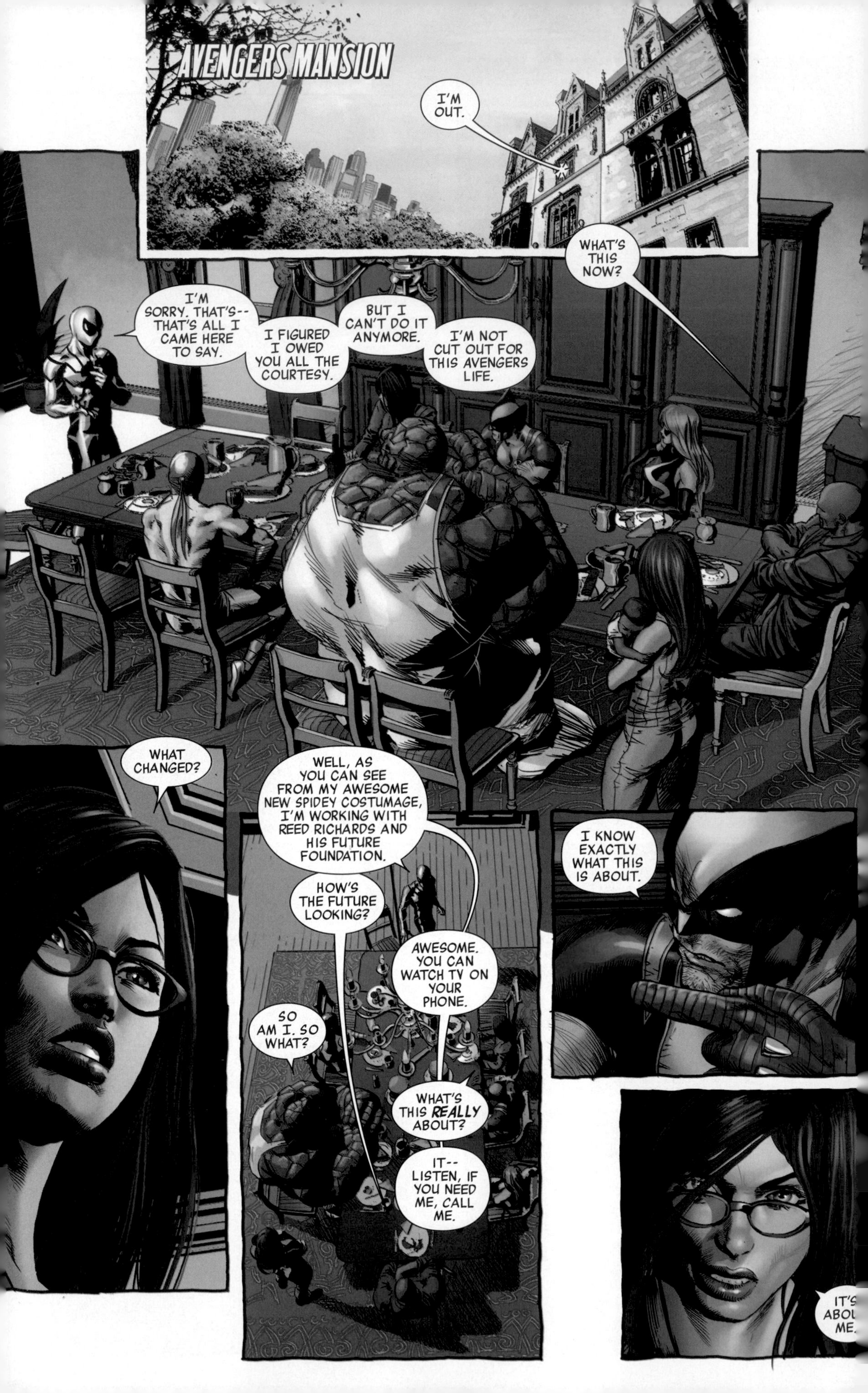
AVENGERS MANSION
I'M OUT.
WHAT'S THIS NOW?
I'M SORRY. THAT'S-- THAT'S ALL I CAME HERE TO SAY.
I FIGURED I OWED YOU ALL THE COURTESY.
BUT I CAN'T DO IT ANYMORE.
I'M NOT CUT OUT FOR THIS AVENGERS LIFE.
WHAT CHANGED?
WELL, AS YOU CAN SEE FROM MY AWESOME NEW SPIDEY COSTUMAGE, I'M WORKING WITH REED RICHARDS AND HIS FUTURE FOUNDATION.
HOW'S THE FUTURE LOOKING?
AWESOME. YOU CAN WATCH TV ON YOUR PHONE.
SO AM I. SO WHAT?
WHAT'S THIS REALLY ABOUT?
IT-- LISTEN, IF YOU NEED ME, CALL ME.
I KNOW EXACTLY WHAT THIS IS ABOUT.
IT'S ABOUT ME.

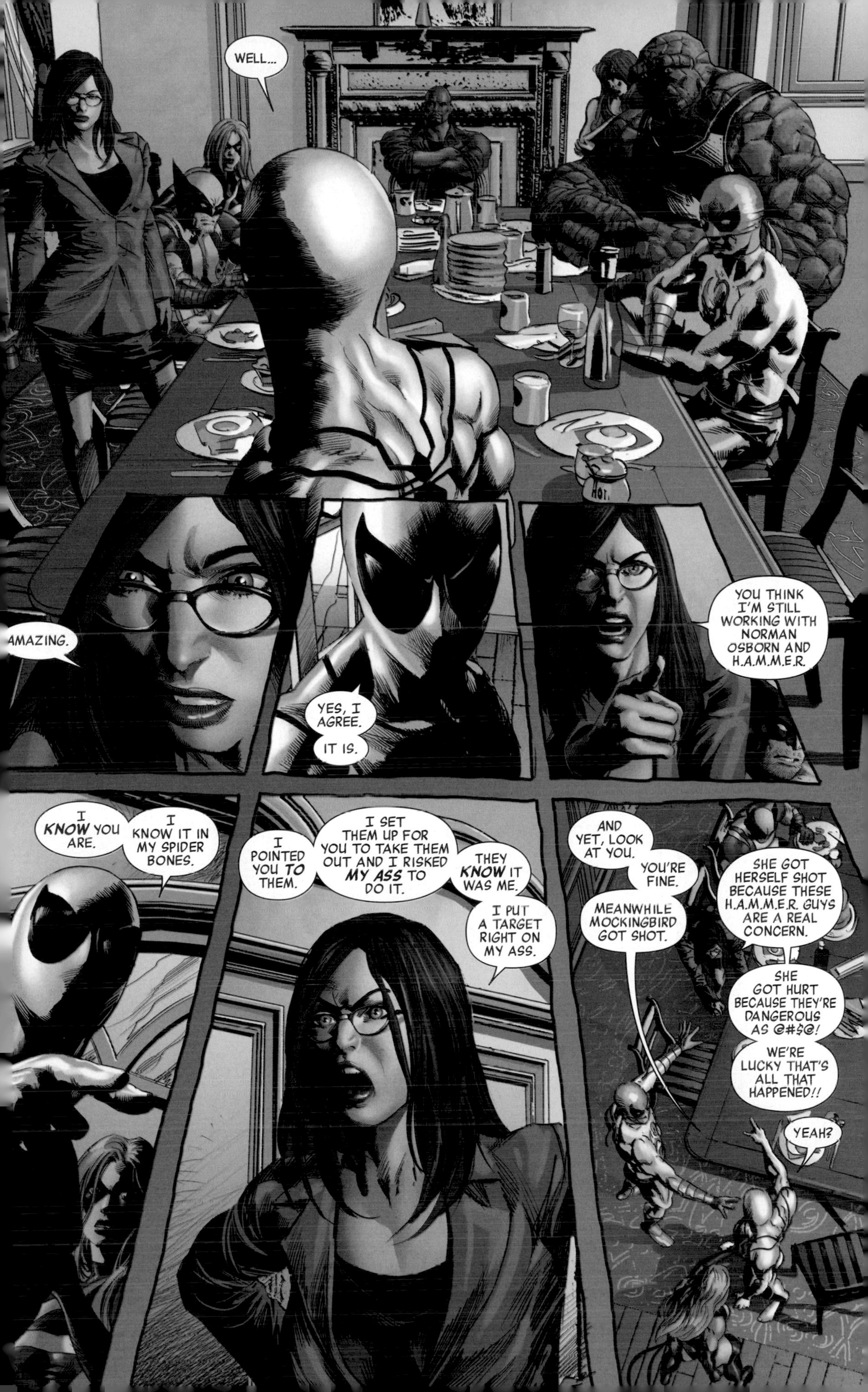

WELL...
AMAZING.
YES, I AGREE.
IT IS.
YOU THINK I'M STILL WORKING WITH NORMAN OSBORN AND H.A.M.M.E.R.
I KNOW YOU ARE.
I KNOW IT IN MY SPIDER BONES.
I POINTED YOU TO THEM.
I SET THEM UP FOR YOU TO TAKE THEM OUT AND I RISKED MY ASS TO DO IT.
THEY KNOW IT WAS ME.
I PUT A TARGET RIGHT ON MY ASS.
AND YET, LOOK AT YOU.
YOU'RE FINE.
MEANWHILE MOCKINGBIRD GOT SHOT.
SHE GOT HERSELF SHOT BECAUSE THESE H.A.M.M.E.R. GUYS ARE A REAL CONCERN.
SHE GOT HURT BECAUSE THEY'RE DANGEROUS AS @#$@!
WE'RE LUCKY THAT'S ALL THAT HAPPENED!!
YEAH?

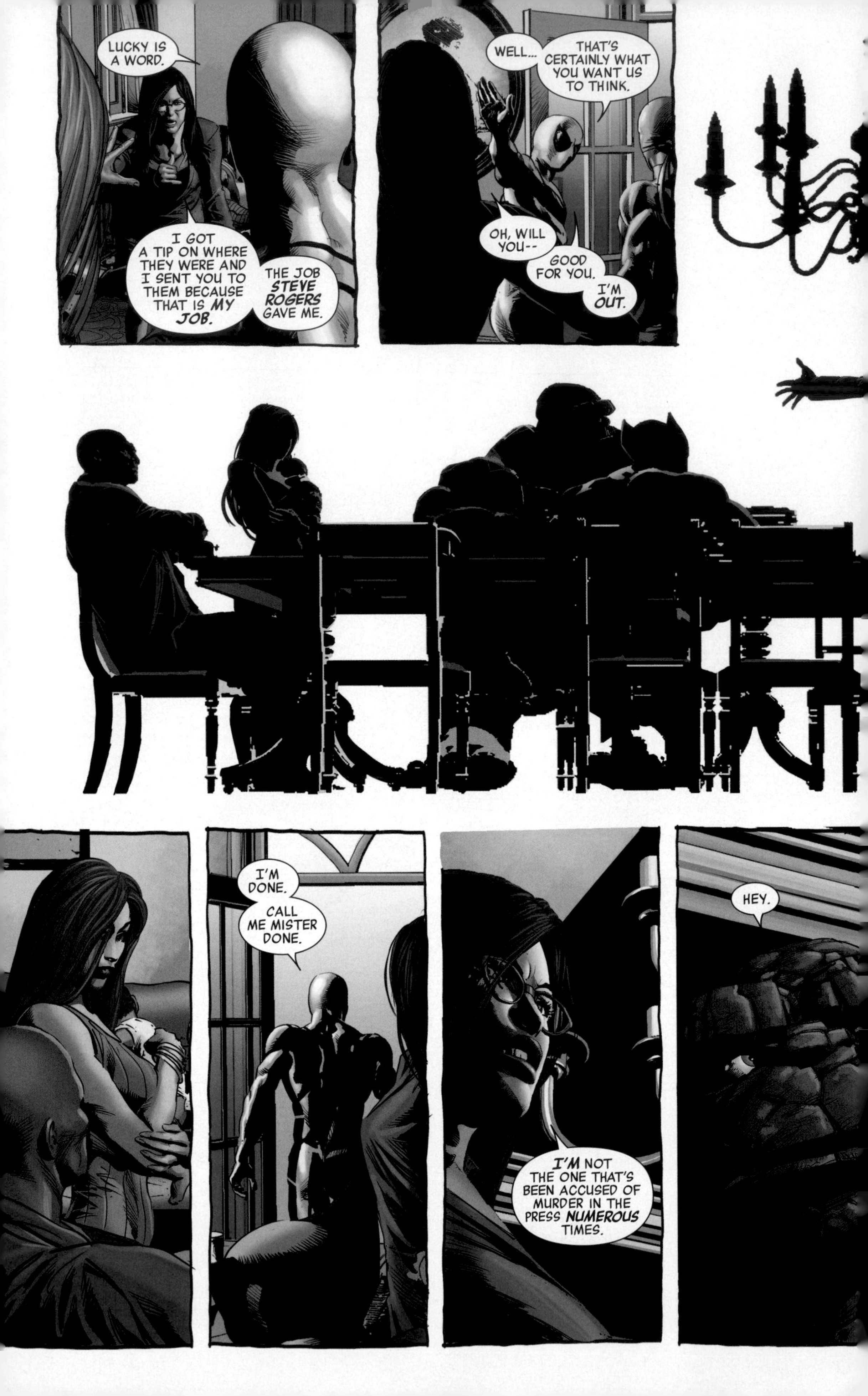
LUCKY IS A WORD.
I GOT A TIP ON WHERE THEY WERE AND I SENT YOU TO THEM BECAUSE THAT IS MY JOB.
THE JOB STEVE ROGERS GAVE ME.
WELL...
THAT'S CERTAINLY WHAT YOU WANT US TO THINK.
OH, WILL YOU--
GOOD FOR YOU.
I'M OUT.
I'M DONE.
CALL ME MISTER DONE.
I'M NOT THE ONE THAT'S BEEN ACCUSED OF MURDER IN THE PRESS NUMEROUS TIMES.
HEY.

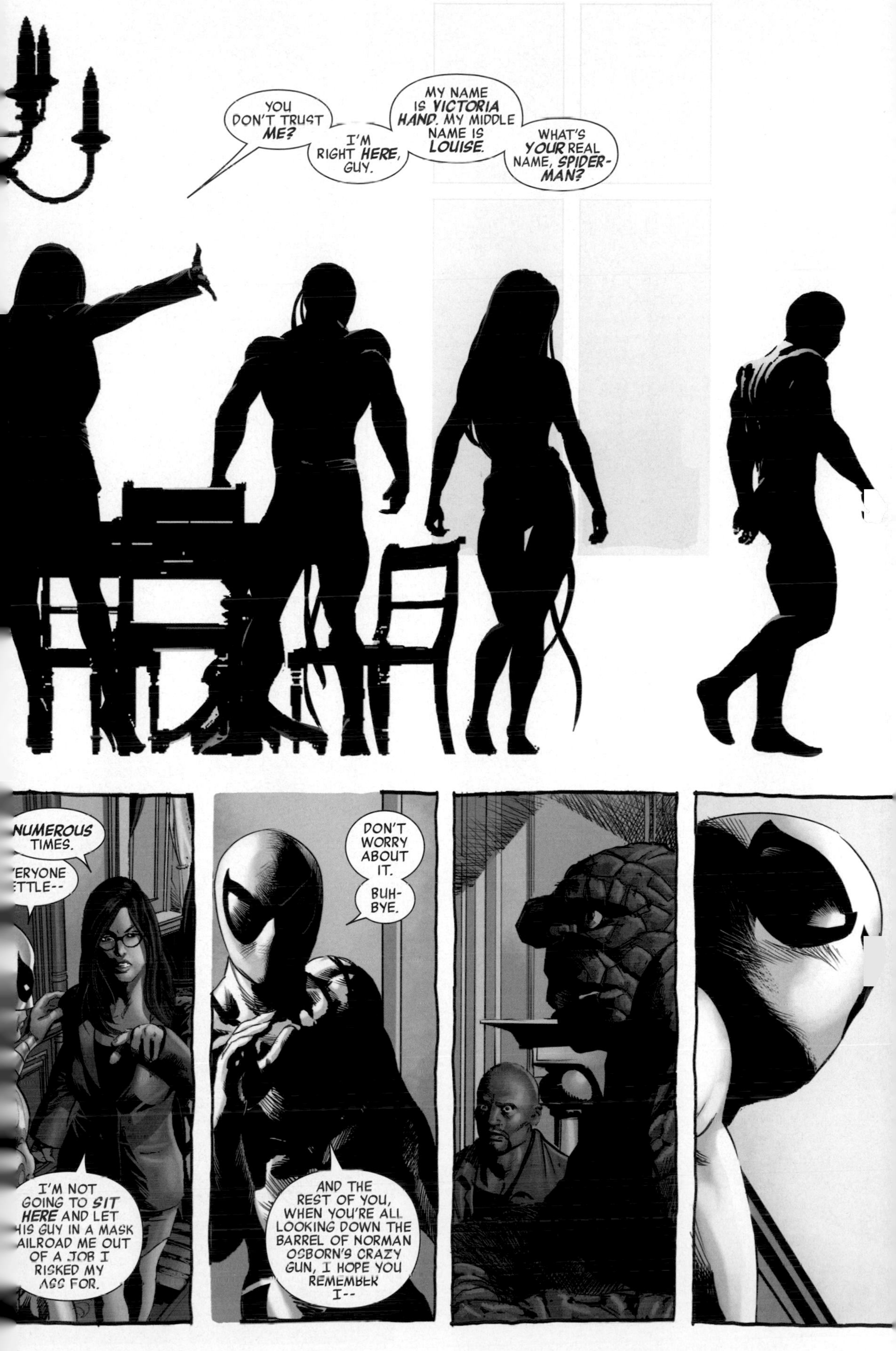
YOU DON'T TRUST ME?
I'M RIGHT HERE, GUY.
MY NAME IS VICTORIA HAND. MY MIDDLE NAME IS LOUISE.
WHAT'S YOUR REAL NAME, SPIDER-MAN?
NUMEROUS TIMES.
ERYONE ETTLE--
I'M NOT GOING TO SIT HERE AND LET HIS GUY IN A MASK AILROAD ME OUT OF A JOB I RISKED MY ASS FOR.
DON'T WORRY ABOUT IT.
BUH-BYE.
AND THE REST OF YOU, WHEN YOU'RE ALL LOOKING DOWN THE BARREL OF NORMAN OSBORN'S CRAZY GUN, I HOPE YOU REMEMBER I--

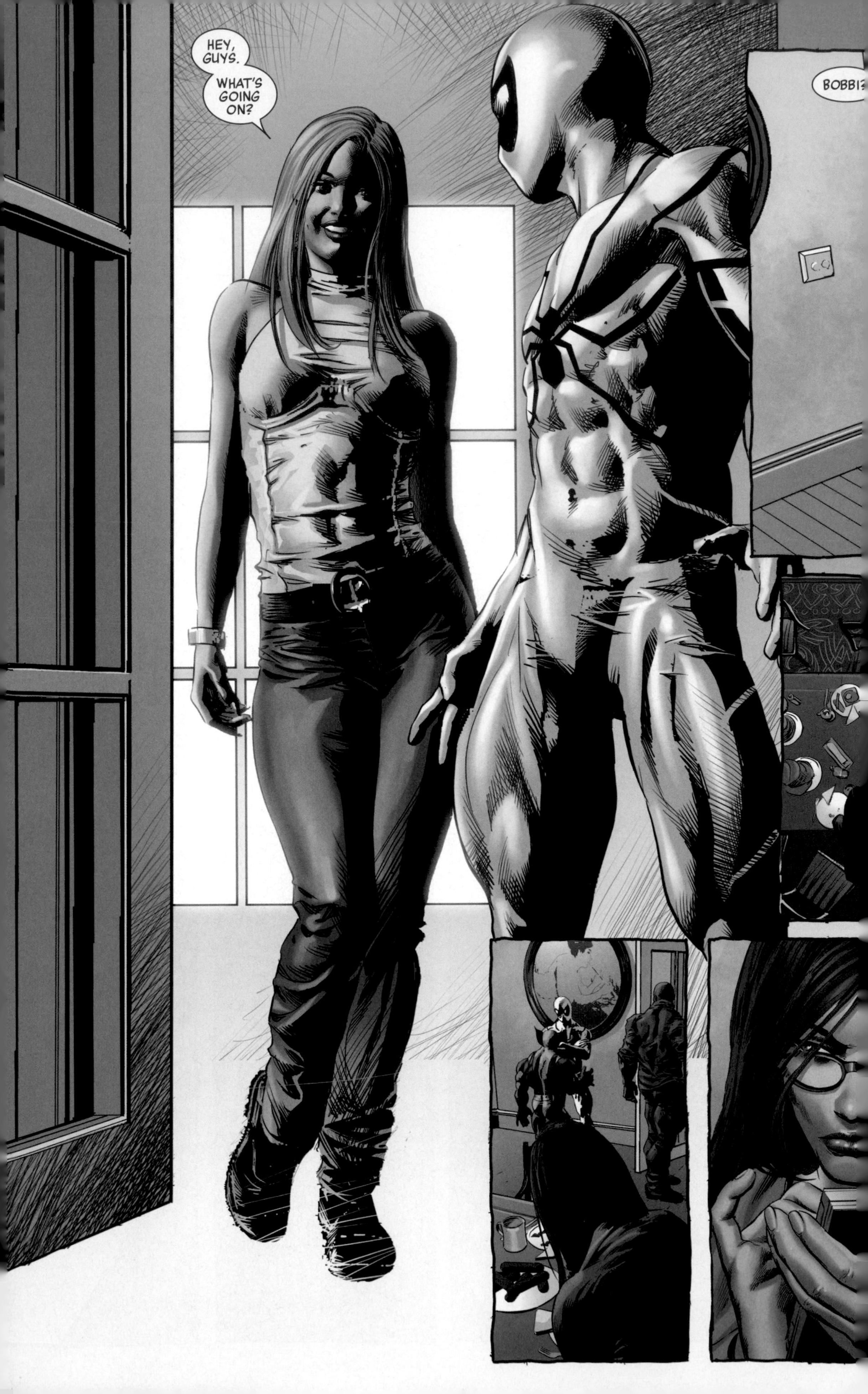
HEY, GUYS.
WHAT'S GOING ON?
BOBBI?

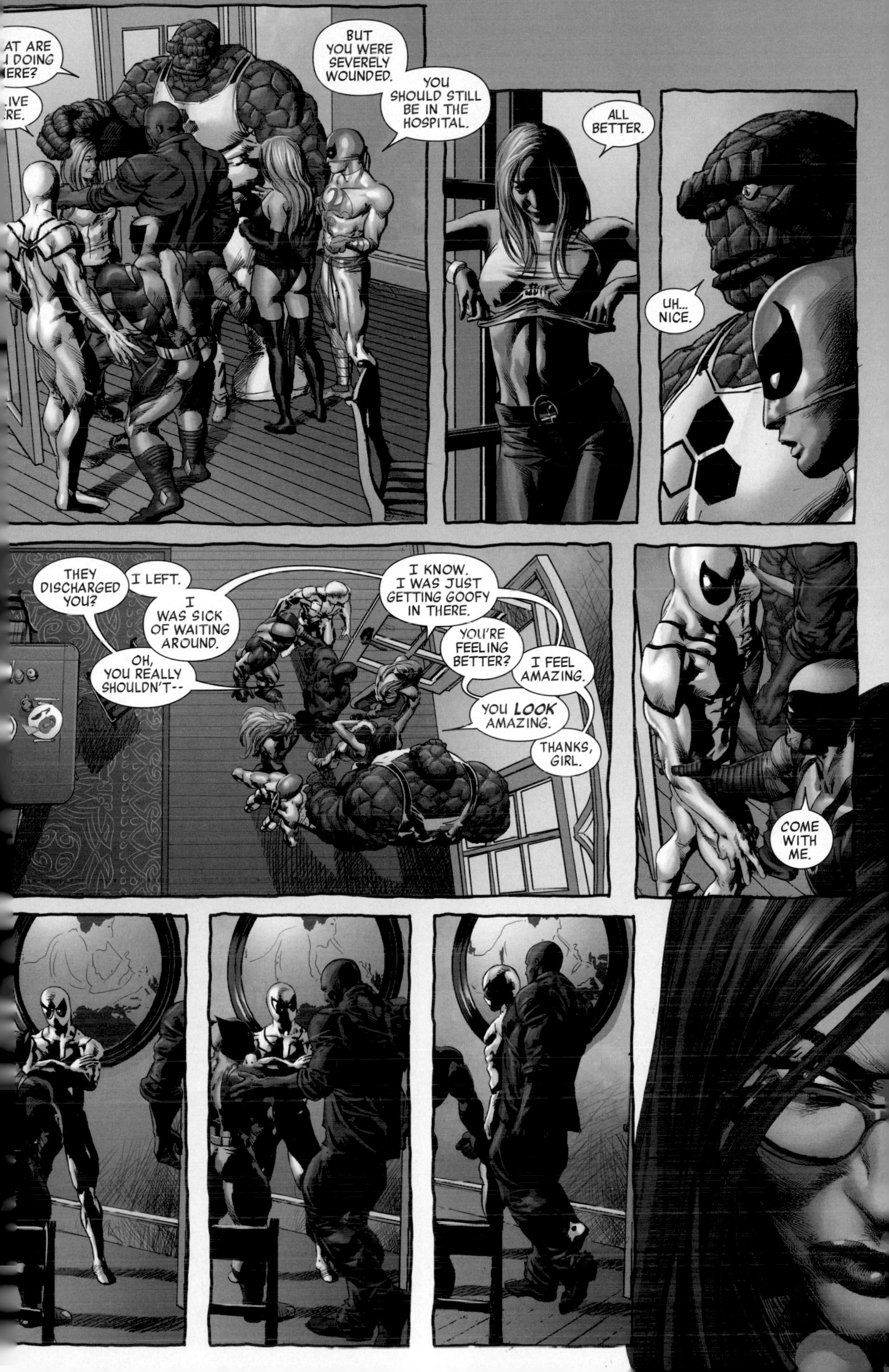

AT ARE
I DOING
HERE?
LIVE
ERE.
BUT YOU WERE SEVERELY WOUNDED.
YOU SHOULD STILL BE IN THE HOSPITAL.
ALL BETTER.
UH... NICE.
THEY DISCHARGED YOU?
I LEFT.
I WAS SICK OF WAITING AROUND.
OH, YOU REALLY SHOULDN'T--
I KNOW. I WAS JUST GETTING GOOFY IN THERE.
YOU'RE FEELING BETTER?
I FEEL AMAZING.
YOU LOOK AMAZING.
THANKS, GIRL.
COME WITH ME.

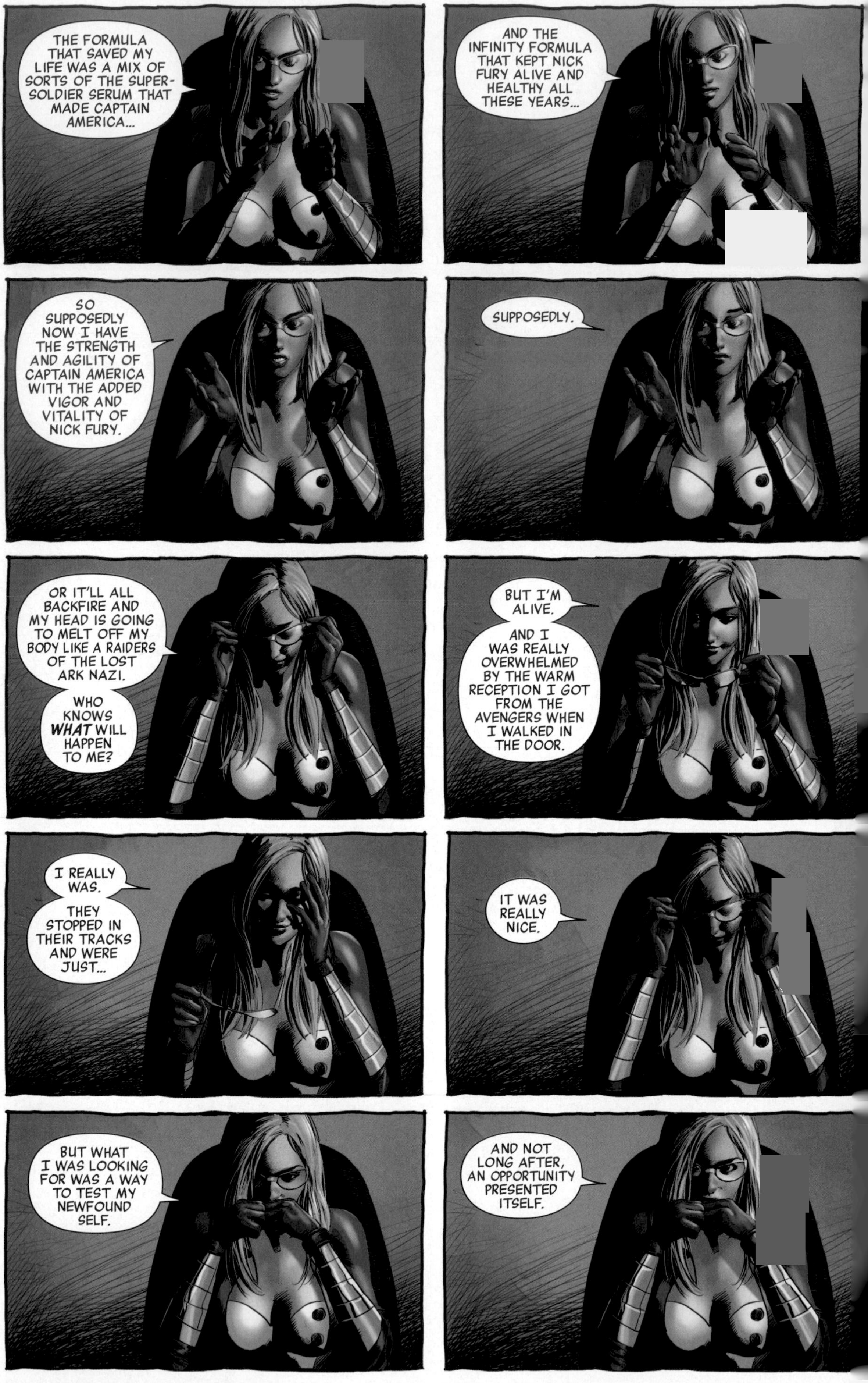
THE FORMULA THAT SAVED MY LIFE WAS A MIX OF SORTS OF THE SUPER-SOLDIER SERUM THAT MADE CAPTAIN AMERICA...
AND THE INFINITY FORMULA THAT KEPT NICK FURY ALIVE AND HEALTHY ALL THESE YEARS...
SO SUPPOSEDLY NOW I HAVE THE STRENGTH AND AGILITY OF CAPTAIN AMERICA WITH THE ADDED VIGOR AND VITALITY OF NICK FURY.
SUPPOSEDLY.
OR IT'LL ALL BACKFIRE AND MY HEAD IS GOING TO MELT OFF MY BODY LIKE A RAIDERS OF THE LOST ARK NAZI.
WHO KNOWS *WHAT* WILL HAPPEN TO ME?
BUT I'M ALIVE.
AND I WAS REALLY OVERWHELMED BY THE WARM RECEPTION I GOT FROM THE AVENGERS WHEN I WALKED IN THE DOOR.
I REALLY WAS.
THEY STOPPED IN THEIR TRACKS AND WERE JUST...
IT WAS REALLY NICE.
BUT WHAT I WAS LOOKING FOR WAS A WAY TO TEST MY NEWFOUND SELF.
AND NOT LONG AFTER, AN OPPORTUNITY PRESENTED ITSELF.

BLITZKRIEG, U.S.A.:

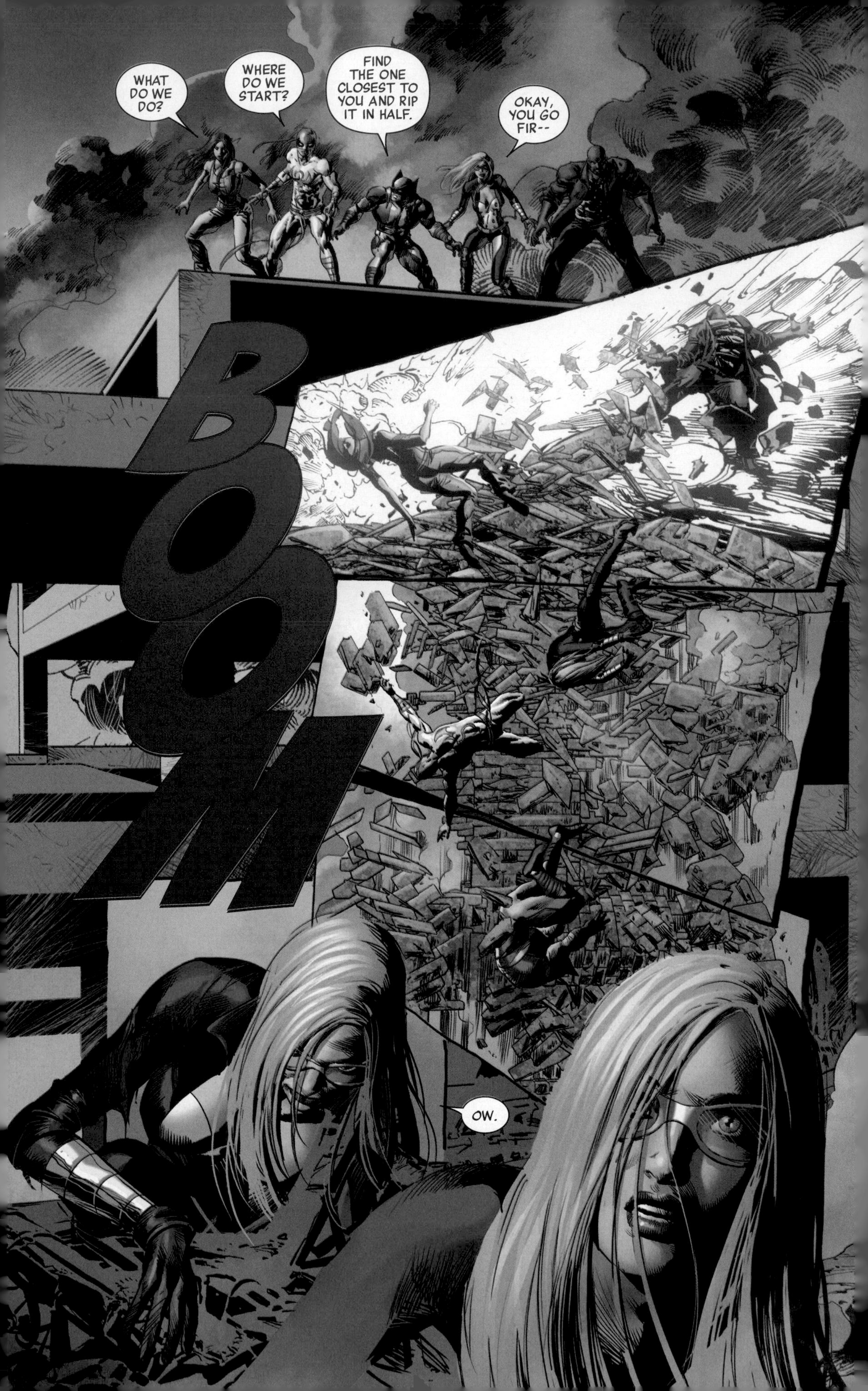
WHAT DO WE DO?
WHERE DO WE START?
FIND THE ONE CLOSEST TO YOU AND RIP IT IN HALF.
OKAY, YOU GO FIR--
BOOM
OW.

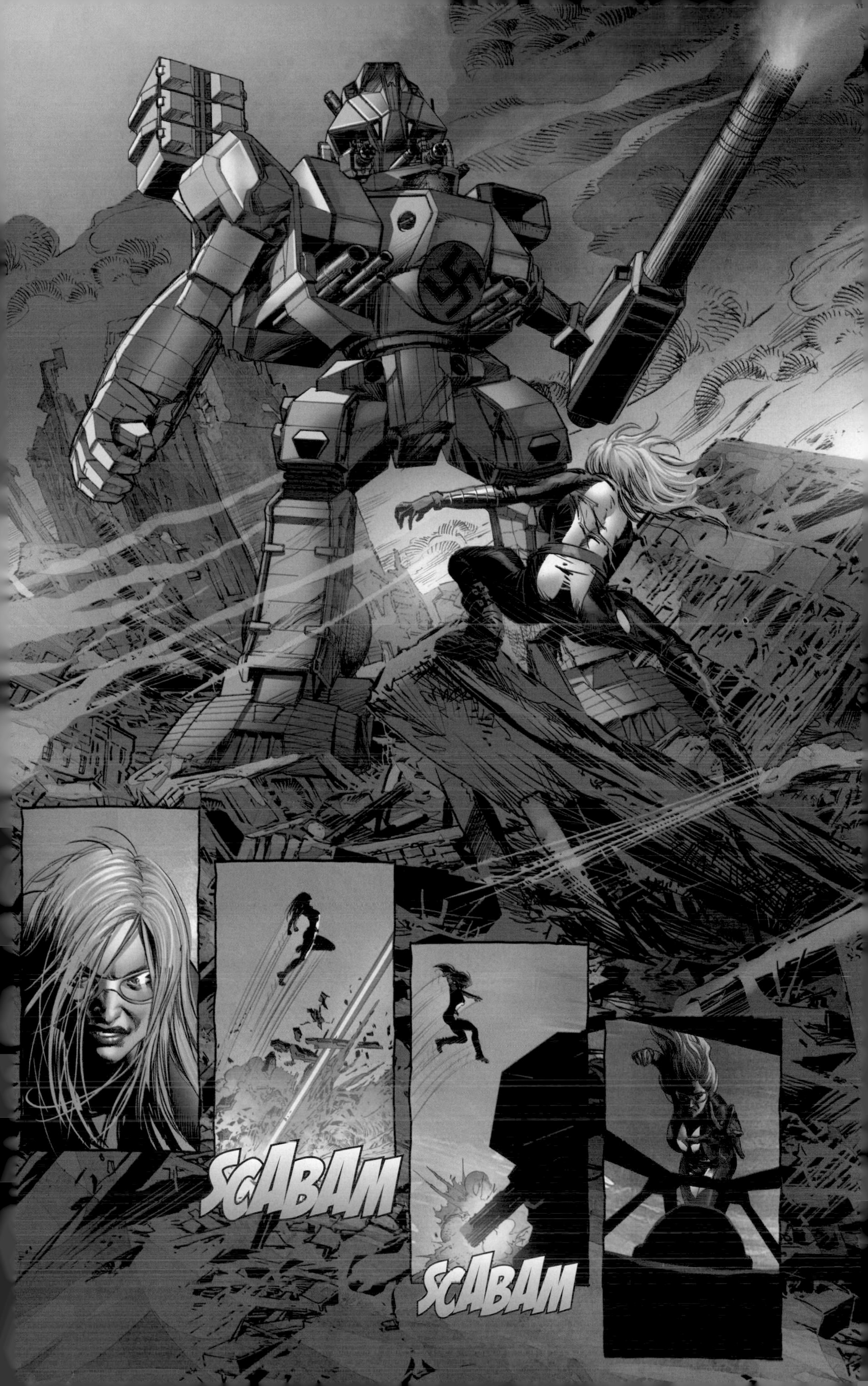
SCABAM
SCABAM

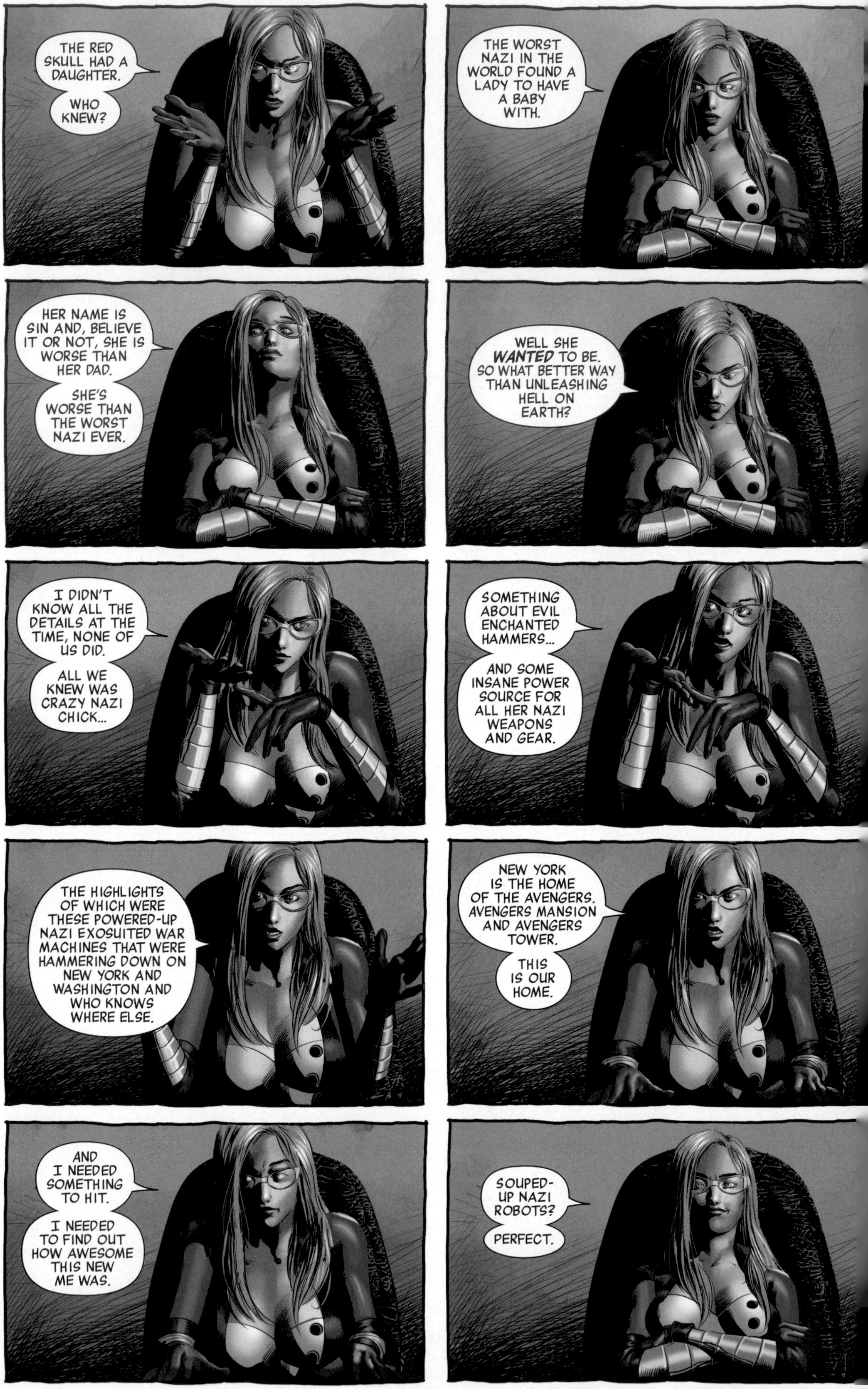
THE RED SKULL HAD A DAUGHTER.
WHO KNEW?
THE WORST NAZI IN THE WORLD FOUND A LADY TO HAVE A BABY WITH.
HER NAME IS SIN AND, BELIEVE IT OR NOT, SHE IS WORSE THAN HER DAD.
SHE'S WORSE THAN THE WORST NAZI EVER.
WELL SHE WANTED TO BE. SO WHAT BETTER WAY THAN UNLEASHING HELL ON EARTH?
I DIDN'T KNOW ALL THE DETAILS AT THE TIME, NONE OF US DID.
ALL WE KNEW WAS CRAZY NAZI CHICK...
SOMETHING ABOUT EVIL ENCHANTED HAMMERS...
AND SOME INSANE POWER SOURCE FOR ALL HER NAZI WEAPONS AND GEAR.
THE HIGHLIGHTS OF WHICH WERE THESE POWERED-UP NAZI EXOSUITED WAR MACHINES THAT WERE HAMMERING DOWN ON NEW YORK AND WASHINGTON AND WHO KNOWS WHERE ELSE.
NEW YORK IS THE HOME OF THE AVENGERS. AVENGERS MANSION AND AVENGERS TOWER.
THIS IS OUR HOME.
AND I NEEDED SOMETHING TO HIT.
I NEEDED TO FIND OUT HOW AWESOME THIS NEW ME WAS.
SOUPED-UP NAZI ROBOTS?
PERFECT.

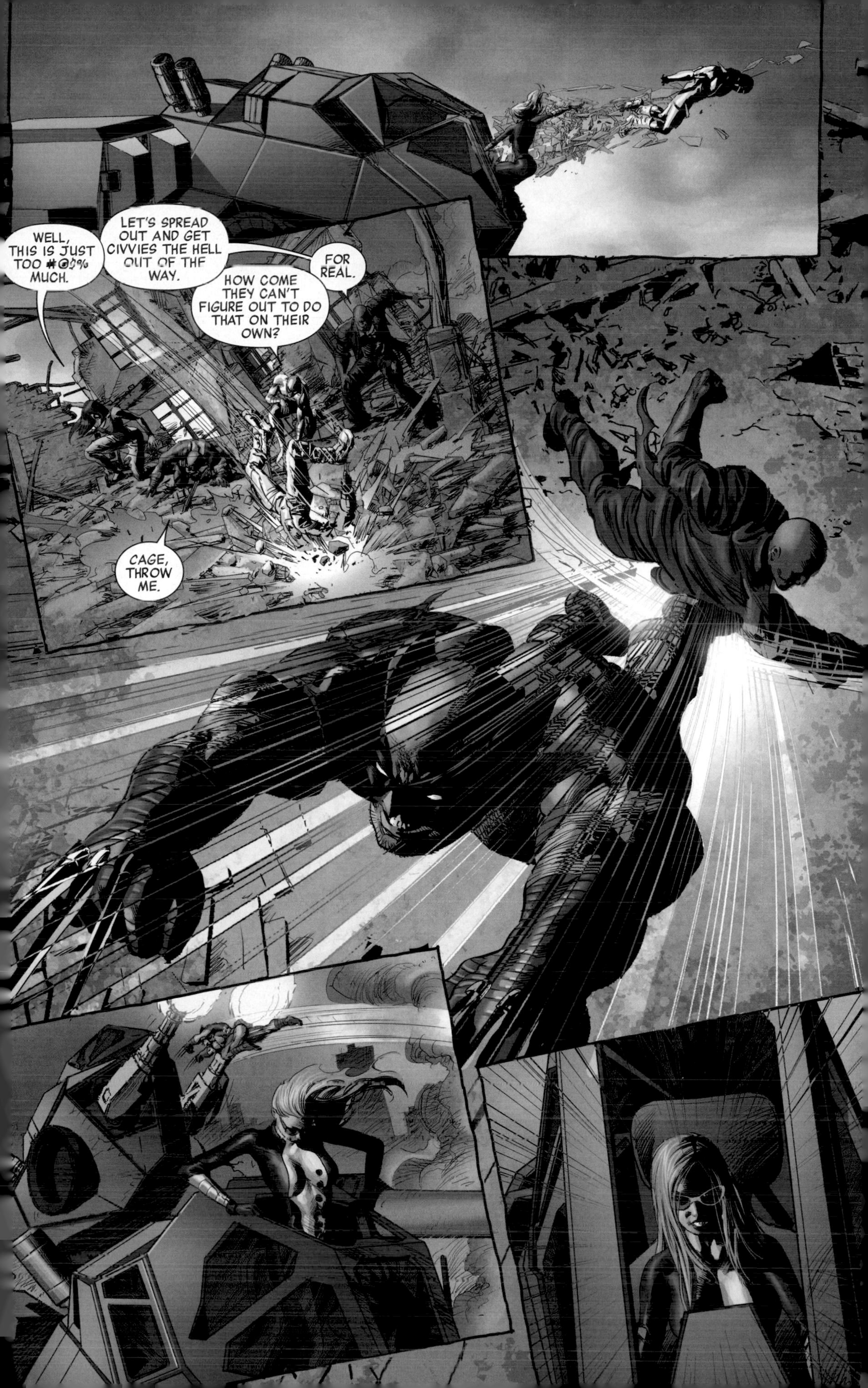
WELL, THIS IS JUST TOO #@?% MUCH.
LET'S SPREAD OUT AND GET CIVVIES THE HELL OUT OF THE WAY.
FOR REAL.
HOW COME THEY CAN'T FIGURE OUT TO DO THAT ON THEIR OWN?
CAGE, THROW ME.

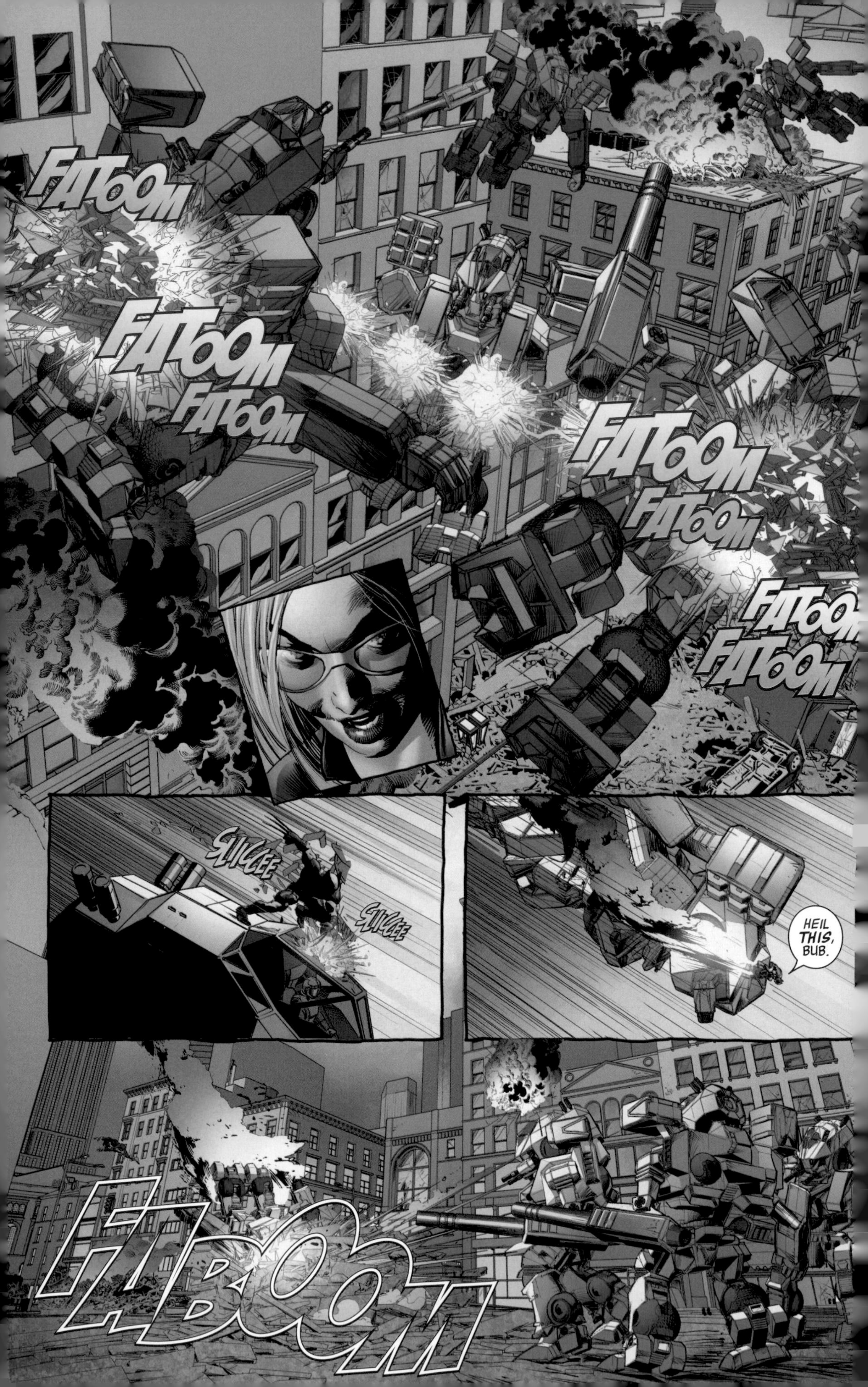
FATOOM
FATOOM
FATOOM
FATOOM
FATOOM
FATOOM
FATOOM
SLICCEE
SLICCEE
HEIL THIS, BUB.
FABOOM

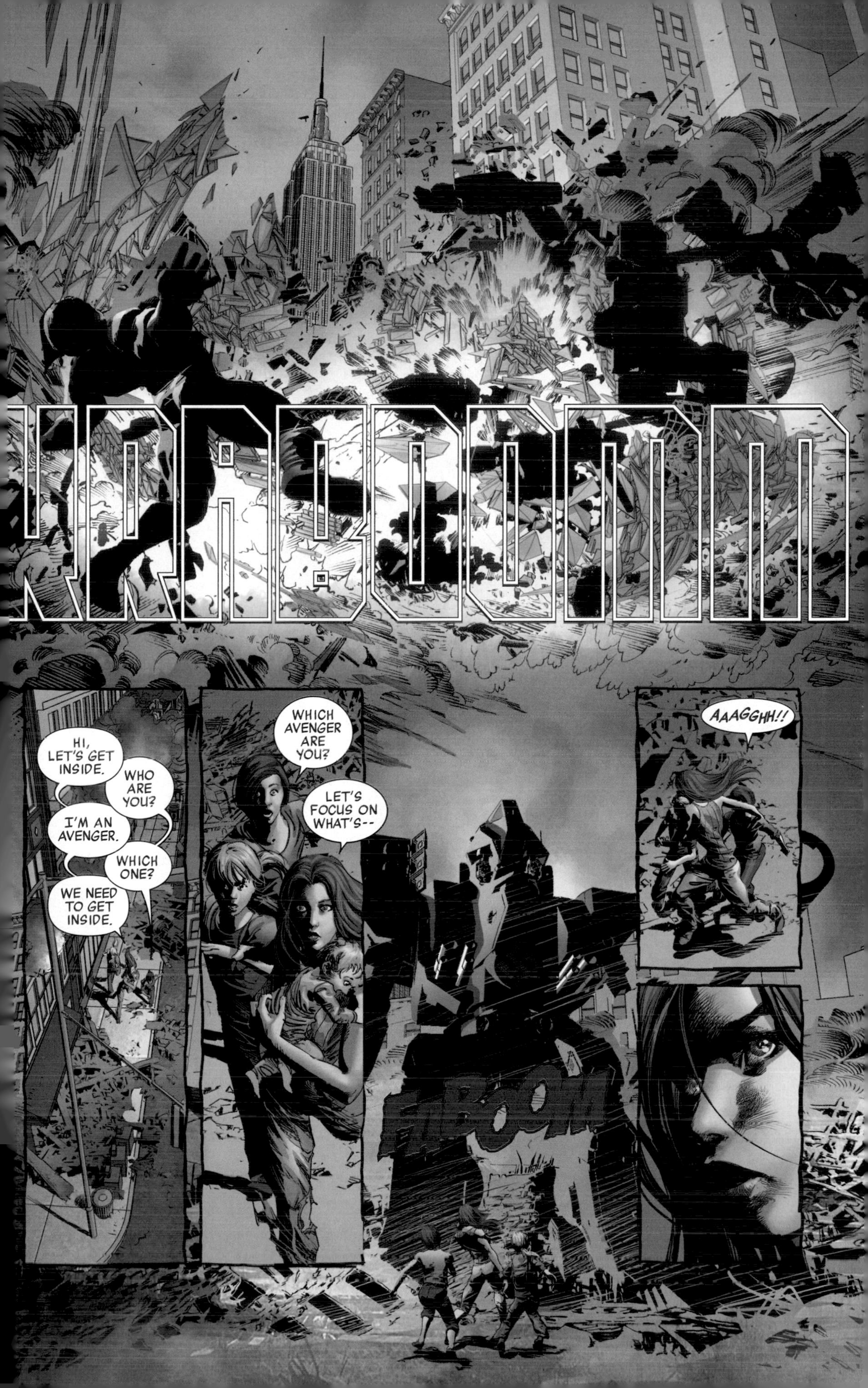
KRA-BOOM
HI, LET'S GET INSIDE.
WHO ARE YOU?
I'M AN AVENGER.
WHICH ONE?
WE NEED TO GET INSIDE.
WHICH AVENGER ARE YOU?
LET'S FOCUS ON WHAT'S--
FROOM
AAAGGHH!!

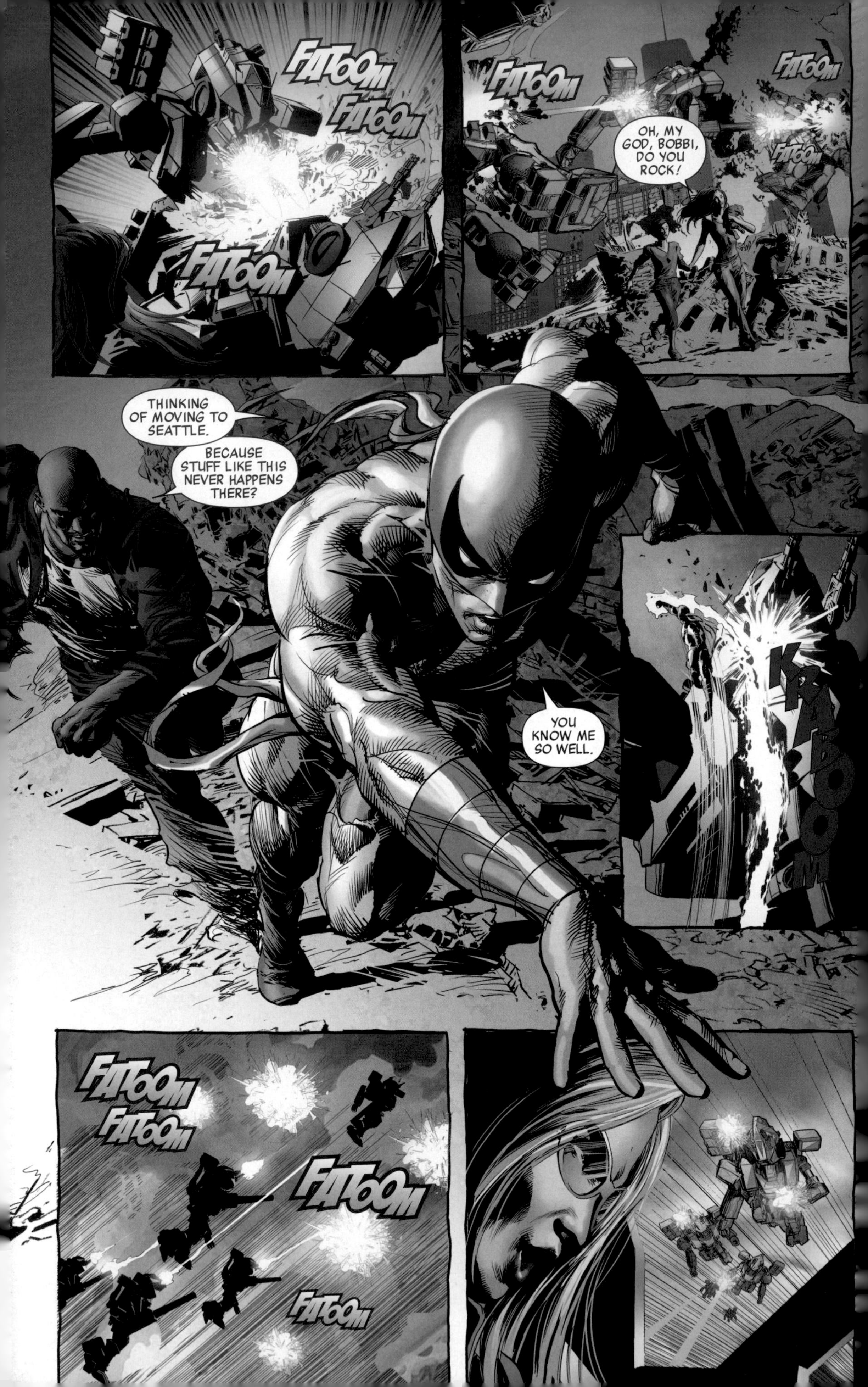
FATOOM
FATOOM
FATOOM
FATOOM
FATOOM
OH, MY GOD, BOBBI, DO YOU ROCK!
FATOOM
THINKING OF MOVING TO SEATTLE.
BECAUSE STUFF LIKE THIS NEVER HAPPENS THERE?
YOU KNOW ME SO WELL.
KRABOOM
FATOOM
FATOOM
FATOOM
FATOOM

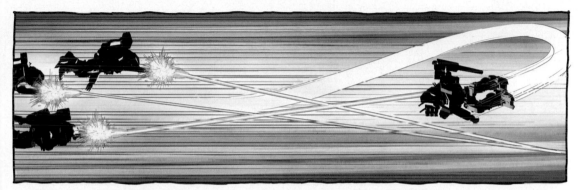

FATOOM
FATOOM
FATOOM

SLBOOOM

OH, I LIKE THE NEW ME.

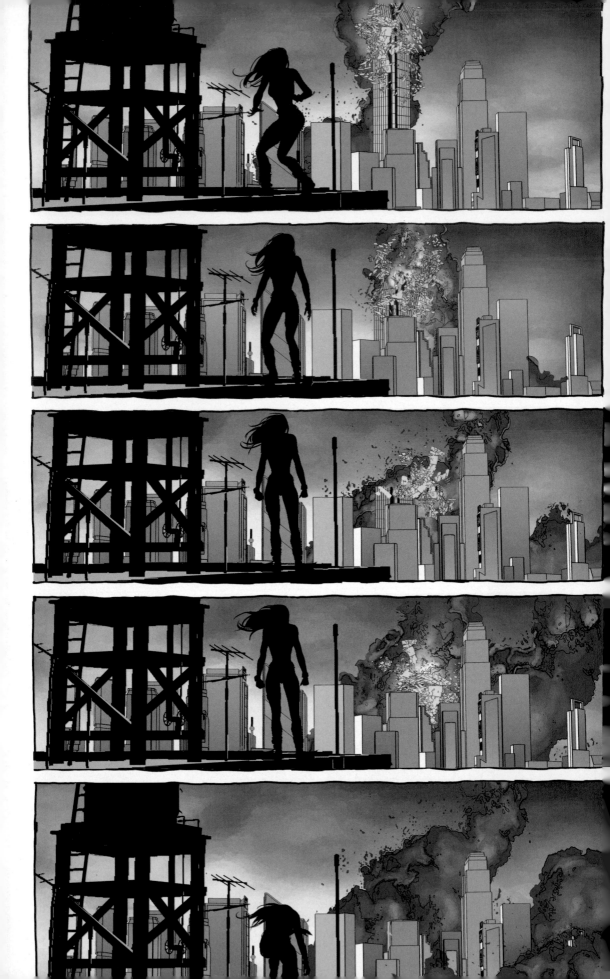

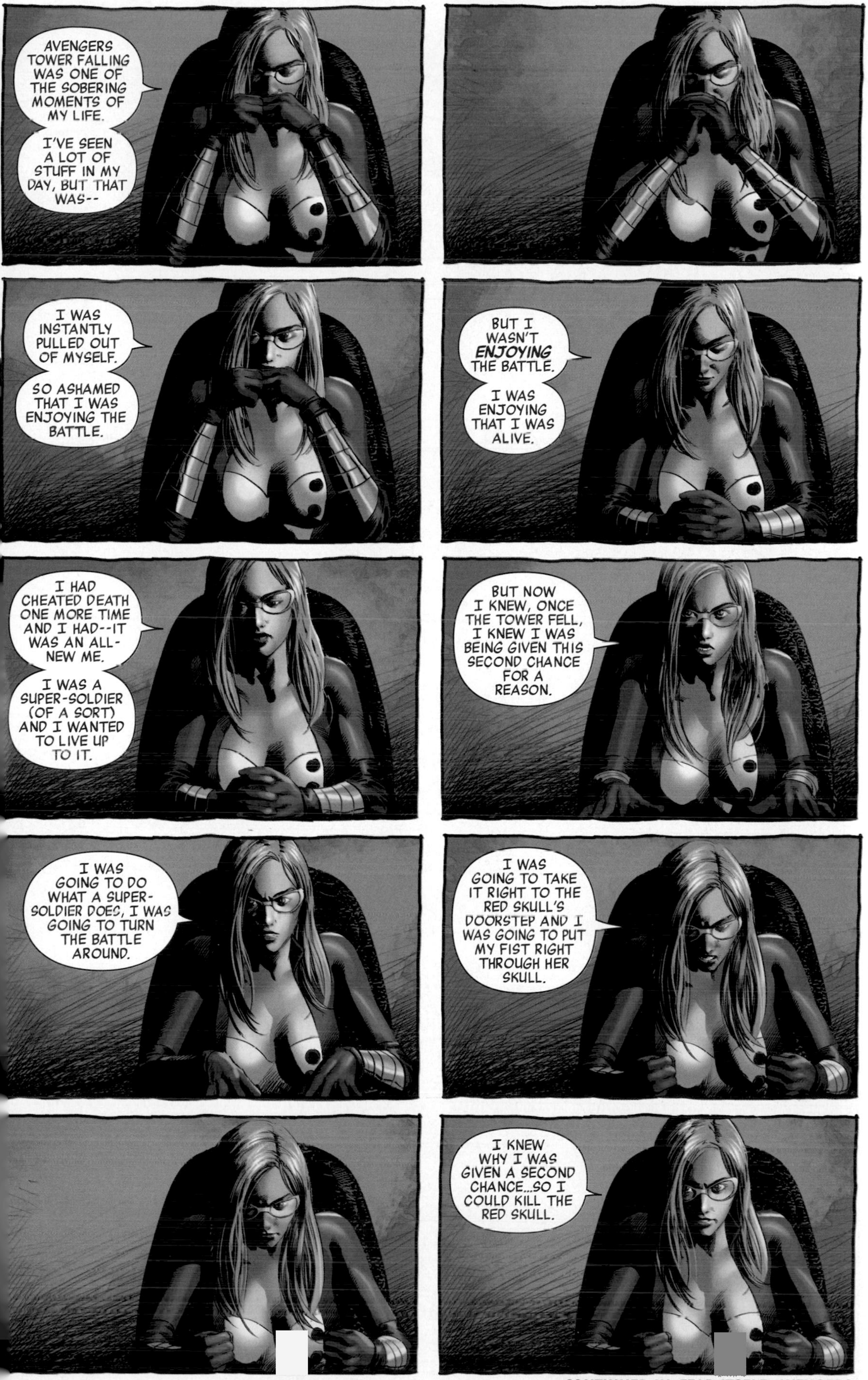
AVENGERS TOWER FALLING WAS ONE OF THE SOBERING MOMENTS OF MY LIFE.
I'VE SEEN A LOT OF STUFF IN MY DAY, BUT THAT WAS--
I WAS INSTANTLY PULLED OUT OF MYSELF.
SO ASHAMED THAT I WAS ENJOYING THE BATTLE.
BUT I WASN'T ENJOYING THE BATTLE.
I WAS ENJOYING THAT I WAS ALIVE.
I HAD CHEATED DEATH ONE MORE TIME AND I HAD--IT WAS AN ALL-NEW ME.
I WAS A SUPER-SOLDIER (OF A SORT) AND I WANTED TO LIVE UP TO IT.
BUT NOW I KNEW, ONCE THE TOWER FELL, I KNEW I WAS BEING GIVEN THIS SECOND CHANCE FOR A REASON.
I WAS GOING TO DO WHAT A SUPER-SOLDIER DOES, I WAS GOING TO TURN THE BATTLE AROUND.
I WAS GOING TO TAKE IT RIGHT TO THE RED SKULL'S DOORSTEP AND I WAS GOING TO PUT MY FIST RIGHT THROUGH HER SKULL.
I KNEW WHY I WAS GIVEN A SECOND CHANCE...SO I COULD KILL THE RED SKULL.

CONTINUED IN *FEAR ITSELF: AVENGERS.*

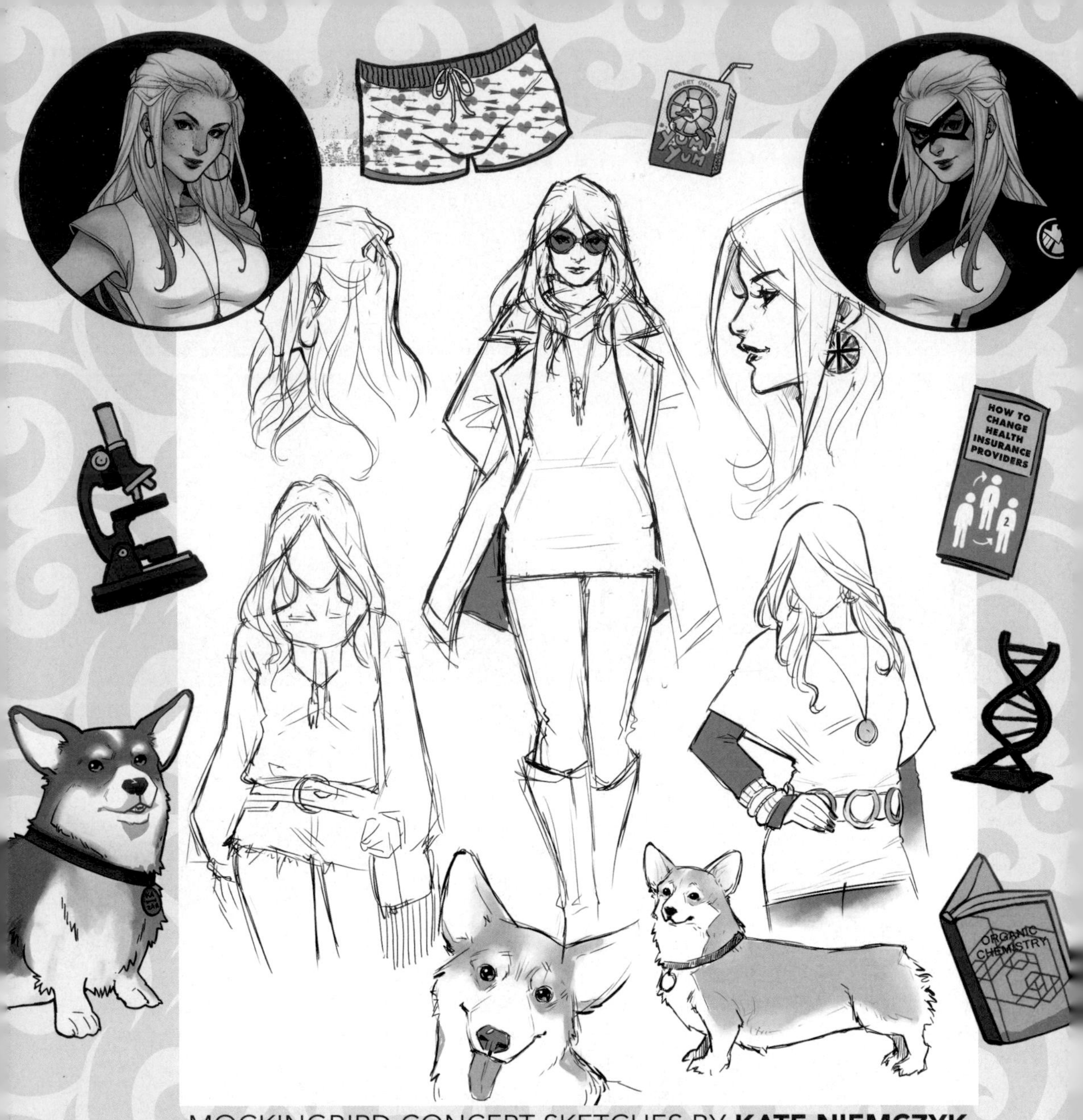
HOW TO CHANGE HEALTH INSURANCE PROVIDERS
ORGANIC CHEMISTRY

MOCKINGBIRD CONCEPT SKETCHES BY **KATE NIEMCZYK**

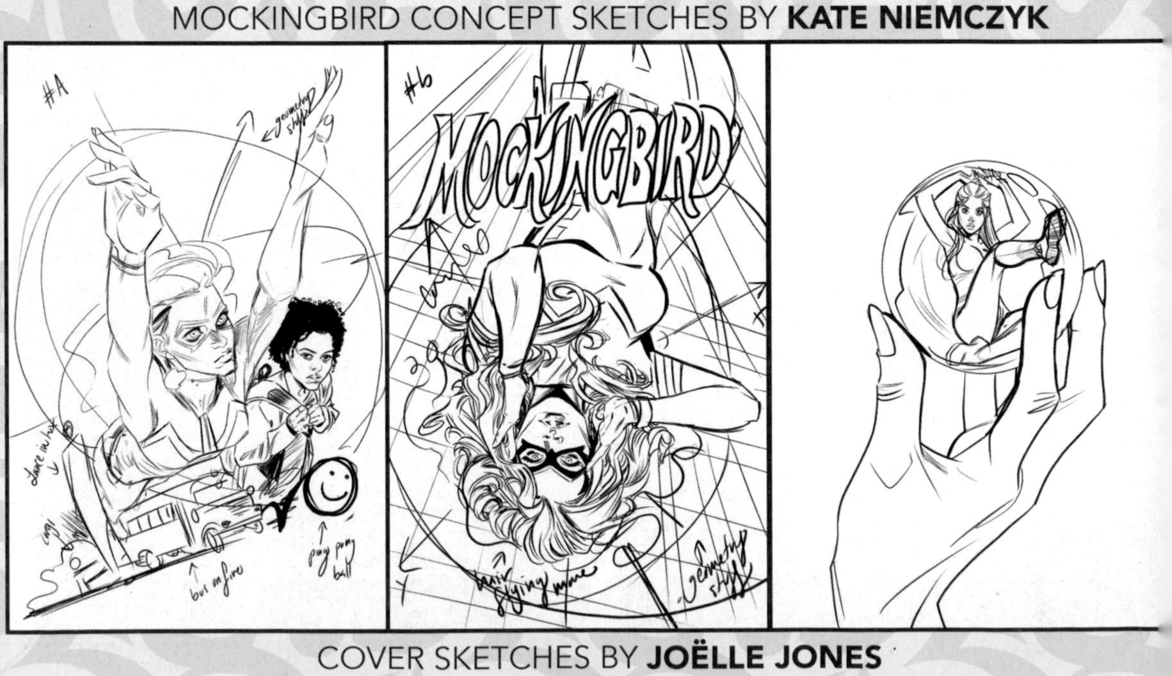
#A
geometry style
bus on fire
ping pong ball
#b
MOCKINGBIRD
geometry style

COVER SKETCHES BY **JOËLLE JONES**